D0875542

A HANDBOOK
TO THE SEPTUAGINT

BY

RICHARD R. OTTLEY, M.A.

AUTHOR OF
"ISAIAH ACCORDING TO THE SEPTUAGINT"

METHUEN & CO. LTD.
36 ESSEX STREET W.C.
LONDON

First Published in 1920

VXORI DILECTAE

L.

CVIVS MEMORIA

PACEM IAM CONSECVTAE

SEMPER DVLCIS EST

PREFACE

THIS handbook deals with the oldest translation of the Hebrew Scriptures; older than the New Testament, and written in the same language. Very naturally, therefore, the Old and New Testaments in Greek came together to form the Bible of the early Christian Church. For five centuries or so this version of the Old Testament was dominant; translations into other languages were, as a rule, made from it, and not from the Hebrew, until the Vulgate appeared. It is only the Bible's due that the better translations of it have ranked, side by side with original works, among the world's great literature; but the Septuagint counted for generations of men almost as the sacred original itself. Yet its makers, excepting only the grandson of the author of Ecclesiasticus, are anonymous and unknown; they have won no such personal repute as Jerome, Wiclif, Luther, or Coverdale. But their work exercised for long years an influence which it is hardly possible to over-rate, until the Vulgate prevailed, not directly over the Greek Version itself, but over its Latin daughter-version. And when, after the Dark Ages, the revival of learning brought Greek literature westward again, the hold of the

Vulgate upon the Latin countries was too strong to be dislodged or even shaken, and the Northern nations demanded translations from the original into their own tongues. So vanished all chance of the Septuagint regaining its former place as a popular possession. It has lived on only as a field (but there was treasure hid in that field) for a narrow circle of students.

Of late, however, it has begun to seem possible that this circle might be to some extent enlarged. Greek scholarship is not, so far, extinct in this country, and may yet survive for some time. But the Septuagint was not fully intelligible to every Greek scholar as such; and only lately has the help that he needed been forthcoming, in the shape of an improved text, and aids to the understanding of it. There still seems room for the present book, which demands from the reader, as a minimum, only a fair knowledge of the Greek language, and of the Old Testament; and begins, as far as possible, at the beginning.

In recent years, several of those to whom reference is made in this book have been taken away. My friend Professor James Moulton succumbed to the results of the pirate methods of the German Empire; I cannot write of it unmoved.

> 'His virtues
> Will plead like angels, trumpet-tongued, against
> The deep damnation of his taking-off:'

I leave my references to his work unaltered, as I believe he would have wished.

Professor Swete has also passed away, honoured by all who knew him, and by many who knew only his writings. I owe him far more than I may here set down. As, doubtless through his kindness, my name appears on the title-page of the latest edition of his *Introduction*, I may perhaps explain that I feel my part in it to have been quite subordinate. The merits of the work remain his.

To my friends, Professor Burkitt and Mr. H. St. J. Thackeray, I have on former occasions been much indebted and very grateful. That this is still the case, the plentiful references in the following pages will show.

In such a handbook as this, dealing largely with names, facts, and dates, a writer who works alone can hardly hope to avoid slips, and is lucky if he can steer clear of more serious blunders. I am the more grateful, therefore, to Messrs. Methuen's reader and to the printers for their watchful accuracy and care.

The object of this work is to induce people to read the Septuagint. I hope that as they do so, they will feel themselves drawing a step nearer to the original. While scanning the pages, perhaps, with greater ease than if the Hebrew were before them, they will come to perceive its terms of expression, and even its wording, under the Greek surface. They will be able to enjoy the simple, unpretending language; and will have the satisfaction of reading the Old Testament as in the oldest surviving documents that contain it.

R. R. O.

December 1919

CONTENTS

CHAPTER I

WHAT IS THE SEPTUAGINT? A FIRST SURVEY

CHAPTER II

EARLY HISTORY OF THE SEPTUAGINT (TO A.D. 500)

CHAPTER III

MODERN STUDY OF THE SEPTUAGINT (FROM A.D. 1500)

CHAPTER IV

THE TEXT OF THE SEPTUAGINT

CHAPTER V

THE CHARACTER OF THE TRANSLATION: THE GREEK AND THE HEBREW

CHAPTER VI

THE APOCRYPHA AND PSEUDEPIGRAPHA

CHAPTER VII

THE LANGUAGE AND STYLE OF THE SEPTUAGINT

CHAPTER VIII

SOME PASSAGES EXAMINED. REMARKS ON GRAMMAR

CHAPTER IX

THE VALUE OF THE LXX. HOW TO WORK AT IT

CHAPTER X

BOOKS FOR STUDY. MSS. OF THE SEPTUAGINT

Note.—*Biblical references are generally given according to the English Version.*

A HANDBOOK TO THE SEPTUAGINT

CHAPTER I

WHAT IS THE SEPTUAGINT? A FIRST SURVEY

Our four great MSS. of the Bible in Greek—How is this?—Age of the Greek version, and of MSS.—Names of books—Contents of the Greek MSS.—The Apocrypha—Order of books, and of passages—Differences of detail—Character of the translation—Textual and "inter-textual" criticism—Confusion of letters—Quotations from LXX. in N.T.—The language of the LXX.—Proper names—Differences between MSS.—Summary.

AMONG the greatest treasures of civilised and Christian Europe are four great manuscript books: the four oldest copies of the Bible, once complete or nearly complete, that are known to exist. They are housed in the principal libraries of Rome, Petrograd, London, and Paris. Two of the four are a little less, and two, probably, rather more than fifteen hundred years old. So highly are they valued, that when Napoleon was master of Rome, the copy in the Vatican Library there was carried off to France among the spoils of war; and, when his empire fell, and peace was made in 1815, it was reclaimed. Of the four, two are still nearly complete; but of the other two, only portions remain. Originally, they contained the Old and New Testaments, and something more besides. Now, none of them has the Old Testament quite complete, and only one, with barely a third of the Old Testament left, has the New Testament entire. They are all in Greek.

But how comes this? The New Testament, we know, was written in Greek; or, at any rate, if any part of it was originally composed in another language, the Greek is all that has come down to us, and the existence of anything before it is, at most, a matter of inference. But the Old Testament was written in a Semitic language, nearly all of it in Hebrew; many Hebrew manuscripts of it exist to-day, printed editions in Hebrew are common, and have been issued for four hundred years past. How then can the oldest Bibles known be all in Greek? and what has this to do with the first question that anyone, coming fresh to the subject, would naturally ask, namely, What is the Septuagint?

However, in answering one of these questions, we shall very nearly answer the other. Very long ago, the Old Testament was translated from Hebrew into Greek; as long ago as from the third to the first century B.C. Now it so happens, that as the Jews' practice was to renew their Hebrew manuscripts with extreme care, rather than to preserve the older ones, these leading MSS. of the Greek version are from four to five centuries older than any existing Hebrew MSS. of the O.T. (some Hebrew MSS. are believed to be of the ninth century; the oldest *dated* one belongs to A.D. 916). And the 'Septuagint' is, roughly, the O.T. in Greek; with a little more accuracy, it is a translation of the O.T. into Greek, with certain additional books, some, doubtless, translated, some originally composed in Greek. It is called the 'Septuagint' (usually abbreviated 'LXX.') because of a tradition that it was made by seventy, or more precisely seventy-two Jewish elders, at Alexandria, in the reign (284–247 B.C.) of Ptolemy Philadelphus, King of Egypt.

Any visitor to the British Museum can look, from a respectful distance, at one of the great volumes of the Codex Alexandrinus, as the manuscript of the Greek Bible there is called. It is written in 'uncial' or capital letters, and the words are not divided by spaces; so that an unpractised person might find it difficult to read, though it is far easier than the later 'cursive' or running-hand MSS. But it would be better, for practical purposes, to get a printed copy of the Septuagint, which can easily be done; and we will turn it over, and examine its contents, to gain some first ideas about it. Possibly we may want to compare it with the Hebrew; the Authorised Version in English, made from the Hebrew, will serve some of our needs, though not all. Let us then take our copy of the LXX., or O.T. in Greek, and see what it is like.

Looking through its contents, we see, first, that the books are not quite as we are used to see them. After Judges and Ruth, we come to 'Basileion A', that is, '1 Kingdoms'; and there appear to be four books of Kingdoms. We may, however, remember that the Authorised Version gives a second title to the Books of Samuel, 'otherwise called, the First (and Second) Books of Kings'; and similarly, our 1 and 2 Kings 'commonly called the Third and Fourth . . .' It would be natural to guess that there is some connexion between these names and our Septuagint titles, and the guess would be right. The Septuagint it was that (probably) divided Samuel and Kings (as well as Chronicles) each into halves, and called them the four books of Kingdoms; the Latin Vulgate calls them 1-4 Regum; and later the name of Samuel was restored to the former two.

The name 'Chronicles' is a rendering of the Hebrew 'Words (or 'events') of the Days'. This is changed to Paraleipomena, 'Things left out'. After this our printed copy most likely follows the Vatican MS., and continues with Esdras A, Esdras B, Psalms; the Petrograd follows Esdras B with Esther; our British Museum copy goes on here to the Prophets. Thus the MSS. differ as to the order of the books, and not one of them agrees with the order of our English Bible. We might have supposed that the English version followed the Hebrew; but on turning to the Hebrew Bible, we find that our familiar order differs no less from that; for there the Prophets follow next after Kings, and Chronicles stands last of all.

Nor do our names for the books follow the Hebrew with exactness. On the contrary, if we look back, we see that our names Genesis, Exodus, etc., come from the Septuagint: also Psalms. The Hebrew only names the five books of the Law as minor divisions, from the principal opening words of each:

B'reshith (In the beginning), V'elleh Sh'mōth (And these are the names), and so on.

We now come to Esdras A. On looking closer, it may be seen that this is not our 'Ezra', but that Ezra and Nehemiah together form Esdras B. This Esdras A is not in our English O.T. at all. If, however, we look at the Apocrypha, we shall find it there, as 1 Esdras. (2 Esdras of the Apocrypha is not known in Hebrew or Greek, but only in a Latin version; and the Vulgate arrangement of these books is different again. From one source or another, as many as six so-called Books of Esdras are reckoned; but we cannot discuss this here.) And now, looking on, we find that the Septuagint contains the other books of the Apocrypha, except 2 Esdras and the 'Prayer of Manasses'; dispersed in one order or another among the remaining books are Tobit, Judith, Wisdom (of Solomon), Wisdom of Sirach (Ecclesiasticus); and there follow, in one or other of our MSS., not only two, but four books of Maccabees. The additions to Esther, found in our Apocrypha, are here embodied in the book, in their natural sequence; the Song of the Three Children comes in its place in Daniel, as sung by Shadrach and his companions in the 'burning fiery furnace'; and 'Susanna' and 'Bel and the Dragon' follow at the end of Daniel. Similarly, Baruch, Lamentations, and the 'Epistle of Jeremy' follow Jeremiah in that order. These books of the Apocrypha, then, are not in the Hebrew Old Testament, but may be said to belong properly to the Septuagint.

Here it had better be said, that there are some hundreds of MSS., containing parts, greater or less, of the Septuagint. A few contain the whole of the O.T., some the N.T. as well; about thirty are written in uncials, these, as usual, being generally the older. Many small portions on vellum or papyrus have been unearthed in recent times, some of them even older than our four great Bibles. Speaking broadly, the uncials date from the fourth to the ninth century, the cursives from the ninth century to the establishment of printing. But no uncials, except the four, survive, which contained, so far as we know, the complete Bible in Greek. For the present it may be convenient to give a few facts concerning the four; a fuller list is given towards the end of Chapter X.

Codex Alexandrinus, in London, British Museum. Written in the fifth century A.D. Contains the O.T. nearly complete: small gaps in Gen. i. ii., a verse or two elsewhere. 1 Sam. xii. 18–xiv. 9, and Psalms xlix. 19–lxxxix. 10 are missing altogether. (Matt. i.–xxiv. wanting in N.T.) In England since 1627. Generally referred to by the symbol A.

Codex Vaticanus. Rome, Vatican Library. Fourth century. Genesis down to xlvi. 28, a few verses of 2 Samuel (2 Kingdoms), and Ps. cvi.–cxxxviii. are missing; the MS. never contained any book of Maccabees. In the Vatican Library since fifteenth century, except 1809–15. Is considered on the whole the best MS. of the LXX. Referred to as B.

Codex Sinaiticus. Petrograd, Imperial Library (part at Leipzig). Fourth century, perhaps later than B. Contains small fragments only of Genesis and Numbers, some chapters of 1 Chronicles–2 Esdras, but most of the Poetical Books and Prophets; not Hosea, Amos, or Micah. Brought from Sinai by Tischendorf in 1844 and 1859. Referred to as א (Aleph), or sometimes as S.

Codex Ephraemi rescriptus. Paris, National Library. Fifth century. Of the O.T. only fragments of Prov., Eccles., Song, Job, Wisdom, and Sirach remain. The MS. is a 'palimpsest'; *i.e.*, the writing was scraped or washed out, and other matter, in this case some works of St. Ephraem the Syrian, in a Greek version, was written on the parchment. The older writing underneath can still be read, but with difficulty. In France since sixteenth century. Referred to as C.

[It should be added that Cod. Basiliano-Vaticanus, at Rome, which contains considerable portions of the O.T. from Leviticus to Esther, and Cod. Venetus, in St. Mark's Library at Venice, which is nearly complete from Job xxx. to the end of the O.T., with four books of Maccabees, are now generally thought to be the corresponding parts of one MS. of the whole O.T. The Vatican MS. is known as N; the Venice as V, or as 23, because Holmes and Parsons, who compiled a great edition of the Septuagint, supposed it to be a cursive. (Uncials are generally known by capital letters, cursives by numerals, or small letters.) Eighth or ninth century.]

Some MSS. contain also a book of the 'Psalms of Solomon'; Cod. A, though it does not contain them now, names them at the end of its list of books. Also, Cod. A, and some other MSS. contain, after the Psalms, what may be called Hymns; *i.e.*, certain poetical passages, such as the Song of Miriam from Exod. xv., the Song of Moses from Deut. xxxii.,

Jonah's prayer, Hezekiah's prayer from Isa. xxxviii., and the Psalm of Habakkuk; as well as the *Magnificat, Nunc Dimittis*, and *Benedictus*, which belong correspondingly to the N.T. These passages therefore occur twice over in A. Lastly, there is a 'Morning Hymn', put together from Luke ii. 14, various Psalms, a few words based on Dan. iii. 52 (ver. 3 of the Song of the Three Children, in the Apocrypha); and a few lines of doxology and of prayer, some of which are found in the *Te Deum*. The greater part of this composition is recited in our Communion Service (as in the Mass), and is familiar under the name of *Gloria in Excelsis.*

There is a 151st Psalm in the Septuagint, which Cod. A however clearly marks as 'outside the number'. It seems to be founded on passages of Kings and the Psalms; but as it does not closely follow the LXX. of those passages, and is not in the Hebrew, its origin is doubtful.

If we now look through the Old Testament again, this time with an eye to smaller details, we shall find the Greek and the Hebrew occasionally differing in the order of chapters and parts of chapters, within the books. Full details cannot be given here; but we may notice some verses transposed, as in Gen. xxxi. 46–52; the Sixth Commandment in Ex. xx. follows the Eighth; the account of the Tabernacle, Ex. xxxv.–xl., differs much in order; verses are transposed, Ezek. vii. 3–9, Mal. iv. 4–6. So are the chapters, 1 Kings xx., xxi. The numbering is also somewhat different; the Psalms, without the extra one, number 150, but are differently divided; Psalms ix. and x. are joined together, so that the LXX. Psalms are mostly numbered one behind the Hebrew and English. There are other slight differences, so that only for the last three Psalms do the numbers coincide again. In Jeremiah, from chap. xxv., the transposition is extensive, and the references consequently differ; the main principle is that the prophecies against the foreign peoples are moved back from chap. xxxii. to xxv., and also differently arranged among themselves.

Further than this, the Septuagint sometimes contains less, sometimes more than the Hebrew text. These additions and omissions vary much in character, and cannot all be put down to one cause, either accident or design.

As the MSS. of the LXX. are considerably older than any existing Hebrew MS., and the actual date of the translation much older again, it has often been thought that the LXX. may represent, or bear witness to, an older text than the Hebrew Old Testament. This question must be dealt with later. For our present purpose, it will be convenient, without pre-judging, to regard the Hebrew as the standard (represented generally very fairly by the English translation), and to mark how the Septuagint deviates from it. In the Pentateuch we shall find generally less difference than elsewhere. There are reasons for this. The Law was regarded as specially sacred, and the Jews guarded and preserved the text most jealously. Even the Sadducees, who in the later history were the party most inclined to admit foreign, especially Greek, influence and culture, professed to hold fast by the Law, for all their cosmopolitanism, which, for Jews, was considerable. The Pentateuch, too, was almost certainly the first portion of the Old Testament to be translated, and the work is better done than the rest, and much better than some parts of it. Its translators were more at home than their successors, both with the original language, and generally, it would seem, with Greek. Their local—Egyptian—knowledge was also of some service. Evidence, largely internal, has been discovered, showing that the other books were not all translated at the same time, nor by the same hands.

[To this we may add, that our great MSS. seem to vary in character, in different books or groups of books; chiefly, it would seem, because they were copied, directly or indirectly, from originals which were produced at different times or places. To this we must return later.]

Even in the Pentateuch, however, we find divergences between the Hebrew and the Greek. For instance, in Genesis, the ages of the Patriarchs differ; the LXX. generally adds a hundred years to the age of each when his first son was born, and subtracts the same from the remainder of his life (Gen. v. xi.). This, if accepted as correct, alters the chronology, which here depends entirely on the statements of age, to a considerable extent, lengthening the periods from Adam to Noah, and from Noah to Abraham. Minor verbal divergences are often to be found. To give a few instances only; in Gen. vii. 3, LXX. adds 'which are clean' to the fowls, as though to correspond to the clean beasts just above. In Gen. xi., the chronology is further altered by inserting one Cainan (cf. Gen. v. 9–14) between Arphaxad and Salah. With this, it may be noticed, the list in Luke iii. (ver. 36) agrees. In Gen. xlix., as in most of the poetical and more difficult passages, the divergence is more marked;

many lines are apparently paraphrased. In ver. 10, we find 'a ruler' for the 'sceptre' or 'marshal's staff'; 'thighs' or 'loins' for 'feet'; and instead of 'Shiloh', 'that which is laid up for him', with a variety of readings in the MSS.; the verse ending with 'And he (is) the expectation of nations'. Wide as the divergence appears to be over 'Shiloh', the translators are evidently trying to render something very close to our Hebrew text, and may be near the right track; moreover, the Hebrew is difficult and uncertain. (There is a curious resemblance to this passage in Ezek. xxi. 27.) Other versions have some likeness to LXX. here.

In Exodus, among the transposed chapters, xxxv.–xl., some verses are altogether absent from the Greek; as xxxv. 8, and several verses in the two following chapters. In Deut. xxxii., ver. 43 is expanded into a kind of eight-line stanza, ending with 'and the Lord will purify the land of His people.' Here lines 1, 3, part of 6, and 8 correspond to the Heb.; the verb in the last line probably represents the same text. The parallelism of the Greek is obvious. So, throughout the translation, here and there a verse is expanded, shortened, or omitted; and words or phrases are added, omitted, or varied. For instance, the Greek adds a further list of towns to Josh. xv. 59; in Josh. xxiv., it adds a verse in the place of 31, and gives the Heb. 31 after 28. In 1 Sam. xiii., ver. 1 (where Heb. is not clear) is omitted; ver. 2 agrees with the Heb., which begins with 'And.'

In Psalm xiv., the Septuagint, besides inserting 'where no fear was' in ver. 5, as in the parallel Psalm liii., has also three extra verses, which we know from Romans iii. 14–18, and even more familiarly from our Prayer-Book version of the Psalms. These verses appear to be a compilation from other Psalms, and from Isa. lix. 7 (=Prov. i. 16); and it is to be noticed that this verse of Proverbs is absent from the better MSS. of the LXX. The Greek both adds and omits several verses in Proverbs. In Isaiah, ii. 22, xxxviii. 15, lvi. 12, and practically xl. 7, are absent from the Greek; other verses are shortened, and the additions throughout the book are very small. These are but a few instances of what is found.

Large portions of the version appear to be decidedly literal; the Hebrew order of words is often exactly preserved, which of course would not be possible in English, as it is in Greek. Thus, in Gen. ii. 4–9, though there are slight differences in the translation, it is still almost word for word in the same order. In ver. 4, LXX. have given the more usual order, 'heaven and earth', perhaps by inadvertence and force of habit; in ver. 5, they could not begin the clause with *γάρ*. In ver. 9 *ἔτι* is inserted, and in ver. 11, *ἐκεῖ οὗ* . . . they have changed the Heb. order and idiom, though in similar phrases they often follow it. But the slightness of these exceptions shows how closely the general order is followed. This practice makes it easier, in many cases, to see what the translators thought the Hebrew before them was.

A few books are rendered with more tendency to paraphrase: *e.g.*, Job, and much of Proverbs. Esdras A and Daniel (see below) are regarded as paraphrases; and in each case there is extant a more literal version as well. The Psalms generally are rendered with an attempt to be literal. So are the Prophets; when there seems to be paraphrase, it is probably because the translators found themselves in difficulties, and could not achieve literal exactness.

In comparing passages of no special difficulty, the Authorised Version in English will be found of great use, because its most careful use of *italics* shows at a glance what words are supplied, as not being expressed in the Hebrew. In Gen. i. 2, *was*, in 4 *it was*, in 9 *land*, are so marked; and in each case we see that the Greek can render without supplying additional words. We learn also, if we did not know it before, that the verb 'to be' is often unexpressed in Hebrew.

The best edition, beyond doubt, of the Septuagint for ordinary use is the Cambridge 'manual' edition, *The Old Testament in Greek*. This gives the text according to B (or A, in Genesis, where B is deficient); and in footnotes it gives the readings of a few other uncial MSS. At the beginning of Genesis there are D (the 'Cotton Genesis'; only fragments now remain, preserved at the British Museum, but many of its other readings are known) and E (the Bodleian Genesis, at Oxford); D is probably of the fifth or sixth, E of the ninth century. Here we see that in Gen. i. 14 AD read εἰς φαῦσιν, E has ὥστε φαίνειν: the wording differs, but the sense is the same. In vi. 2, we find that A (though doubtfully) and E have the interesting reading 'the angels of God' for 'the sons of God.' We know that MSS. of ancient authors usually differ to some extent in readings. What we have to notice here is, that many of the important differences between MSS. of the Septuagint seem due not so much to corruption of the Greek text by accidental errors of copyists, as to other causes. The copyists here (as also in the New Testament) appear very often to have written down their different words deliberately, and with some reason for doing so; and, as a rule, they have not written mere unintelligible corruptions, such as are found in MSS., say of Æschylus (where, for instance, *Choephoroe* 544, an iambic line, is written ουφεισεπασαστταργανηπλειζετο). Where the Septuagint is unintelligible, as it does sometimes seem to be, there *may* be corruption in the Greek; but it is oftener due to other reasons, connected rather with the translation than the copying. We cannot now give many details about this; a few examples must serve to show the kind of differences and difficulties that occur.

[The study of the differences between MSS. of a book, with a view to finding the best reading, is called Textual Criticism. Where it is a question, not merely of MSS. of onc book, but involving different books, different versions of a book, or an original book and one or more translations of it, I have ventured to call it Intertextual Criticism. This is, of course, constantly required, where the Hebrew O.T., the Septuagint, and perhaps other versions also, have to be compared.]

In Gen. xxii. 13, Heb. has, 'behold, a ram behind (him)': LXX. has, 'behold, one ram', ἰδοὺ κριὸς εἷς. Now Hebrew marks its vowels only by dots or points above or below the consonants, except that a weak consonant, Aleph, Vav, or Yod,[1] carries a vowel, so to speak, sometimes, especially at the beginning of a word; and these 'points' were not invented till long after the Septuagint was made, and even after our

[1] Aleph is a mere breathing, ' : Vav is v or w : Yod is i or y. See Appendix, Heb. alphabet.

older MSS. of it were written. Disregarding vowels, therefore, except at the beginning of words, the Heb. for 'behind' is AHR, and for 'one' it is AHD. In Heb., D and R are very much alike; so that there can hardly be a doubt that LXX. read the word, rightly or wrongly, with D; and in fact several Hebrew MSS. read it so also, as well as other versions. We shall have to return to this matter of D and R; but first, look at the end of the sentence in the Greek, σαβὲκ τῶν κεράτων. We know no such Greek word as σαβέκ. Moreover, if we take ἐν φυτῷ as it almost must be, as equivalent to 'in a thicket', the word is superfluous. But look at the Hebrew; there we find that the word for 'thicket' is SBQ, with the very same consonants (as Greek has no Q). Here, then, the LXX. has 'transliterated' the word—copied it in Greek letters—as well as endeavoured to translate it. There is a 'doublet' or duplicate; either due to the translators, if they put what they thought to be the meaning, and, not being quite certain, added the Heb. word as a kind of security; or else, as is more probable, inserted from another Greek version. One later translator was prone to 'transliterate' thus; and it is most likely from his work, and has been inserted in LXX. manuscripts from some copy which contained both versions.

On the question, above, between 'behind' and 'one,' the Vulgate (Jerome's translation from the Heb., about A.D. 400) is against the LXX., and has *post tergum*. But in Gen. xiv. 14, Vulg. and LXX. agree; that Abram 'counted' or 'numbered', Heb. that he 'let loose' (A.V. 'armed', margin and R.V. 'led forth') his servants. This is another case of D and R; Heb.

has YRQ, the versions probably read YDQ. So, in Ex. xxi. 29, 36, Heb. speaks of the man 'keeping in' the dangerous ox, S^{H}MR; LXX. of 'destroying' it, S^{H}MD. So in the list of Javan's sons, Gen. x. 4, Heb. has 'Dodanim,' LXX. has Ῥόδιοι, with which the corresponding list, 1 Chron. i. 7, agrees. But the ordinary texts of the Vulgate have *Dodanim* in both places. The LXX. has Ῥοδίων again for 'Dedan' in Ezek. xxviii. 15. The confusion, or the doubt, between this D or R recurs constantly. Other letters also give rise to confusion; especially the semi-vowels Vav and Yod, and some others. In Isa. viii. 12, Heb. has 'Say ye not, Conspiracy, to all to whom this people shall say, Conspiracy' (cf. 2 Kings xi. 14). But the LXX. have σκληρόν, twice; so that they drift away from the meaning, and with another slight alteration give 'Say ye not a stubborn thing; for everything that this people speaketh is stubborn.' Now 'stubborn' would be in Heb. QS^{H}H, and 'Conspiracy' is QS^{H}R; there can be no doubt that LXX. read the former, and it looks very like the Hebrew. Therefore no support is given by LXX. to some who wish to read QDS^{H}, though the resemblance is fairly close. [In Heb. S^{H} and one S are the same letter, differently dotted; and these also are easily confused; without the dots, there is no difference.]

The LXX. version of 'Precept upon precept, line upon line', Isa. xxviii. 10, 13, is 'Receive affliction on affliction, hope on hope.' Here ^{T}ZV has been read as ^{T}ZR, and the next word, QV, wrongly interpreted, as it is several times in the chapter; till the sense is quite lost, and some verses are scarcely coherent. This, we saw before, happens more often in poetic and prophetic passages, where the Heb., with flights of eloquence and abrupt transitions, is harder to follow than in narrative, where the context, and sometimes general knowledge of the story, makes clues easier to find and to hold.

It may have struck the reader before this, that the New Testament quotes many passages from the Old; and it may be as well to look at a few, and compare them in each place. Let us try the Psalms: Ps. ii. 1 is quoted in Acts iv. 25; and ver. 7 of the same Psalm in Acts xiii. 33, and Heb. i. 5, v. 5. On looking them out, we find that the N.T. agrees exactly with the Greek of the LXX.; which cannot be chance; for the Heb. might be rendered in many ways in Greek; while the form of the Greek word for 'rage furiously' occurs nowhere else.

Ps. viii. 2, again, is quoted in Matt. xxi. 16 strictly according to the LXX., and it will be found that this is the case with the majority of quotations. On the other hand, Zech. ix. 9 is quoted, Matt. xxi. 5, in words which agree nearly with LXX. at the beginning, but nearer Heb. at the end; in John xii. 15, with no close resemblance to LXX. Clearly, if LXX. gives a close rendering of the Hebrew, it can only be recognised by the wording of the Greek; if not, it is at once evident whether the N.T. writer used it or not. If the quotation is not from LXX., nor from any other known Greek version, it must be examined to see how far it tallies with the Hebrew; for the age of our present Hebrew text is an important question.

Isa. vi. 9, 10 is quoted five times in the N.T., in Matt. xiii. 14, Mark iv. 12, Luke viii. 10, John xii. 40, Acts xxviii. 26. Here Matt. and the Acts quote direct from the LXX., while Mark and Luke can hardly be said to depart from it, though they have shortened the quotation. But John quotes freely, approaching the LXX. only towards the end of the passage; though the resemblance to the Heb. is not very close (unles it can be supposed that the writer was influenced by Aramaic forms; see Bp. Lightfoot, *Biblical Essays*, p. 137). Many quotations made direct from the LXX. occur in the Epistle to the Hebrews; as Ps. xl. 6–8 in Heb. x. 6, with the purely Septuagintal reading, 'a body hast thou prepared me', which is possibly due to corruption of the Greek text. So also Prov. xi. 31 appears, 1 Pet. iv. 18, in its Septuagint form, 'if the righteous scarcely be saved, where shall the ungodly and the sinner appear?' which divulges markedly from the Hebrew.

This matter of N.T. quotations from the O.T. can be conveniently studied with the help of Westcott and Hort's edition of the Greek New Testament, which, besides giving a full list, marks O.T. allusions and quotations by special type. See also Prof. Swete's *Introd. to O.T. in Greek*, part iii. chap. 2.

We can scarcely have examined the Septuagint even so far as this, without noticing that the Greek in which it is written is mostly somewhat different from the 'classical' language, as written by Thucydides, Plato, or Demosthenes. It is more like that in which many books of the New Testament are written, and may remind some readers, from time to time, of Polybius, the historian of the second century B.C. Of late years a great quantity of writing, chiefly on papyrus, has been discovered in Egypt;

and the general verdict of scholars who have examined these papyri is, that their language, the current Greek in Egypt of the two or three centuries before and after the birth of Christ, strongly resembles the Greek of the Septuagint. Still, some are struck by what had been noticed long before these papyri were studied; namely, the Hebrew colouring and constructions, found mainly, of course, in the *translated* books which form the greater part of the Septuagint; the other view, however, is gaining ground. Yet the short sentences, due to the style of the original, and the absence of variety in their modes of connexion, do remind a reader of the Hebrew; and some constructions and phrases are distinctly Hebraic in cast, even though the papyri may contain similar sentences; for instance, *δύο δύο*, Gen. vii. 2, 3, etc., *προσέθηκεν τεκεῖν*, iv. 2, *ἀνὰ μέσον τοῦ φωτὸς καὶ ἀνὰ μέσον τοῦ σκότους*, i. 4, *ἡ γῆ ἐφ' ἧς σὺ καθεύδεις ἐπ' αὐτῆς*, xxviii. 13. Such expressions, too, recur constantly in the Septuagint. The *ideas* are often, necessarily, rather Semitic than Greek; to give one instance, 'thy desire shall be to thy husband,' Gen. iii. 16; and the translators, doing their best to be literal, have produced a rendering which might have puzzled an ordinary Athenian.

Many forms of words occur, as we may see, characteristic of later Greek than the classical period; and some constructions, which, though not Hebraic, are not strictly classical Greek. But more conspicuous is the disappearance of many Attic constructions and devices. The optative mood has disappeared from almost all dependent clauses, and from indirect speech; indicative tenses follow *ὅταν*, as Gen. xxxviii. 9, and ὡς ἄν, as Gen. vi. 4. New augmented forms are used, as ἠνεῴχθην, Gen. vii. 11, viii. 6, ἀπεκατέστησεν, xxiii. 16; 3rd persons plur. in imperfects and second aorists end in -σαν, as εγεννῶσαν, Gen. vi. 4, ἐφάγοσαν, xviii. 8, εἰσήλθοσαν, Ex. i. 1, and in optatives, as αἰνέσαισαν, Gen. xlix. 8. We now find σκότος, ἔλεος, and a few other such words as neuters (3rd decl.); the neut. sing. σωτήριον is common; conversely, λογός is now the usual form; νῖκος takes the place of νίκη. The vocabulary is much changed, and on the whole, enlarged; many words have taken on an altered or special meaning, to suit the new ideas with which the Greek language had hitherto been little concerned; ἄγγελος, εἴδωλον, ἐκκλησία, are instances of one kind, ἔθνη of another.

The Proper Names in the Septuagint will also attract notice. As both text and footnotes will show, the MSS. have often made havoc of them, when unfamiliar. Many names of *persons* are indeclinable; others have been furnished with Greek terminations and forms of declension. Thus Hebrew names ending in -iah have it changed to -ias. From the New Testament we are familiar with *Esaias* and *Judas*, and the uninstructed have sometimes been confused by *Jesus* in Acts vii. 45, Heb. iv. 8. Names of *places*, apart from their form, often raise questions as to their identity. Some receive their correct Greek equivalents, as *Azotus* for Ashdod, 1 Sam. v. 1, etc., *Tanis* for Zoan, Numb. xiii. 22, etc., *Syria* as a rule for Aram, *Ethiopia* for Cush, and so forth. The practice varies in different books or parts of books; thus Tyre, Heb. Tzor, is sometimes Σόρ, sometimes Τύρος. Some equivalents given are doubtful, some clearly wrong: *Cappadocia* is for Caphtor, Deut. ii. 23, Amos ix. 7; *Carchedon*, the regular Greek for Carthage, stands for Tarshish in Isa. xxiii., cf. Ezek. xxvii. 12, xxxviii. 13; while 'Persians' for Sinim, Isa. xlix. 12, seems to be a mere guess without probability. In 2 Chronicles the *Troglodytes*, xii. 3, the *Amazones*, xiv. 15, and *Alimazones*, xxii. 1, argue either too much or too little knowledge on the translators' part, since there is no sign of them in the Hebrew; for the *Minaeans*, xxvi. 7, cf. xx. 1 and 1 Chron. iv. 41. In Isa. iii. 22, LXX.'s 'Laconian gauzes' might seem a gratuitous anachronism.

There are some simple instances of corruption in the Greek of proper names, where the letters are alike in shape, as Dael for Lael in Num. iii. 24. In 1 Chron. iv. 21 Laadah is represented by Ἀαδά in A and Μαδάθ in B. Remembering what was said about Heb. D and R, it is not surprising, if *Aram* and *Edom* are sometimes confused in the Hebrew; as in 2 Sam. viii. 12. On the other hand the slip between *Judaea* and *Idumaea* is purely a matter of the Greek: Amos i. 9, 11; Isa. vii. 6, etc.

Sometimes the forms in which names occur in the LXX. are due to the difference between the Hebrew and Greek alphabets and sounds. Hebrew is rich in sibilants and gutturals, which the Greeks found impossible to distinguish or to pronounce. (English has some advantage over Greek, in separating S from Sh; how could LXX. have rendered Judg. xii. 6 adequately? but Greek can distinguish Zechariah and Tzephaniah, though it fails with Amo(t)z and Amos.) The Tz of Tzor and Tzidon has usually become T in one, S in the other. The only Hebrew guttural that

Greek can indicate capably, is Cheth, the strongest, by χ, as in Ἀχαάβ, Ἀχειτόφελ; Aleph and He are generally unrepresented, except at the beginning of words. Here English is but little better in its practice; *Abraham* has its proper h, which Greek omits, but *A(h)aron* has not, and *Achab* is unusual and possibly misleading; in *Isaac*, *Jacob*, and *Esau*, the gutturals are lost altogether, which is scarcely to be regretted, as no scientific method could comfortably naturalise Yishchaq, Ya'aqob, and 'Esav. The difficult letter Ayin is sometimes represented by the Greek smooth breathing, as in *Ezra*, *Amalek*, *Abednego*, *Uzziah*, and *Eber*, while in *Hebrew* the aspirate is used (though see 1 *Hen. IV.* II. iv. 198); but γ sometimes appears, especially before ο, as in Γοθονιήλ, Γοθολία, and in *Gomorrah*, where English has adopted it, also in *Gaza* (*Azzah* in Deut. ii. 23, etc.), and in the middle of words, as Χοδολλογόμορ, cf. Θαλγά, Gen. xiv. 1; Βεελφεγώρ, Num. xxv. 3. A few confusions may be noticed: *Omri* (initial Ayin) is not distinguished, in the older MSS., from his predecessor *Zimri*, and both appear as Ζαμβρεί, see 1 Kings xvi. 16; Mic. vi. 16; *Ophir* is usually Σουφείρ, though not in Gen. x. 29; cf. B's Σεμιούδ, Σουφί, Num. xxxiv. 20, 23. There is also an apparent tendency to add or strengthen final consonants; Σαλωμών, Εὐειλάτ = Havilah, Φάλεκ = Peleg, Θολάεκ and Φούτ, 1 Chron. vii. 1, 'Ελιβέμας, Φόγωρ, Gen. xxxvi. 14, 39.

The LXX. seems to have influenced the forms of many names in the English Bible. See the Appendix on the Hebrew alphabet.

Turning over the pages once more, and looking at the foot-notes, we see that in Judges, though the readings of only one MS. are quoted, the quantity of notes is very large. When this is noticed earlier, as in some chapters of Joshua, it may be due to the lists of proper names, or some exceptional cause; but in Judges it is constantly the case. Looking closer, we see that many of these notes, instead of being concerned with small variants, involve complete changes of words and phrases. The difference between A and B is, in fact, here so large that they are considered to give distinct 'recensions' or editions of the Greek, if not two different versions. (In the larger Cambridge edition both texts appear, on opposite pages, each with the variants of the MSS. that mainly support it. A separate edition of A's has been issued, for comparison with the 'manual' edition.) The merits of the two texts have not been finally determined; but the opinion prevails that B is not, in Judges, of such relative excellence as in many, or most, of the other books. In 1 Sam. (1 Kingdoms) xvii., xviii., a long foot-note shows us that B omits many verses, which A supplies; the same occurs at 1 Kings (3 Kingdoms) ix. 15. Passing over some smaller differences of a similar kind, we see that at 1 Kings xii. 24 B has a long passage—23 verses of much more than average length—which A, in its turn, omits. There is also a shorter passage at xvi. 28 inserted by B and not by A.

Now, firstly, we may notice that B's narrative amounts to a rather different version of the stories, fairly consistent as it stands, if not entirely free from difficulties. Secondly, we see that A, on the other hand, agrees generally with the English version, that is, with the Hebrew. Thirdly, if we read the passages which A, but not B, inserts, we may see signs that the style is not quite that of the general run, so far, of the Septuagint. It is difficult to be sure at first; but in 1 Kings ix. 15, we find the word σύν before an ordinary accusative of the object, and the same thing occurs again two or three times below. Now this curious, apparently meaningless, insertion of σύν is known to be a practice of one Aquila—he had his reasons—who translated the O.T. from the Hebrew very literally into Greek, about A.D. 130; considerably later than the Septuagint, but well before the date of our MSS. Some fragments of his work have been discovered of late years, and some MSS. of the LXX. give extracts in margin or text, and sometimes attribute them to him or to other later translators. He seems to have worked from a Hebrew text very like our present one. We may surmise, then, that these A passages do not belong to the original LXX., which may never have contained them; apparently it did not, as B omits them altogether, and A supplies them in this different style. Closer examination, especially in Kings, will show some more slight traces of Aquila in A, and a few even in B. But these traits of style are found regularly in Ecclesiastes; and the Greek version of that book is now suspected of being Aquila's work, possibly an early draft of his translation, as the extracts we possess elsewhere of Aquila's Ecclesiastes do not tally exactly with it.

On somewhat similar grounds the work of another later translator, Theodotion, is identified here and there in Job and Jeremiah. In Daniel, we know from the writings of Origen and Jerome that

Theodotion's version superseded the Septuagint; and the Greek MSS. now extant contain only Theodotion's Daniel, excepting one cursive, which is supported by a Syriac version. It is this Theodotion who occasionally 'transliterates' a word instead of translating it; otherwise his style is not unlike the later books of the LXX. Some editions print the two translations side by side.

The book of Tobit is also found in two editions, Aleph (S) differing considerably from AB. A third edition of some passages is said to occur in a few cursives. Ecclesiasticus also is found in a shorter version in the great uncials, and a fuller one in some important cursives. The A.V. follows the latter, R.V. the former.

We may now sum up the results of our first survey. Its object has been, not to answer questions and solve difficulties, but to see what the questions and the difficulties are; to gain some notion what the Septuagint is like, and why it is worth studying.

The LXX., then, was made in Egypt, from the third to the first century B.C. Our oldest MSS. of it (neglecting small fragments) date from about A.D. 350 to near 500; four to five centuries before the oldest Hebrew MS. Thus the question arises, does the Septuagint possibly represent an older and purer text of the Old Testament than that obtained from the Hebrew MSS.?

Some of the names by which we call the books are taken from the LXX. Our familiar order of the books, from Judges onward, is neither that of the Hebrew, nor that of the LXX.; but the Greek rearrangement seems to have been carried further, the books grouped according to the nature of their contents, with an attempt at chronological order within the groups.

The Septuagint contains every book of the Hebrew, and also some others, which are interspersed among those of the Hebrew list. These others the English Bible sets apart, and most of them form our Apocrypha. Several of them show signs of having been translated from a Semitic language; some were, doubtless, originally composed in Greek. Our MSS. contain yet a few other books, and some poetical passages (O. and N.T.) used as canticles, besides the *Gloria in Excelsis.* Here appears a link between the LXX. and our Book of Common Prayer.

The Septuagint diverges, in many ways, from what an exact Greek translation of the Hebrew, as we know it, would be. The order of some passages differs; there are additions and omissions; there are verbal disagreements, greater and less. The amount of divergence varies in different books; it is least, on the whole, in the Pentateuch, which is the best part of the version, and doubtless the oldest. In some books, as Kings, Job, Proverbs, Jeremiah, the omissions and insertions are numerous and important. In Psalm xiv. are inserted three verses, made up from other passages of the Bible, which occur (as a quotation?) in Romans iii., and have found their way into our Prayer-Book version. There is thus an evident connexion between our Prayer-Book Psalter and the LXX., though Ps. xl. 6 shows that there is independence also.

The character of the translation is often closely

literal; it also preserves, in most places, the Hebrew order of the words, to an extent which English cannot. It paraphrases at times, but in many books this seems only to be done when the translators were uncertain as to the exact meaning. Often it represents the Hebrew closely enough for a skilled scholar to be able to reconstruct much of the original from it. Clearly, therefore, it affords valuable side-lights upon the Hebrew, and though further from it in some ways, in others it gives us a nearer approach than any English translation can.

The MSS., like those of most ancient works, vary one from another, at times considerably. (The Hebrew MSS. of the O.T. are peculiar in resembling one another closely.) They diverge only occasionally because of corruption in the Greek itself; more often because those which we possess were copied, directly or indirectly, from others which represented various recensions of the text. The explanation must then be sought in the history of the Septuagint, which, as we shall see in the next chapter, is complex. Nor were our MSS. copied from entire Bibles, which can seldom have existed; their originals must have been rolls containing each a single book, or a small group of books. Thus each of our large MSS. may, in fact usually does, differ in character of text in different parts.

Still, the divergence between the LXX., so far as we can determine its true text, and the Hebrew as we have it, is much more marked than that between the Greek MSS. Of all the principal versions, the LXX. differs most from the Hebrew. There is divergence of every kind and of every degree; in some few verses it may be said that not a word in Heb. and Greek agree. The questions, why the texts differ, and which is preferable, must be faced later. It is harder to reconstruct the history than in the case of the LXX. itself alone. But we shall probably find grounds for a working hypothesis, that, on the one hand, the LXX., comparatively early in date, may sometimes be right, and must regularly be considered, in questions of order and arrangement, perhaps also where the *matter* differs decidedly; but that, on the other, though in theory the LXX. may have preserved, in some details, a better text, yet, when practically studied, the tendency to trust it against the Hebrew in matters of a letter, a word, or a phrase, is discouraged by observing how often the Greek translators misread, or misunderstood their original. Their support, when they agree, counts in some ways far more than their divergence. It must be remembered that, whatever view be taken of the Hebrew, the Septuagint can lay no claim to inspiration.

We can often see what the translators took their original to be, and compare it with the extant Hebrew; and it is seldom preferable. This is a broad statement, with which some would disagree; mostly, perhaps, those who have not studied the Greek specially and continuously, but have devoted themselves chiefly to Semitic studies, and are inclined to treat the Hebrew with boldness and freedom, using the LXX. as a make-weight against it. It is quite possible, certainly, that the LXX. may, in some non-Hebrew readings, point to old traditions; many such, if not probably right, may yet be interesting. Even their mistakes are often instructive; and few of their readings should be discarded and lost sight of as altogether without possible value.

Quotations made by the N.T. writers from the O.T. are frequently, though not always, in exact or fairly close verbal agreement with the LXX.; even when this differs markedly from the Hebrew. The N.T. writers vary in their practice, which can be ascertained and summarised.

The language in which the LXX. is written is, briefly, that which was used throughout the Greek-speaking world after Alexander's conquests had produced their effect. It is often called the *κοινὴ διάλεκτος*, or simply the *κοινή*. It has also been known as 'Hellenistic' Greek. Opinions differ, to some extent, on the point how far the Greek of the LXX. is affected by Hebrew idioms. The modern study of the papyri has led many to think that the influence of Hebrew is slighter than was formerly held to be the case.

The Proper Names show in various ways the relations between the Hebrew and the Greek alphabets. They also throw light on the translators' knowledge of history, geography, and traditions connected with the O.T. Their Egyptian knowledge is frequently perceptible.

In some books, *e.g.*, Judges, Daniel, Tobit, more than one version seems to have been current; in others, as Job, a shorter version seems to have been supplemented from later sources. Traces appear of later Greek translations, fragments of which are found in the margin and notes of some MSS., and have also sometimes intruded into the text. This, and the fact that the LXX. was more than once edited in early time, make its textual criticism a complicated matter.[1]

Such are, briefly, the results of our opening survey; it is at any rate clear that there is room for plenty of study. Various questions have been raised, which this book cannot attempt to answer fully. It will now be necessary to return to them separately, and try to get the student a few steps further on his way; first tracing the history of the Septuagint, so far as it is known, or reasonably inferred. This history, especially the earlier part, should throw light on some of the questions that have been brought to our notice.

[1] As an eminent authority once put it in private talk some years ago, 'The one thing certain about the Septuagint at present is, that it is—not the Septuagint.' This paradox-epigram of course purposely overstates the case; he meant that the true text can only be extracted with difficulty, and sometimes with uncertainty, from the mixture which is found in our MSS. Also, it has come to seem decidedly likely that some books are not the Alexandrian version at all, but the work of Aquila and Theodotion.

CHAPTER II

EARLY HISTORY OF THE SEPTUAGINT (TO A.D. 500)

The 'Letter of Aristeas'—Date and place of the making of the Septuagint—Evidence of the N.T. writers, etc.—Spread and range of the LXX.—Its popularity—Adopted by Christian Church—Hostility of the Jews—Aquila, and other translators—Origen and the Hexapla—The three editions that followed Origen—Versions in other languages—Mostly made from LXX.—The Old Latin—Jerome, and the Vulgate—The LXX. ceases to be generally used—Ways in which its influence survives.

THE traditional story of the making of the Septuagint has already been mentioned. It runs somewhat as follows. Ptolemy Philadelphus, King of Egypt, who encouraged the extension of the great library founded by his father, desired, on the strength of suggestions made by his librarian, Demetrius of Phalerum, to obtain a copy of the Jewish Laws for the library, and, to this end, to have the necessary Greek translation made. The King, accordingly, after inquiring into the subject of these laws, sent an embassy to Eleazar, the high priest at Jerusalem; with a letter, stating that as great numbers of Jews had been brought to Egypt by the Persians, and others, more lately, as prisoners, by his own father, he was setting them free. As a favour to these Jews in Egypt, and others scattered through the world, he wished their Law to be translated into Greek. He asked, therefore, to have sent to him six elders of each tribe, capable of making this translation. With this letter were sent handsome presents and offerings to the Temple, which are described in detail. Eleazar, answering cordially, despatched the seventy-two elders, whose names and tribes are given. He bade them an affectionate farewell, and in answer to questions from the envoys, discoursed to them at some length on the regulations of the Law. When the elders arrived at Alexandria, the king gave them a magnificent welcome, and feasted them on seven days; putting questions, before each day's banquet, to ten or eleven of the number, which are recorded, with the wise answers made to him by each elder. After this, they were taken to a quiet house by the seashore, where they carried out their work; which was finished, and their renderings agreed upon, by a happy coincidence, in seventy-two days, Demetrius himself acting as scribe and secretary. On the conclusion of the work, the Jews of Alexandria were assembled, and the translation was read to them, and applauded; and it was decided, that as it had been executed 'well, and piously, and with perfect accuracy,' it should remain, under penalty of a curse, unaltered and unrevised. The king was informed, and the whole work was read to him; he ordered that the books should be carefully guarded, and bade a cordial farewell to the translators, giving them handsome presents, and sending great gifts to the high priest Eleazar.

Such is the story, as told at length in the 'Letter of Aristeas to Philocrates.' 'Aristeas,' the narrator, represents himself as a Greek attached to the court of Philadelphus, and as a member of the embassy to Eleazar. His story is repeated, or referred to, by Aristobulus, an Alexandrian writer quoted by Eusebius; by the Alexandrian Jew Philo, and by Josephus; and by Christian writers, Irenaeus, Clement of Alexandria, Augustine, and Epiphanius, who give currency to sundry embellishments of the story, as that the translators worked in pairs, shut up in cells, and that their translations of the whole, thus separately made, were found to be in exact verbal agreement. The author of a work known as *Cohortatio ad Graecos* (according to some, Justin Martyr) claims to have seen the remains of the cells where the work was done. Jerome, however, dismisses the cell story, pointing out that Aristeas and Josephus say nothing of it.

If abundance of detail, and of supporters of the tradition, were all that could be required, this account might well have ranked as history. But modern critics have dealt unsparingly with it, and it has not emerged unscathed. In the sixteenth century it began to be doubted whether 'Aristeas'' letter was all that it professed to be; and in 1684 Hody, afterwards Professor of Greek at Oxford, showed that it was not. It is now generally agreed that the author betrays himself to be in reality a Jew, and no Greek courtier; his history is faulty, for Demetrius was never librarian, was not in favour with Philadelphus, and died in exile very early in his reign. A success referred to as won at sea over Antigonus, took place nearly forty years after the death of Demetrius; unless a battle, earlier indeed, but still not early enough, has been manufactured into a victory from a defeat! There are phrases apparently borrowed from the very Septuagint whose origin he is describing; and others which seem to betray the writer as later than Philadelphus, and not his contemporary. There are possibly references to the prologue of the Greek Sirach; and in two places there are, as in Aristobulus, what seem to be allusions to some earlier renderings of the Hebrew Scriptures into Greek. It is hardly now regarded as possible to contend that 'Aristeas to Philocrates' is either a genuine letter, or written at the time when the supposed events happened.

On the other hand, it is recognised that a foundation of truth underlies the tale, rejecting, of course, the embellishments of Epiphanius, and any anachronisms proved to be such. Jew though the real author be, he draws skilfully upon non-Jewish sources for the geography of Palestine, and the wisdom displayed in the king's questions to the elders, and their answers; while his knowledge of the Alexandrian city and court seems to be exact and trustworthy. We may believe, then, without hesitation, that the Law—the Pentateuch—with which alone Aristeas is concerned, was translated at Alexandria, probably within fifty years of the date indicated in the 'Letter.' The translation of the remaining books followed, bit by bit, during the next century and a half. In some cases, one book of a group may have been translated first, as 1 Kingdoms among the historical books, or Isaiah among the prophets; or again, some separate passages, used as lessons in the synagogue, may have been, first interpreted, when these lessons were read, then committed to writing, and later used as instalments of the translation of those books in which they occur. Various hands would of course be employed in the work, as it extended over several generations; and the books which do not belong to the Hebrew Old Testament, whether original or translated, were added, from time to time, to the Alexandrian collection. In the case of the younger Ben-Sira (Sirach) we have the translator of one of these books avowing himself as such; and it is conjectured that he may have taken part in other translations also. The date of his arrival in Egypt is generally agreed to have been 132 B.C.;[1] so that his work may reasonably be placed in the next ten to fifteen years. By 100 B.C. or thereabouts, the Greek Bible must have been nearly complete. It is not necessary to believe that the work of translation must have owed its beginning to Philadelphus, his librarian, or his courtiers. In the story told by 'Aristeas,' we can scarcely separate the part played by the king, the embassy, and the high priest from the visit of translators from Palestine to Egypt. Now the best authorities perceive no clear signs of Palestinian knowledge or influence in the translation generally; while on the other hand they point to an occasional Egyptian word, to Egyptian influence on the spelling (though this may be due to copyists), and to signs of Egyptian local knowledge. But as the name of Alexandria perpetuates to this day, above all the other like foundations, the conqueror's memory; so the great city stood at the head of all the outlying Greek culture which he had spread

[1] For a different view, see below, p. 142.

abroad, and of the diffused Greek speech which accompanied that culture. The conquered Jews and the conquering Greeks were both dispersed among the 'nations' and the 'barbarians.' Over the regions where these two dispersions coincided — roughly speaking, the countries covered by St. Paul's known journeys, with Egypt, Cyrenaica, and a large tract eastward to Babylonia and Parthia—there was no greater centre than Alexandria, where Greek influence was of the strongest, and where there was for many generations a large and generally thriving Jewish element. These Jews, the more when concentrated in a Greek city, naturally came to learn the Greek language, and in time to forget their own; and the result was, that they came to have absolute need of a Greek version of their Scriptures. To this need, probably, more than to the encouragement of literature at the court of the Ptolemies, is due the origin of the Septuagint. To it, certainly, is due its continued spread and use; the practical encouragement which consists in reading, and the consequent multiplying of copies.

Thus we find, that by the time of the Apostles, the Septuagint was widely used and known; and it seems to have been generally welcomed, by all classes that used it. We have already seen how it is quoted, though not exclusively, by the writers of the New Testament; Philo (*fl.* A.D. 40) makes constant and copious use of it; Josephus knows the Greek version, as well as the Hebrew; and fragments of other less known writers have been preserved, which tell the same tale, and carry it rather further back in time; the Alexandrian historian Demetrius, and the poet Ezekiel, quoted by Clement of Alexandria, are instances. Close study of some of the later books of the LXX. also makes it clear that, while the translators are not the same as those of the earlier ones, they used their predecessors' work. Isaiah's translator seems to have known something of the Greek Pentateuch; the author of Wisdom uses Exodus, perhaps other books of the Pentateuch, and also Isaiah; 4 Maccabees quotes from several books; 2 Maccabees has one clear quotation, and even the translator of 1 Maccabees has possible references (*e.g.*, to Judg. vii. 3). Ben-Sira seems to have known many of the earlier books. The use of the Septuagint is so far a tradition, gradually accumulating; and among Greek-speaking Jews it had hardly a serious rival, up to the close of the first century after Christ.

There were, however, in Palestine, still some who spoke Aramaic, and held to the Semitic idiom, as to their ancestral customs. When Christianity arose, and its converts came from among the Hellenist Jews, the Dispersion, and the Gentiles, the LXX. rapidly became the Bible of the Christian Church. So few Christians had any knowledge of Hebrew, that they could scarcely test, and did not doubt, the correctness and faithfulness of the version; if corruptions had by now arisen in the text, they were in no position to criticise. Eventually, when the Faith spread to regions East, West, and South, where even Greek was not well enough known, the Western and Southern regions had Latin and Coptic translations made, not from the original Hebrew, but from the Septuagint, behind which they could not go. In the East, the Syriac version of the O.T., circulating among a comparatively isolated people, was made from the Hebrew; but even this Semitic version was not entirely free from the LXX.'s influence. The great Greek version spread widely, and where it spread, men believed in it, almost as the inspired original. The Christians had no wish to doubt, and no knowledge to detect any reason for doubting.

But, when Jerusalem had fallen, and Christianity was becoming a force which none could ignore, the Jews, conquered, dispossessed, and embittered, concentrated themselves upon anything national that remained to them. This cause alone might have set them against the Septuagint; but beside this, as they knew, and were even now carefully analysing, their Scriptures in Hebrew, they were aware of the discrepancies between the Hebrew and the Septuagint, which was, moreover, often quoted against them by Christians. They were on the way to establish an officially received text; and however the discrepancies had arisen, this, as we know, differed considerably from any Hebrew which the Septuagint might appear to represent. They thus passed to antagonism against the LXX., and when controversy arose, accusations were made, which faintly echo to this day, of texts purposely falsified. But, as the Hebrew could not be understood by most whom they hoped to reach, they found means to combat the Septuagint on its own ground.

Aquila, of Sinope in Pontus, connected by marriage, it is said, with the Emperor Hadrian, was converted to Christianity. But later, having quarrelled with the

Christian teachers, he became a Jewish proselyte. After studying under eminent Rabbis, he made from the Hebrew text of his day a new Greek version, in which he aimed at completely literal representation of his original, in opposition to the widely divergent LXX. Every word, every particle, was to be faithfully and consistently represented; hence his use of σὺν to represent the particle ETH, identical in form with a preposition meaning 'with,' but serving simply as a prefix marking the objective case. The resulting Greek is, in places, scarcely tolerable; but the merits of the translation as absolutely literal, which are not without value to-day, were highly esteemed by his Jewish contemporaries; it suited the ideas of the teachers of the time, and came to be used by almost all Jews who understood Greek better than Hebrew. The Christians mostly held to the Septuagint; but the learned ones who understood Aquila's thorough fidelity to the letter of the original found profit in him. Origen and Jerome, the two most learned of early Christians whom we know, are the two that have most to say in his favour.

It must have been about A.D. 130 that Aquila accomplished his task. Some fifty or sixty years later, Theodotion, probably a Jew from Ephesus who had become a Christian, and said by some to have been an Ebionite, produced another version of the Old Testament in Greek. It is a question whether his work was not based upon the existing LXX.; it is so near it in style as hardly to be distinguishable from it in some places; but the Hebrew text he used was much nearer to Aquila's, and to ours, than that which the LXX. appears to represent. We have already seen that his version of Daniel appears, instead of the LXX., in all Greek MSS. but one; and it is now thought that parts, at least, of some historical books are his work. A puzzling thing is, that the Book of Daniel appears to be quoted with the text, or with some readings, of Theodotion, before his time; *e.g.*, by Irenaeus, Justin, Clement of Rome, and Barnabas; and even in the N.T., see Mark xiv. 62, Heb. xi. 33, Rev. ix. 20, xii. 7, xiii. 7, xix. 6. At present the only explanation given is, that two forms of the LXX.'s Daniel may have existed, of which Theodotion chose one for a revision, not very drastic; while the other continued to be known as the LXX.; but the revised version spread rapidly, and the other has barely survived. The matter needs further consideration.

A fourth version was produced by Symmachus, probably an Ebionite, writing a short time after Theodotion. His Greek style was better than his predecessors', and his translation more in accordance with modern ideas; but the remains of it are fragmentary, and its value for textual evidence rather less. Symmachus seems to have used all previous Greek versions, making Aquila, perhaps, his basis for revision, but aiming at an opposite effect to Aquila's literalism. The history of these versions has to be be recorded, because they came to influence the LXX.

The *Quinta*, *Sexta*, and *Septima* are for the most part little more than names; the very existence of *Septima* has been questioned; its remains are at best very small and uncertain. Fragments of *Sexta* are found in several books, and accounts of its discovery by Origen are given, though not very clearly, by

Eusebius and Jerome, and still more hazily by Epiphanius.[1] *Quinta* is associated with *Sexta* in these accounts; fragments of it exist, chiefly in 2 Kings and the poetical books; its style has been commended above all the other versions. But it has been argued[2] that variants passing as *Quinta* in 2 Kings are marginal readings entered in the Hexapla (see below), and may be, in some cases, the genuine LXX.

At least two other translators appear to be referred to, 'the Hebrew' and 'the Syrian', but nothing can fairly be said to be known of either. The 'Graecus Venetus' is a mediaeval version, perhaps of the fourteenth century, made from the Hebrew, by a Jew, with an attempt at Attic elegance. The Aramaic portions of Daniel are given in Doric! It has been well edited by O. von Gebhardt, but is of little practical value. It contains the Pentateuch, Ruth, Prov., Cant., Eccles., Daniel. Only one (Venice) MS. of it is extant.

These versions, from Aquila to *Sexta*, seem to have been produced between A.D. 130 and 200 (roughly). About this latter time begins the working life of one of the chief makers of the history of the Septuagint.

Origen (A.D. 186-253) became a student and writer when quite young, and devoted himself largely to the study of the Old Testament. Almost alone among Gentile students of his time, he set himself to learn Hebrew. When able to read the Hebrew Old Testa-

[1] Eusebius, *Hist. Eccles.*, vi. 16: Jerome, *De Vivis Illustr.*, 54; Epiph., *De Mens. et pond.*, 18, 19. See Dr. G. Mercati in *Studi e Testi*, No. 5, p. 28 ff.

[2] By Prof. Burkitt, *Proc. Soc. Bibl. Archæology*, June 1902.

ment, he came to comprehend the divergence between it and the LXX.; and proceeded to do all in his power to put the Christian Church in possession of the best possible equivalent for the original. In carrying out his plan, he proposed to make use of Aquila's version, on account of its literal faithfulness, which he recognised; and also the other later versions; and to mark clearly the differences of order and matter between the Hebrew and the LXX., so that the LXX. might be, not superseded, but amplified, and, where clearly needing it, corrected. Using a system of critical marks or symbols which he adopted from the Alexandrian librarian Aristarchus, who had edited Homer four centuries before, he marked all additions or omissions in the LXX. as compared with the Hebrew, which he assumed to be the true and original text. Eventually his work took shape in a parallel arrangement of the Hebrew and the principal Greek versions, which, being generally in six columns, became known as the Hexapla. The first column contained the Hebrew; the second, the Hebrew in Greek letters; the third, Aquila, as nearest the Hebrew; the fourth, Symmachus, regarded as a revised Aquila; the fifth, the Septuagint; the sixth, Theodotion. The Hebrew order was followed; and critical marks showed displacements of the order in the LXX. The additions in the LXX. were marked as such; the omissions were supplied from the later sources, mainly Aquila or Theodotion. Where Origen considered the LXX. to be clearly corrupt, he appears to have mended it from any preferable readings he could discover, and failing these, from the later versions again. His fifth column, therefore, consisted of the best text of the LXX. that he could command, arranged according to the Hebrew order, slightly emended, and brought, with the aid of the other Greek versions, into as close agreement with the Hebrew as he could achieve. Critical marks accompanied all changes of the LXX., except, apparently, the emendations.

Such, at least, is the view which has been generally held since the appearance of F. Field's great work on the subject, which included a collection of all the fragments of the Hexapla then known (1875). It has, however, been lately suggested[1] that the text of Origen's fifth column was an unrevised text of the LXX.; not a critical work, but simply the foundation for it. It is pointed out that no critical marks are found in the Hexapla-fragments recently discovered; that they were less needed in the Hexapla, where the texts were side by side, and perhaps better away; and that few or no specimen readings can be pointed out, which show that the fifth column really contained a revised text. The witness of Eusebius on this point is non-existent, and Jerome has been cited on both sides. But Field's long experience had convinced him that there were "innumera loca" to prove his view; the absence of marks in the Hexapla-fragments proves little as to the original Hexapla, for they are probably only a copy of the Psalter, and not certainly exact; it is agreed that the marks were often imperfectly reproduced, or absent, in copies.

[1] By Dr. Mercati, who has discovered certain Hexapla-fragments, and Prof. Lietzmann (in *Göttingische gelehrte Anzeigen*, May 1902). Dr. Mercati's suggestion that the Tetrapla, not the Hexapla, contained the critical marks is ingenious, but seems arbitrary.

Again, if this critical apparatus of signs was not in the Hexapla, where was it, and whence did the MSS. known as Hexaplaric obtain it? It requires us to suppose further work on Origen's part. Moreover, we have been led to think that it was just when the LXX. was recopied, alone, from the fifth column that the signs tended to drop out.

The Tetrapla is the name given to a smaller edition of the Hexapla, containing the four Greek versions only, and not the Hebrew. It is not known for certain whether the Tetrapla was earlier or later than the Hexapla; but the latter was the principal work, and references to it are more frequent. Occasionally the notes in MSS. mention also the Pentapla, Heptapla, and Octapla. This is generally supposed to mean that here and there, especially in the Psalms, the number of columns varied, to include the *Quinta* and *Sexta*, or at times to drop a column; but the only reference to the five is at Isa. iii. 24. The Octapla and Hexapla are not mentioned together at any passage; and the idea that they could be separate works is almost disproved by the practical difficulty. The Hexapla alone must have been enormous; at a very moderate estimate—probably much too low—it must have required from six to seven thousand large pages.

The result of Origen's labours was successful, in so far as he accomplished a comparison between the Hebrew and Greek texts. He preserved for the time a mass of material, of which, but for him, we should probably now have possessed much less than we do. Also, he succeeded in constructing a Greek version, composite, but still mainly LXX., nearer to the

Hebrew than had ever existed before, unless we consider that the original LXX. and the Hebrew of, say, 150 B.C. really tallied closely. (Most authorities think that this is not likely; the difficulty of supposing that the M.T. was developed from such a text is in their view too great. How the discrepancies arose is a different matter.) It is true that the subsequent treatment of the LXX., on the basis of his composite text, by men who were probably roused to labour by his example, but were not equal to him in attainments, has made it difficult to recover the original Greek text from the resulting mixtures. It is also true that a modern scholar would probably have worked on a different method; but he should not therefore speak patronisingly of Origen's work, nor with censure for its indirect consequences. To do so is to commit the moral fault of ingratitude, which is worst when shown towards those into whose labours the ungrateful have entered; and the intellectual mistake—which should be confined to the lower order of so-called practical minds—of judging by results.

Origen died about A.D. 253, and within two generations of that time we find other steps being taken to edit the LXX. It is usual to attribute to him the impulses which led to this; and he had doubtless furnished the means for some of what was done. But the history of the New Testament text, which follows a somewhat similar course, tends to make it a probable presumption, that had he not existed, the LXX. would sooner or later have undergone treatment. As it is, Theodotion worked before him.

After Origen, the thread of the history becomes threefold. About A.D. 300, Pamphilus (martyred in 310) and Eusebius (Bp. of Caesarea, died 338) took up the idea of reissuing Origen's revised text of the LXX. Apparently they thought not only that this text agreed with the Hebrew, and therefore must be right, but also that it represented the original LXX. They endeavoured to reproduce the critical signs, but it seems doubtful whether they really grasped their full bearing on the text. Their edition, therefore, actually gives a text mixed with later versions; and as copies were made, the signs were occasionally misplaced, as it was hard to check them accurately in the single text; sometimes they were omitted, and soon they tended to vanish altogether. Some MSS. now extant (as G, Cod. Sarravianus of the Octateuch) give approximately the text of Origen, or of Pamphilus and Eusebius, with critical marks; others give a mixed text in which some readings from this source appear, as A in Kings. From this mixture very few MSS. are altogether free. Some again give readings from the later versions, and even 'according to the Hebrew,' in their marginal notes; these are primarily due to Origen's work, even when the MS. that gives them does not reproduce his text. MSS. with these readings are generally known as 'Hexaplaric,' and form one of the three classes into which our MSS. are (provisionally) divided.

Much about the same time that Pamphilus and Eusebius were working in Palestine, where their text mainly circulated, Lucian of Samosata (martyred about 311) was similarly engaged at Antioch. One of his principles in revision was, as it seems, to insert as much as possible from divergent readings, harmonising or fusing them together. He seems also to have taken some account of the Hebrew. Not merely has his result been compared to the 'Syrian' text of the N.T., which Westcott and Hort held to be due to revision, but the idea that Lucian himself was concerned in the N.T. version,[1] mooted long before the time of WH by Hug, has recurred from time to time, and has adherents now. In the O.T., Lucian's edition is valued, because there appears to be a decidedly ancient element preserved in it, of which we should else have had very little direct Greek evidence; it has some kinship with the Old Latin version (see below). So far it has been chiefly studied in the books of Kings. In the Psalter, Prof. Rahlfs of Göttingen (*Septuaginta-Studien*, ii. pp. 230, 236) holds that Lucian's edition had a career, as well as a character, like that of the 'Syrian' text of the N.T., and, prevailing over other texts, sooner or later won its way to general acceptance, even in the West, and into liturgical use ('Kirchtext'). As regards the O.T. generally, it was used at Antioch, and passed thence to Constantinople,[2] circulating generally in the intervening districts of Asia Minor. Lucian's edition was identified by Field from marginal notes in the Syro-hexaplar version, and by Lagarde by comparison of certain MSS.: from which he reconstructed a Lucianic text, from Genesis to Esther; this was published in 1883, but his death prevented its further progress.

The third of the editions that followed Origen's

[1] Hort, *The N.T. in Greek*, Introd. p. 138.

[2] 'Antioch is the true ecclesiastical parent of Constantinople.' Hort, *Introd.* p. 143.

work was produced, again about the same time, in Egypt, the Septuagint's original home. Its author, Hesychius, is supposed to have been a martyr, perhaps a Bishop; but nothing is known for certain. He seems to have made a careful revision of the Egyptian texts of his day, with attention to grammatical and literary detail, but no extensive alteration; and generally with little notice, if any, of the Origenian text, or of the Hebrew. His version may thus best represent the text as current in Egypt before Origen's day; but its characteristics are faintly marked, so that though many MSS.—including, in parts of the O.T., especially the Prophets, some of our great uncials—may preserve a more or less Hesychian text, yet it is hard to recognise with certainty. As might be expected, the Hesychian text continued in use mainly in Alexandria and Egypt; and the resemblance to Westcott and Hort's 'Alexandrian' text in general character is noticeable.

We have now nearly reached the time when our oldest MSS. were produced. No existing MS., so far as we know, contains a pure text, without mixture, of any of the editions described above, or of the text from which Origen began his work: the *κοινὴ ἔκδοσις* or vulgate edition of the LXX. Hexaplaric readings, in themselves a mixture, are found, in greater or less quantity, in MSS. whose general text is of a different character: MSS. mainly Hesychian have corrections from Lucianic sources, or a mixture of Lucianic readings, and the converse also happens. From these mixtures the original text, if it is to be reached, has to be disentangled.

The later history of the text of the LXX., for ten

or twelve centuries, consists simply in the production and copying of MSS., until the time of the earliest printed editions. As a living version of the Bible, it was destined before long to be superseded by a younger rival in another language; the day of its widespread supremacy among Christians was over. This, it will be seen, was due less to its failings than to political changes—the break-up of the ancient civilisation, and the coming of the new nations.

We must now look back, in point of time, to notice the early versions of the Bible in other languages than Greek. This is not a side-issue, nor irrelevant, as it might at first sight seem to be. These early versions are, in fact, often important witnesses on questions of the LXX.'s text. For the strongest proof of the prevalence and success of the Septuagint is the fact that the other early versions were mostly made from it, and not from the Hebrew. As has already been seen, the LXX. in early Christian history counted with its readers almost as an original; and it was so completely trusted that the ancient world, with few exceptions, received their Bible either in Greek, the Septuagint itself, or in secondary versions made from it.

The one important, but isolated, exception is the remarkable Syrian Church of the Euphrates valley.[1] Its metropolis was Edessa, east of the Euphrates, about half-way between Samosata and Carrhae: not part of the Roman Empire until A.D. 216. This church possessed a version of the Old Testament

[1] See Prof. Burkitt's *Early Chistianity outside the Roman Empire.* Cambridge, 1899.

made direct from the Hebrew; there were many Jews among the population. This version, known as the Peshiṭta, has therefore a different history and character in the Old and in the New Testament. In some parts of the O.T. it shows decided traces of the LXX.'s influence; but substantially it is an independent version from the Hebrew, and, strictly speaking, we have no concern with it here. The Apocryphal books, which belong to the LXX., were added to it later.

Apart from this Syrian Church, we have now to regard the countries where Christians, requiring versions of the Scriptures, were to be found, from A.D. 100 (roughly) to A.D. 400. It is barely necessary to remark that these countries were all included in the Roman Empire at the beginning of this period, and were nominally under its sway throughout the whole of it. The more civilised portions of the Empire spoke either Greek or Latin; the dividing line between the two languages, both in Europe and Africa, corresponded nearly with the 19th meridian of East longitude. Thus the three languages of the Inscription on the Cross sufficed for those who stood by. Greek was more widely spread than Latin, and traders carried it to every seaport of the Empire, and up many river valleys; the higher and educated classes at Rome spoke and wrote it constantly and familiarly, and it went with them to provincial seats of government and pleasure resorts. Latin however prevailed in Italy, especially in the country districts and toward the north; in Gaul and Spain, and in the Roman province of Africa, of which Carthage was the principal city. Still, the fact that the early Latin versions were made from the LXX. reflects the historical truth that Christianity, in its origin Semitic, came to the Western churches through Greek channels.

It was, indeed, only because Christianity, unlike a fashionable cult or philosophy, appealed to the lowest as well as the highest classes, that any other versions than the Greek and Latin (and Syriac) were demanded. As it is, the only others, dating before A.D. 400, of which we have any surviving fragments, are those in the dialects of Egypt. The lower classes of Egypt, Upper or Lower, outside Alexandria, did not commonly speak Greek; certainly it was not their familiar tongue. Accordingly, we find Egyptian (Coptic) versions existing, both of the Old and New Testaments; of which considerable remnants are preserved, in two principal dialects, and two or three less important. The British Museum, according to a catalogue dated 1905, has nearly a thousand Egyptian Biblical MSS.; some are but fragments, but some contain as many as five books, though incomplete, and there is a whole volume of the (Sahidic) Psalter. The principal dialects are the Bohairic (or Memphitic, a name now passing out of use) spoken in the Delta, and the Sahidic (Thebaic) of Upper Egypt. The Middle Egyptian, the Fayumic and Akhmimic, are at present of less importance. The two chief versions may date from the third, possibly before the end of the second, century. The Bohairic appears to have a text akin to that of the Hesychian MSS., but not altogether free from Lucianic readings, or at least readings found in Lucianic MSS. The Sahidic shows traces of Hexaplaric readings in some books; and in Job, where it was thought to have a pre-Hexaplar text, Professor Burkitt[1] pronounces that it was more probably made from the text as revised by Origen, but omitting most of the additions marked with an asterisk; which were known in Upper Egypt, as one MS. contains them. These versions are valuable, in so far as they throw light on the text-history of the LXX., or if not that, then upon the local distribution of the varieties of text.

The *Old Latin* version, as it is called, is yet more important, both for its textual evidence, and for its share in perpetuating the influence of the LXX., even up to the present day, as will presently be seen. It was probably made before the end of the second century, for the use, in the first place, of the African Christians in Carthage and its neighbourhood—where the need was greater, as Greek was less spoken, than at Rome, or in Italy and Southern Gaul. At a slightly later time Italy also possessed its Latin version; but the relation between the Old Latin texts, which vary considerably, is not yet very clearly ascertained, especially as regards the O.T. The African text is doubtless the oldest, and made from a Greek text which is older than the Hexapla. Therefore, especially as it is very literal, it gives valuable evidence as to the text of the LXX. before the alterations and additions made by Origen and his successors. Thus it is theoretically possible, and in some instances appears to be demonstrably the case, that the O.L. sometimes preserves the right reading, when most or all extant Greek MSS. have lost it. (Thus Prof. Burkitt points out—*Tyconius*, p. cx

[1] In *Encycl. Biblica*, art. 'Text and Versions,' vol. iv. col. 5027.

—that in Ezek. xxviii. 7 the O.L. has *vulnerabunt* = τρώσουσιν, supported by the chief Egyptian versions; the Greek authorities have the corruption στρώσουσιν.) It seems also that the underlying Greek text is from an Egyptian source. The O.L. may therefore show some resemblance to Hesychian texts, based on Egyptian MSS.; and a similar text appears to have been used by Lucian among his materials, and to have been perhaps the oldest and purest of them. On the other hand, corruptions are found in it, due to misreading of the Greek, or to mistakes in the Greek MSS. used. Thus Isa. xlv. 1 appears as *Sic dicit Dominus Christo meo Domino*, evidently reading Κυρίῳ for Κύρῳ. It has been suggested that this was an alteration made with a purpose; but more probably the misreading was due to accident, possibly aided by the remembrance of Ps. cx. 1. Another instance is Ezek. xxxviii. 13, where the corruption is purely Latin, *iuvenis* for *tu venis*. In Isa. xxix. 3, the LXX. reads ὡς Δαυείδ for 'like a circle,' D for R; and *sicut David* has become in one Latin text *sicut avis*.

The Old Latin, unfortunately, is not extant for the O.T. in a complete form. In the N.T. there exist some very old MSS. of it, almost rivalling the Greek uncials for age; but those of the O.T. contain only parts of the Bible, and are generally fragmentary; the oldest are of the fifth and sixth centuries. The quotations in the Latin Fathers are valuable, but not like continuous texts, and they need careful examination, as there is risk that quotations may be copied according to later, more familiar, readings. The best sources are the *Testimonia* of Cyprian, the *Rules* of Tyconius, and the *Speculum* (attributed, doubtfully, to Augustine); there are many quotations in Tertullian, of yet earlier date, but opinions differ as to the value of this evidence as it stands. The Old Latin Psalter must be regarded somewhat apart from the other books: Prof. Rahlfs finds here (cf. above, p. 47) something analogous to the 'Western' text of the N.T.

From the Old Latin we pass on to Jerome and his work. But it will be convenient first to deal briefly with the other ancient versions of the Old Testament, namely:

1. *Later Syriac.*—Paul, Bishop of Tella, produced a version of the O.T., at Alexandria, as it is said, in A.D. 616. This is an extremely literal version from the LXX. More than that, it is made from Origen's revision, the fifth column of the Hexapla, with the critical marks preserved. Consequently it is one of the principal authorities for the Hexaplar text, and to that extent, for the Septuagint. It is commonly known as the *Syro-hexaplar*.

Another version, the Palestinian Syriac (or Aramaic), is extant in considerable portions. It was made from the LXX., and is quoted in the larger Cambridge edition; but its importance is not equal to that of the Syro-hexaplar. It is only of late years that it has been recovered and used.

Other Syriac versions were made; one, made under the direction of Philoxenus, Bishop of Mabug, in the fifth century, is referred to in the margin of the Syro-hexaplar. But they are of little practical importance.

2. *Ethiopic.*—Mainly, at any rate, from the LXX.,

until the Reformation, and is still the authoritative Bible of the Roman Communion. In the main, it put an end to its predecessor's supremacy; but indirectly, here and there, especially in the Psalter, it perpetuated its influence.

For the Gallican Psalter (a revised Latin translation, as has been said above, from the Hexaplaric Septuagint) held its ground, and stands in the received Vulgate to-day. The reader will be reminded of our own Prayer-Book Psalter, which is to most Englishmen, although less accurate than the Authorised or Revised Version, far more of a familiar friend. Liturgical use is of course mainly responsible for this; and it may be said in passing that liturgical influence upon texts deserves more attention than it has yet received. But the Gallican Psalter and the Septuagint have a connexion with our Prayer-Book Psalter, closer than mere analogy. The Prayer-Book Psalter 'followeth the division of the Hebrews, and the translation of the great English Bible, set forth and used in the time of King Henry the Eighth and Edward the Sixth'. Now the Great Bible (1539-1541) is Miles Coverdale's revision of Matthew's Bible, which is in the earlier books and the New Testament Tyndale's, but in the later part of the O.T., including the Psalms, mainly Coverdale's own version of 1535, from the German and the Latin. In his revision, Coverdale made much use of Sebastian Münster's Latin version from the Hebrew, which had appeared too late for him to use before. He was not Hebraist enough to make a thoroughly independent version, and his work is rather a compilation from existing authorities. Based largely, though indirectly, on the Hebrew, it was greatly influenced by the Vulgate; and, as issued in the Great Bible, the Psalter had (after the manner of Origen!) indications and marks to show that certain words and clauses were not in the Hebrew, and to point out 'diversity of reading'. These, as in other instances, fell gradually out of use in ordinary later copies. Our Prayer-Book Psalter, then, though based on the Hebrew, shows traces of the influence of the Vulgate, *i.e.*, the Gallican Psalter, derived from the LXX. There are also a few cases, not important, of agreement with the LXX., even against the Vulgate; but in a Psalter produced as Coverdale's was, it is hardly possible to say with certainty how these came about.

At the risk of prolonging a digression, a few examples may be given of Septuagint renderings preserved in the P.B. The additional passage in Psalm xiv. was noticed above. In xxii. 17, 'they pierced my hands and my feet', *they pierced* is practically LXX. and Vulgate (with Syriac); a slight difference from the ordinary Hebrew reading 'like a lion', though a few Heb. MSS. have the verb. In the previous verse (P.B.), 'many' is LXX. Vulg., not Heb.; so is 'the Lord' in the last clause of the Psalm. In xl. 6, P.B. follows Heb. In xxxi. 17, 'my times' appears to be from Heb.; LXX. may have here corrupted καιροί into κλῆροι, Vulg. *sortes*; but the Roman Ps. has more correctly *tempora mea*. In xxxvii. 29, 'the unrighteous shall be punished', is LXX. and Vulg.; Heb. does not contain the clause, and here the psalm, which is an acrostic, is without a verse beginning with the letter

Ain. In xxxviii. 7 the Vulg. has escaped (through the O.L.?) the Greek corruption ψυχή (for ψόαι), and so P.B. rightly 'loins'. Here the Roman Ps. has *anima.* In lxxxix. 21 P.B. 'oil', and Vulg., have avoided a Greek corruption in LXX. In cv. 28 is a curious case; Heb. has 'and they rebelled not against his words', the margin having 'word', singular. Vulg. has *et non exacerbavit sermones suos*: Roman Ps., *quia exacerbaverunt verbum eius*: LXX., καὶ παρεπίκραναν τοὺς λόγους αὐτοῦ: and P.B., 'and they were not obedient unto his word'. Here P.B. and LXX. agree in sense against Heb. and Vulg.; but the verbs employed give rise to a suspicion that it is the negative that has slipped out in LXX., and that the P.B. version has confused the renderings.[1] (Omission, even addition of a negative is not unknown in LXX., as against Hebrew; generally making havoc of the sense.)

From the time that the Vulgate made good its hold upon Western Christendom, the Septuagint almost ceased to be a living Bible in those regions; where, in the Middle Ages, the knowledge of Greek was almost as rare as that of Hebrew. There was not much temptation to make efforts to consult a version which no longer commanded the same trust and reverence as of old. Manuscripts of it were copied from time to time; but till the revival of Greek learning and the introduction of printing, there is a wide gap in the history of the Septuagint, and its later fortunes are very different.

[1] For further agreements of P.B. with LXX., see xxxvi. 13, lxviii. 25; with S. Münster, see xxxix. 14, lxiii. 4.

CHAPTER III

MODERN STUDY OF THE SEPTUAGINT (FROM A.D. 1500)

The blank of a thousand years—Earliest printed editions—Work at the Text—Grabe—Holmes and Parsons—Other branches of study—The nineteenth century—Tischendorf, Lagarde, Field—The Cambridge O.T. in Greek—The Oxford Concordance—Recent and living workers.

TO resume, then, after a blank space of, roughly, a thousand years: when the LXX. had branched into the various recensions that followed Origen's work, its career as a Bible in actual use was, for the West, nearly at an end. While Jerome was doing the work that was to replace it and its direct Latin representative, the barbarians were closing in on the Empire: during the next century the old order was breaking up apace. Teutonic tribes filled the Latin lands, and wedges began to be thrust in between Latin and Greek Christendom. Then followed the ages of violence and chivalry, when the new nations were struggling into light and taking shape out of what was without form, void, and dark. Any chronological chart will show the intellectual blankness of this period, when men fought the Saracen, resisted the Turk, and warred incessantly with these and with one another. The wonder is that so many monuments of the previous civilisation were preserved, and in the case of literature even copied.

When we resume the story, Constantinople has fallen, America is just discovered, and the nations of Europe, save for the Turk, have entered more or less securely into their own. Fugitives from the East have brought their learned treasures westward; and the new studies have been fortified by the invention of printing. The Vulgate, naturally, was among the first books to be printed: sixty years after it, in 1517 (but the work had been nearly twenty years in progress), the first printed Septuagint was ready for issue. Some light is thrown on the position it then held, by the fact that it appeared only as one version of a Polyglot Bible. The Jews had printed their own Bibles a generation before; but the Complutensian Bible was the first edition of the Hebrew undertaken by a Christian scholar, and also the first of the Septuagint. This great book was published in 1521, at Alcalá (Complutum) near Madrid, and Cardinal Jimenez (Ximenes) was responsible for its issue; under him worked Greeks, converted Jews, and the picked scholars of Spain. On the Old Testament pages, the Hebrew, Latin and Greek appeared in that order; the Vulgate having the place of honour, 'inter synagogam et orientalem ecclesiam . . . tanquam duos hinc et inde latrones, medium autem Iesum, hoc est Romanam sive Latinam ecclesiam, collocantes'.

The text of the Complutensian Septuagint is considered to be Lucianic in its general colouring. Some of the MSS. used in forming it (Holmes and Parsons' 68, 108, 248) are pretty certainly known. However interesting—the N.T. volume is one of the most beautiful of books—it is of little practical importance to-day, for the study of the text. The same may be said of the Aldine edition, printed after, but published two years before the Complutensian, in February 1518-9. Aldus himself was dead by this time, but the reputation of his press, under his father-in-law, Andreas Asulanus, still stood high. It is not known for certain what range of MSS. was at command; if those to be found in Venice were used, it is curious that 68, again, was probably among them; it is thought that 29 and 121 may also have been used.[1] The text is approximately Hesychian in character. Both Complutensian and Aldine served as foundations for later editions, even into the seventeenth century.

The third great edition is that commonly known as the 'Sixtine', published at Rome in 1587 under Pope Sixtus V. (who also took measures for the issue of a revised Vulgate); it was printed to appear in 1586, the date being altered by hand. The Roman authorities had the advantage of using Cod. B, whose importance they recognised; but they also consulted other MSS., among them Cod. Venetus (V = 23). The greater part of Genesis, missing in B, is said to have been supplied by 19, a Chigi MS.;[2] the source for the missing Psalms cvi.-cxxxviii. is not known. The editors (Cardinal Carafa, assisted by P. Morinus and others) modified or corrected their MS. text in many places; so that their text is not an exact copy of B, though mainly based upon it. In the Book of Isaiah,

[1] According to M. L. Margolis, *Amer. J. of Semit. Lang. and Lit.*, Jan. 1918, the MSS. used were 18, 64, 121 and a fourth not identified.

[2] Nestle, *Sept. Studien*, i. p. 9.

for instance, an ordinary edition reprinting the Sixtine text will be found to differ from B in fully 300 places, and the variations for the whole of the O.T. have been estimated at 4000. A large proportion of these, it is true, are but slight: matters of spelling and accents, of the order or division of words; some readings of a later corrector, as against the original hand, of B are found, a few omitted words are supplied. On the whole, the alterations are generally reasonable, if the point of view of an editor at that time be fairly considered. They are not always right, but they are in the direction that would then have been thought so, as the importance of showing the exact words of the MS., or the exact source of each word in the printed text, was not then recognised. Substantially, the Sixtine edition gives the text of B, and that was, in the main, the best text available. The editors could hardly have foreseen the need for anything better, though the issue of a purer text, in recent years, has been an enormous help to Septuagint study. It is, however, important to remark that each chapter of the Sixtine was furnished with valuable notes, giving variants, and readings from later Greek versions; but in the numerous reprints and later editions based upon the Sixtine, these, as usual in such cases, generally disappeared, leaving any arbitrary appearances in the text to explain themselves. The Sixtine served as the basis for most of the ordinary editions of the LXX. for just three centuries. The great folio was not within the ordinary reader's reach; but Paris, London, Cambridge, Amsterdam, Leipzig, Oxford, all from time to time issued editions based upon it.

That of L. Bos, published at Frankfort in 1709, deserves mention; it gives a slightly corrected Sixtine text, with a quantity of Hexaplar readings from the later versions, and variants from the Complutensian and Aldine editions. The London Polyglot, edited by Brian Walton (Bp. of Chester), 1657, gave the variants of Cod. A.

By this time work was being done in various departments of Septuagint study; but it will be convenient to notice now two more great editions. In 1707 appeared the first volume of an edition by J. E. Grabe, of which the text is based upon Cod. A; but treated after the manner of Origen's Hexapla. It seems that Origen's method, after all, made something like a permanent appeal to such as desired a Greek text coupled with an approach to the matter of the Hebrew. Grabe, in fact, gives a faithful representation of Cod. A's text, and deviations from it are shown as such; while the Greek can be continuously *read*, with the closest possible approximation to the Hebrew. For critical purposes, however, though generally sound, it is not very convenient, and the sources of the Hexaplaric additions and of the corrections of A's text are not given; there are also occasional uncorrected mistakes, and a few unaccountable readings. Still it is a fine edition, and has been found useful even in modern days. The text (again without the critical marks and distinctions of type!) was reprinted at Moscow for the use of the Greek Church, in 1821; also by the S.P.C.K., with Dr. Field for editor, at Oxford in 1859: see below, p. 231. Grabe died in 1712, before his great edition was completed. The fourth volume had followed the first in 1709; the second, ed. F. Lee, and third, ed. W. Wigan, appeared in 1719 and 1720.[1]

The other great edition, almost colossal in size, is that of Holmes and Parsons, and is of a different character to those described above. The text is from the Sixtine, or more particularly, it appears, from Bos's edition;[2] but the variants given below the text are derived from almost every available source. The evidence of 300 MSS., the four great editions, quotations from the Fathers, and about nine versions, is given in the five large folio volumes. Collators were employed all over Europe, and the results of their work, to the extent of 164 MS. volumes, are stored in the Bodleian Library at Oxford. Ten years' preparation resulted in the first volume's appearance in 1798. After Holmes' death in 1805,[3] the work was carried on by James Parsons, who brought out the other four volumes between 1810 and 1827, and survived, it is pleasant to know, for twenty years.

The plan of Holmes and Parsons' work was

[1] Grabe's edition has appeared in a smaller form, as well as in folio. Fifteen years ago I bought the folio edition in London for three shillings and sixpence! It had been sold by a parish library, in defiance of the donor's express wishes. I cannot imagine what the parish can have got for such money as reached them for the sale, to compensate for the loss of this fine volume; the twentieth century compares ill with the eighteenth, over this transaction.

[2] Nestle in Hastings' *D.B.*, iv. 449. See also Swete, *Introd. to O.T. in Gr.*, p. 185.

[3] Robert Holmes was Canon of Christ Church and Professor of Poetry at Oxford. The names of Holmes and Parsons do not seem to have become famous beyond the ranks of Septuagint students. Most biographical dictionaries ignore them; and once, in a great library, I asked an attendant for their work. It was on a shelf in the gallery where we stood; but the answer came, "'Homes and Parsons'; is it a novel?"

magnificent; the excution of it in detail has often been the subject of complaints and adverse criticism. It is equally easy to blame and to account for its shortcomings. The editors of so huge a work were obliged to depend on a large number of collators and collaborators, whose results they could not always control with completeness; and perfect accuracy amid such a mass of details is hardly within human reach. Their text, too, was not quite satisfactory for the purpose. But every student since their time has depended on their work as the great store of textual information; and the modern Cambridge Septuagint, though far more accurate, has been of necessity limited in size and scope compared with it. The treatment of the Syriac and the Hexaplar material is weak; but the information was not then as full as to-day, nor the importance so much recognised. If the work is not perfectly done, it was a notable achievement to have done it at all. The Cambridge edition, though it will supersede it in part, still borrows from it; and such parts of Holmes and Parsons as may not, for long years, be replaced will be more useful when the modern work is also in use.

The other Septuagint work between 1500 and 1850 must be very briefly dealt with, though often of great value in its day. The part that is permanently useful has been so far worked into books by later writers that there is now little need for the ordinary student to consult the older authorities regularly.

Andrew de Maes was the first to make use of the Syro-hexaplar version, in an edition of the Book of Joshua (1574). M. Norberg and C. Bugati, about 1787, edited MSS. of it, followed by H. Middledorpf in 1835. The Old Latin was brought together from some MSS., and largely from the quotations in the Latin Fathers, by P. Sabatier, 1743–1749; the Latin Psalter had been previously dealt with by the other Maurists (Benedictine) Blaupin, Constant, and Guesnie, in their edition of Augustine, 1681. The commentaries, and *catenae*, or commentaries compiled from various sources, which are found accompanying the text in many MSS. of the LXX., were dealt with by B. Corderius (1643) and Patrick Young (Junius), who also concerned himself with the text[1]: by Curter (1580), on Isaiah, with a text constructed from the Aldine edition and Cod. Q; and by T. Ittig, 1707, and J. C. Wolf, 1742.

J. A. Fabricius, who died in 1736, did much for the study of the Apocrypha and other non-canonical books, and some of his work, re-edited some fifty years after his death, is still of service. The fragments of the later Greek versions of the O.T. were collected from the margins of Hexaplaric MSS. by Nobilius, 1588; J. Drusius, 1622; P. Morinus, 1624; and Bernard Montfaucon, 1713, whose work was not superseded for five generations. Bishop Walton's Polyglot, 1657, has been already mentioned; it included the Hebrew, Samaritan, Septuagint with variants of Cod. A, Vulgate, Syriac and Arabic, and the Targums; the author exhibited his general learning in the Introduction. Bishop Pearson, who wrote a preface, 1655, to a Cambridge reprint of the Sixtine, and Humphrey Hody, Professor of Greek at Oxford, 1705, surveyed the field of the study of the Septuagint and its relation to the Hebrew and other

[1] His transcript of Cod. A is still preserved at the British Museum.

versions; J. F. Hug, in the Old Testament as in the New, busied himself with the attempt to sketch the affinities of texts and recensions. Abraham Trom compiled a concordance to the LXX., which, though said to lack accuracy, was the best available for nearly two hundred years, and, in default of a better, decidedly useful if employed with due care. J. F. Schleusner used his wide knowledge of the text in his *Opuscula Critica*, 1812, and *Novus Thesaurus*, 1820, 1829, the latter based upon J. C. Biel's posthumous work of 1780. Z. Frankel and H. W. J. Thiersch, 1841, did what was possible in their day to investigate the language of the Alexandrian version and its character as a rendering of the Old Testament.

A student of to-day will seldom need to consult these works; but they have been the starting-points for the more advanced modern work, and it would be ungrateful to forget their authors. There are others as well, scarcely less deserving of honourable mention; besides commentators on the O.T., such as Bishop Lowth, who, though not primarily students of the LXX., knew and esteemed it. The brief record of names given above is at least enough to show that the study of the Greek Version, since the revival of learning, has never slept, but was pursued by many men whose worldly fame has not equalled their learning and their labour. For though the Septuagint has interested many, its study has scarcely, at any rate till recent years, lain quite in the track of classical or Biblical research; at the same time it includes, or at any rate touches upon, many branches of both. Consequently, the information needed by students has been scattered somewhat thinly over a wide field, and until lately it has been difficult to find any great amount of it in compact form. The language, the Biblical interpretation, the relation to the Hebrew and to many versions, the history and criticism of the text, are, each of them, sufficient subjects for prolonged study, presenting considerable difficulties; and, for a thorough grasp of the problems, both separate and combined treatment are necessary.

Though, as was said, Septuagint study in modern times has never slept, yet perhaps the middle of the nineteenth century marks a halting-place; but not for long, for a new generation of workers was already arising. Tischendorf (1815–1874) spared some of his magnificent energy and equipment to it, as a N.T. scholar of his eminence well might do; but though seven editions of the text were published under his name, the three last and best were issued after his death; and they gave merely a revision of the Sixtine, with variants from the principal uncials. It is almost amusing to find that in the last, under Dr. Eberhard Nestle's direction, the readings of Cod. B, so far as known, were collated with the Sixtine, and the amount of difference made manifest.

Paul Antoine de Lagarde[1] (1829–1891) is the man to whom, probably, living students of the Septuagint most look up to as the leader of modern progress. Incidentally, his contributions to the study of the Syriac, Aramaic, Ethiopic, and Coptic versions were

[1] This estimate was written in the winter of 1913–14. I do not think it fair to modify it (and this applies in other cases also) in view of recent events. Lagarde (originally Bötticher) was a violent Prussian political enthusiast; but I do not see that this concerns us here and now, unless in so far as it might affect our views as to his mental standpoint.

of great value; he did not neglect the Old Latin, and perhaps the best edition of Jerome's 'Hebrew' Psalter is due to him. (Another, by Baer and Tischendorf, appeared in the same year, 1874.) He also directly attacked the problem of reaching a pure text of the Septuagint. For securing this result, he laid down certain general principles of procedure, in his 'Observations on the Greek Translation of the Book of Proverbs,' and other works.[1] Unfortunately he had set himself tasks too great for his strength, or for one man's life; but his principles still live. Of his great scheme for reconstructing the various recensions of the LXX., as a preparation for reaching the original text behind them, he was able to accomplish only the first part, Genesis to Esther, of his Lucianic text, which he put forward as 'in gravioribus omnibus satis fidam.' This, however, has proved of such value that some years since it was described to the present writer as one of the two indispensable books for LXX. study.

The author of the other 'indispensable' book was Dr. F. Field, Fellow of Trin. Coll., Cambridge, whose edition of the extant fragments of Origen's Hexapla was published at Oxford in 1875. All then known of Aq. Theod. Symm. was given, with the corresponding Hebrew, and a most careful record of the evidence of the Syro-hexaplar version. The Latin introduction, still the standard authority, surveys the Hexapla, the versions which preceded, and the

[1] *Anmerkungen zur griechischen Übersetzung der Proverbien*, 1863; *Genesis Graece*, 1868; *Ankündigung einer neuen Ausgabe der gr. Übers. des Alten Test.*, 1882.

recensions which followed it; and much textual help is given in notes.

About this time, 1875–1883, plans were being considered at Cambridge for a new edition of the LXX. It was clear that neither the latest revisions of the Sixtine text, nor the great apparatus of Holmes and Parsons, satisfied modern ideas, so that the time was quite ripe for an attempt to replace them. It was determined to undertake a larger and a smaller edition, with identical texts, representing with all possible accuracy the words of Cod. B: at first from the facsimile of 1881, and later from the photograph of 1890. The smaller 'manual' edition, itself not less than eleven years' work, appeared first in three volumes; the variants of certain principal uncials are given in foot-notes, the *minutiae* of spelling at the end of each volume. The Hymns or Canticles, the Psalms of Solomon, and the Greek text of the Book of Enoch, are now included. The plan is excellent, and the execution worthy of it. Practically, the accuracy is very great, and the source of every word is visible at a glance; and failing an admittedly perfect text, it is difficult to see what better can be desired than an accurate edition on these principles. In the writer's opinion, it is not only the best available edition of the LXX., but perhaps the best edited text of any ancient work in existence. It may be doubted whether, even after the labours of Tregelles, and of Westcott and Hort, the N.T. is really now in a sounder, though of course in a more advanced, textual position than the LXX. The N.T. editions have all along contained, especially in the apparatus, too much editor and too little manuscript. The readings, of course, are (usually) found in one or other MS. or group; but the text is almost invariably mixed, and only Tischendorf, Tregelles, Baljon, and Souter consistently give the readings of MSS., *as such*, in the notes.

From these drawbacks the Cambridge 'Old Testament in Greek' is free; and it can therefore be trusted, through thick and thin, for what it professes to be. It is not surprising that it has given a considerable impetus to the study of the LXX.: and whereas the great works of Field and Lagarde were rather for the inner circle of scholars, this excellent text is of use to readers of every class. The first volume appeared in 1887, the original issue was completed in 1894, and the book continues to pass rapidly through successive editions. The editor, Prof. H. B. Swete, added to his eminent services by writing an 'Introduction to the O.T. in Greek', which brings together a mass of information, mostly within the reach of experts, but difficult for ordinary readers to collect for themselves. This first appeared in 1900.

The larger Cambridge LXX. has the same text as the smaller. The notes, however, give a very large, and at the same time carefully selected, mass of textual evidence. Much fresh material has accumulated since the time of Holmes and Parsons; and the types of text are at any rate better understood now than then. Consequently the editors (Canon Brooke and Mr. N. M'Lean) have been able to limit the number of cursive MSS. whose readings are fully given, and to abandon some versions, wholly or partly, as only complicating, without strengthening, the evidence. They give the evidence of all uncials, of thirty selected cursives, freshly collated, endeavouring 'to represent every group, and every important sub-division of a group',[1] besides special readings from other cursives; of almost every important papyrus fragment, up to the latest discoveries; of the Armenian, Bohairic, Sahidic, Ethiopic, and Palestinian Aramaic, wherever needed, and of the Syro-hexaplar and Old Latin with especial fulness; with Hexaplar matter from the MSS. used. They also give the evidence from quotations in Philo, Josephus, and many Greek and Latin Fathers, according to the best editions available. The work must, of course, be many years in progress, and new materials are used as they come to hand. Genesis was published in 1906; the Octateuch was completed in 1918.

A work like this is difficult to criticise or to appreciate adequately. There has not yet been time for many results to appear from the use of the portions published. The present writer had his doubts at first as to the advantage, unless for saving of space, of abolishing the familiar numbers of the cursives in favour of small letters, and would gladly have seen more of the evidence, say, of the Vulgate and of Tertullian, for comparison and convenience. But he knows that whatever the editors did was done on mature reflection and with the best advice, and that such criticism as the above would not be likely to meet with any general support; while every day's use of the book has left him better pleased with it than before.

Another modern work of great utility is the Oxford

[1] 'The Forthcoming Cambridge Septuagint', art. (by the editors) in *Journal of Theological Studies*, July 1902.

Concordance to the Septuagint, by the late Drs. Hatch and Redpath, the main part of which appeared 1892–1897. It is hardly necessary to describe this in detail; it contains all that can be expected in a concordance, the Greek words in the translated books being referred to the corresponding Hebrew roots. On the whole, it is extremely trustworthy, and has from the first been bearing fruit, as it is easy to use, and supplies in many directions just what is wanted. Various articles by Mr. H. St. J. Thackeray in the *Journal of Theological Studies* during recent years show how in skilful hands this Concordance may be an instrument to make discoveries.

Mr. Thackeray has also produced the first part of a valuable Grammar of the O.T. in Greek; and R. Helbing has done likewise in Germany. The worker is now being provided with tools in far better quantity and quality than heretofore. The 'Letter of Aristeas' has also been edited, and separately translated by Thackeray, and by Prof. Wendland, the editor, with Cohn, of the latest standard collection of Philo's works. It is impossible to name all the workers of the present day, when it has at any rate been said that "il est à croire que les LXX. sont plus que jamais à la mode' (*Revue Biblique*, April 1906). It is equally impossible to omit reference to the work of Canon Charles upon the Apocrypha and Pseudepigrapha, culminating in the publication by the Clarendon Press of two huge volumes, containing English translations, introductions and notes, critical and explanatory. Canon Charles had previously edited several of the books from the Ethiopic, Greek, and other languages, dealing mainly with works of apocalyptic character; in the Oxford *corpus* he has the help of several who have edited other books, and rendered much service in kindred fields of labour. Perhaps it may not be invidious to mention the names of Mrs. Lewis, and Professors Conybeare and Rendel Harris.

Questions of the text, especially in Kings and the Psalter, have been dealt with by Prof. Rahlfs of Göttingen with great clearness and cogency in his *Septuaginta-Studien*, 1904, 1907, 1911. Prof. Deissmann in Germany, and the late Prof. J. H. Moulton[1] in England, have fought manfully for the development of the study of the *κοινή*, and for recognition of the Greek of the N.T. and the O.T. as part and parcel of the ordinary Greek of the time; in which, with the powerful aid of the late Prof. Thumb[2] as a paramount authority on the Greek language through all periods, they have met with great, if not yet complete, success. Materials for this study have been supplied by Drs. Grenfell and Hunt, who have unearthed grand quantities of papyri in Egypt, including valuable fragments of the Septuagint itself; so that O.T. students owe them a special debt, besides their share of the general one. Discoveries have been made also in other quarters; new Coptic MSS. of the Old Testament; the oldest papyrus of Biblical or Apocryphal literature known, an Aramaic fragment of Aḥiḳar, dated by experts as of the fifth century B.C.; fragments of the Hexapla, at Milan, identified by Dr. Giovanni Mercati, now of the

[1] Died from exhaustion and exposure, the boat in which he travelled being torpedoed by the Germans (1917), Deissmann's countrymen.

[2] Died August 1915.

Vatican Library, and from Cairo, recognised by the late Dr. C. Taylor; fragments of Aquila's version of the Psalms, also due to Dr. Taylor, and of Kings, recognised by Prof. Burkitt, who also secured the Sinaitic Syriac of the Gospels, and who has contributed greatly to the textual criticism of the Greek O.T., through the Old Latin, by his study and published text of the African writer Tyconius. As a specimen of other valuable work may be mentioned the Introduction, by Dr. Ceriani of Milan, to the photograph of Cod. Q (1890), one of the chief authorities for the LXX. of the Prophets. A commentary on Ezekiel, by C. H. Cornill, is noteworthy for the use made of the LXX. to emend the Hebrew text. It is not, primarily, an edition of the LXX.; but owing to the attention given to the classification of the Greek MSS., it touches much of the same ground as Ceriani's Introduction, so that their results can be compared. Lastly, for the present, but by no means least, the work of the late Dr. Eberhard Nestle must be named, the more because he expended so much labour in forwarding the work of others, for instance, the Cambridge 'O.T. in Greek'. His articles, *e.g.*, in Hastings' *Dict. of the Bible* and in the *Real-Encykl. für prot. Theologie und Kirche* give, in relatively small compass, an astonishing amount of detail and a wide general view: his *Septuaginta-Studien* furnish the results of great labour on small but important points.

The time since 1850 has certainly been fruitful. Thus, for instance, Montfaucon has been succeeded by Field: Fabricius by Charles: Cardinal Carafa and the Sixtine by Prof. Swete and the Cambridge "manual" text: Holmes and Parsons by Brooke and M'Lean: Trom by Hatch and Redpath. If the earlier work be compared with the later, the gain can be seen to be immense; in some cases the treatment involves such a completely fresh grasp of the subject that no comparative estimate is really possible. In some departments, moreover, the present workers have had no predecessors. The discoverers and examiners of papyri are exploring ground hitherto untrodden; the study of the *κοινή*, its vocubulary and its grammar, has assumed an entirely new aspect. Many documents and fragments of great value, either unsuspected, or thought to be hopelessly lost, have been recovered and made known; and the accumulation of this new material has not hindered the general connexion and consolidation of the study. The ground has been steadily cleared, and there is good hope of a considerable advance toward what all desire—an improved, if not a perfect, text of the Greek Old Testament, and an understanding of it, and of the numerous books that are more or less nearly connected with it.

The age of great Polyglot Bibles is probably over; to be succeeded by more detailed work upon the separate versions, wherein the names of Lagarde, Nestle, and Conybeare are already conspicuous. The work of providing better texts of the Fathers goes steadily on; the editions of Harnack, Zahn, von Gebhardt and Lightfoot, the Berlin series of the earlier Greek, and the Vienna *Corpus* of the Latin writers, are all gifts to be received with thankfulness. It was once a pleasure to note, what the lists of authorities in many a standard work will show, how many nations were contributing in harmony toward the desired ends.[1] Men of Latin and of Teutonic race, on both sides of the Channel and of the Atlantic, have had their share; and it seems to link the millennia together to find that the author of a great lexicon of later Greek bears the name of Sophocles.

[1] There was something delightfully cosmopolitan in seeing an article by J. Psichari in the *Revue des Études Juives*, 1908, in which, if I remember right, the printer had to deal with not less than a dozen languages.

CHAPTER IV

THE TEXT OF THE SEPTUAGINT

Textual Criticism—The necessity for it—Its methods—Special difficulties of the LXX.—Varieties of text, due to corruption, revision, locality—Marshalling of the material—Lagarde's rules—Difficulties in criticising text of a version—Some examples.

WE have now attempted to gain some idea of the problems to be faced when studying the Septuagint. This has been done in two ways: first, by surveying, in a preliminary way, the text itself, to see what we find there; second, by regarding the history of the version, and noticing what work has been done in connexion with it, in ancient and modern times. It is now time to approach the problems for ourselves. As to the order in which to do this, it is perhaps most logical to begin with the matter of textual criticism, that is, of ascertaining what the actual words of the writers were; it is clearly useless to spend time, if we can avoid it, in examining or studying what they did not say. Still, in practice, textual criticism and other study of an ancient text generally proceed side by side; for until some understanding of an author is gained, only the roughest and most elementary study and correction of the text are possible. As, however, the textual study of the Septuagint is peculiar in character, and leads naturally on to other matters of importance, it will be treated here first; though readers who prefer can postpone this chapter till later.

There are many modern books which explain the general course of textual study, and reference will presently be made to some of them; but it will be as well to touch upon principles here, to clear the ground. The works of ancient authors, when printing was yet unknown, were necessarily copied by hand. What we possess now, as the basis of our modern printed editions, are manuscripts, seldom or never the writing of the original author, nor yet the first copies made from that; but copies, generally made several centuries later than the author's time, and with some generations of copies, so to speak, between them and the original. It is by no means unusual for a MS. to be much more than a thousand years later than the author: sometimes the oldest surviving MS. of a work is so. If such a MS. be examined, it is pretty certain that there will be found in it many things which we are sure cannot be the author's real words; there will be obvious mistakes, incoherencies, false grammar, misspellings, and the like. There will probably be other mistakes of less obvious character, which detailed study and knowledge will only gradually reveal. If we have, as is very often the case, more than one, possibly several MSS. of the work, it will soon be discovered that in various places they disagree; one, or more, will contain passages which differ more or less from the other MS. or MSS.; there may be two, three, or even more different 'readings'. Speaking generally, in that case we know that only one of these readings can be right; not necessarily that which appears so at first sight; not necessarily even one which makes some sort of sense against one which appears to make none. Having realised that the people who copied works out frequently varied from the original words, we must try to recover the original, and, as one of the steps toward this, to understand the nature of their mistakes or variations.

A little consideration will show that there are three principal ways in which copyists may come to vary the words:

(1) Sheer mistakes, due to carelessness, weariness, or ignorance: accidental.

(2) Attempts to correct, as they write, what appear to be mistakes in the copy from which they are working; this may be consciously done, or unconsciously ('subconsciously', some might call it).

(3) Alterations, deliberate or even systematic: either (*a*) a more thorough form of (2), attempts to correct the grammar or language; or to improve it; or (*b*), deliberate modification of the words, to alter the meaning in a direction more approved by the copyist.

These might conceivably all occur in the same MS. Generally, according to the nature of the work concerned, and the sort of person copying, one or other will be the more frequent and prominent in a given instance. (3), especially in the form (*b*), is a comparatively special case, and quite rare in many classes of works. On the other hand, (2) and even

(3) (*a*) may frequently occur in the copying from a MS. in which there are already cases of (1). In some instances this may have resulted in cancelling out differences, and restoring the original; in others, it may be feared in most, it may only have ended in departing further from it.

It is not surprising if cases of (1) are frequent in some MSS. The persons who copied them may have been ignorant of the language in which they were writing, or may have been, according to our ideas, illiterate. In such cases they could hardly be expected to copy accurately, as the nature of any mistake they were making would not be apparent to them. The general name for all departures from the original wording, however caused, is 'corruption'. Many 'corrupt' passages may, of course, remain in our texts unsuspected, and therefore untouched; but this will vary with the circumstances of the particular case.

A modern editor, dealing with the text of an ancient author, would begin by collecting as many MSS. of it as possible; or rather, since the actual MSS. are carefully guarded, either careful records of their readings ('collations', *i.e.*, comparisons), or in some cases transcripts, facsimiles, or, if fortunately they can be had, photographs. He notices which resemble one another most among these, and arranges them in groups accordingly. If one MS. has practically all the mistakes that another has, and some more of its own, it is pretty clear that it is, if not a copy of that MS. itself, at least copied from another specimen representing the same class of text. By this kind of reasoning a 'genealogy' of the MSS. is arrived at, if there are enough of them; that is, an arrangement of them in groups, each group depending upon an older MS., whether extant or not, the older ones on MSS. older again (their 'exemplars' or 'archetypes'), and so as far back as possible towards the original author. By this process many of the mistakes in the later MSS. are dismissed, and a purer and more correct text is reached. But where, after going as high up as he can, the editor still cannot reach an intelligible text, or one which, in reasonable probability, may be what the author wrote, or when he has no variety of MSS., and the reading is unsatisfactory, he is obliged to try and 'emend' the text by 'conjecture'; that is, to guess what the author really did write. (Some scholars err on the side of deserting the MS. reading too soon, others on the side of sticking to it too long.) This guessing is not, or at any rate should not be, done at random, by impulse or according to mere fancy; it is guided by knowledge and by certain principles. Practice and study teach, that owing to the resemblances between some letters, mistakes with regard to them are specially likely to occur; these vary according to the language concerned, and even the writing fashionable at each date in the career of a language. If, again, as often happened, MSS. were written from dictation, another series of mistakes may arise, between letters which are alike to the ear in sound, instead of to the eye in shape. There are also slips and lapses to which copyists are prone; if two neighbouring clauses resemble one another, in the run of the letters, especially at the beginning or end, they are apt to let the eye stray from one clause to the similar letters in the other, with the result that if the eye has gone forward, they miss out something, and if backward, they write a syllable, word, or clause twice over or even more; the latter error is generally far easier to correct. These besetting habits of scribes become familiar, and experts are on the look out for them; they even get to know the particular tricks and lapses of individual writers of MSS. There is also some guidance for conjectures, when necessary, in the nature of an author's text. If it is poetry, the metre is a guide; it is no use making a guess which will not fit the hexameter of an epic poet, or the iambic in the episodes of a Greek play. If it is history, a text is hardly admissible which contradicts the facts as given in the context; if it is philosophy, the argument must be considered, and the text should be coherent and consistent. Each kind of writing presents its own difficulties, and requires special study; but in the hands of gifted scholars these very difficulties help to some extent, guiding their conjectures and checking their results.

The difficulty of studying the text of ancient authors varies greatly, according to the quality and quantity of the extant MSS. in each case. There are plenty of MSS. of Virgil, some very good and old; and as a general rule the older the better, because there has been less time for repeated copying to introduce mistakes, and for men to lose the true traditions of the author's words and meaning. The MSS. of Horace are good, but not so old as those of Virgil; still there is a good supply, and though quality is best, quantity also helps, as one MS. may serve to check and correct another. Yet in such cases it is sometimes hard to decide between two rival readings, equally plausible. In contrast to this, the text of some works of Æschylus and Tacitus depends on a single MS., practically or absolutely; so that if the MS. reading is obviously, or probably, corrupt, conjecture is the only chance; and sometimes the MS. is torn, and a piece of it lost; if more than a few letters are missing, the case is hopeless, unless by good luck some other author has quoted the missing passage. Sometimes, again, a passage which does occur in a MS. is quoted elsewhere, but with differences; then the chances of error on either side must be balanced, according to the general accuracy of the MS. and the author who quotes.

Turning now to the case of the Septuagint, let us see how it stands in these respects. We shall find that the MSS. are numerous, old, and, in their way, good. But—they constantly differ: giving us two or three readings between which to choose, each supported by MSS. as old, and as many, as would make up the total stock for many an ancient author. We have, through our survey of the history of the version, a general idea why this is; it is because, besides any corruptions in the ordinary course of copying, the text was revised and worked over by many different hands; and both the ordinary corruption and the revisions went on, more or less independently, over long periods of time, and in different countries. The results of these processes find their way into our MSS., and that not separately, but combined and mixed. Before we can reach the true text, all this mixture has to be disentangled;

each of the processes has to be undone; the revision cancelled, the accidental corruptions corrected; and if the local versions had come to differ before the days of revision, the choice must be made between them, in order to reach the real original.

So far, what has been written might apply almost equally well to the New Testament. The amount of mere corruption may be greater in parts of the O.T. than in the N.T.; but it is not large in either. The revision in the case of the N.T. is historically less established than in the O.T.; but it is the general opinion of the leading authorities that revision did take place, and on somewhat similar lines; at any rate, the appearances of the text-variations are not unlike. The mixture in the MSS., the local divisions of texts, and the general bearing of the secondary versions (Latin, Coptic, etc.) are all fairly comparable. But in the case of the N.T., the textual student may regard the Greek as the ultimate original, beyond which he need not look. Here the Septuagint is on quite a different footing, and a fresh set of complications arises. When (or if) we arrive at the original text of the Greek of the translated books, we have still to consider its relation to the Hebrew. (If they differ, one, at least, of the two must be, in a sense, wrong.) Though it is not for us to correct the translation, and issue yet another revised Septuagint in these latter days, yet it is important to see whether the translator went here and there astray, and if so, how he came to do so. And finally, the question has to be faced, whether the translation, in any places, or in general, represents an older and better Hebrew text than the official received one; which has, and has had for many centuries, comparatively very few variants. Substantially, the received Hebrew text was fixed almost as it is now, at the time when Origen compared it with the Septuagint of his day, and issued his revised text, supplemented from Aquila and Theodotion, who also used much the same Hebrew text. So that the Hebrew encounters us not only at the time when the version was first made, but also, twice over at least, three and four centuries later, when the later translators and Origen (to say nothing of Lucian) used it. Every vicissitude through which the Septuagint passed has left its mark, and caused difficulties with which the modern student must deal in his efforts to recover the original text. Therefore the method of the textual critic must be, in some of his processes, historical.

The extant Greek MSS. have been by now to some extent grouped and classified. Despite the mixture of text, they can be recognised as mainly Hesychian, Lucianic, Hexaplar, or pre-Hexaplar. As in the N.T., this is done partly by comparing them with quotations in the Fathers, whose known dates and places of writing make their affinities pretty clear. Thus Cyril of Alexandria, writing in Egypt (*circ.* A.D. 415), would naturally be expected to use a text of the recension of Hesychius; John Chrysostom's quotations would come from a Lucianic text, such as circulated along the line from Antioch through Asia Minor to Constantinople; Jerome's from a Hexaplar text, though he also had access to the original Hexapla and texts with the critical marks. The pre-Hexaplar text is to be ascertained from the

Greek Fathers of the second century, and also from Philo; while the Old Latin as used in Africa, as late as the fourth century, preserves a pre-Hexaplar form of text. In using these quotations, it is needful to remember that a copyist may at times write a Biblical quotation according to a text more familiar to him than the author's, so that care is needed in drawing conclusions from such evidence, which is, moreover, fragmentary.

Another part of the process is very much that which is described in the *Introduction* to Westcott and Hort's *New Testament in Greek*. From a consideration of the readings in a MS., an opinion is formed of the value and character of its text; this, carried out with MSS. in a group, is extended upward to the archetype of the group. From details of spelling, handwriting, and other small clues, the character of this archetype is obtained, and working further up, still considering texts together, the parent of two or more such archetypes is to a large extent mentally reconstructed and analysed. Working up as far as possible, and then downward again,[1] the MSS. fall into a kind of genealogical tree, and the knowledge thus gained helps to form an improved judgment on readings, both by closer acquaintance with the characters of the individual MSS., and by its being now clear in many cases whether a given reading has departed from that of the archetype or not. On this process, in the case of the N.T., Westcott and Hort laid great stress. When its results

[1] Though Hort did not say so, this process bears some analogy to the Platonic method of ascending from the study of the particulars to that of the ideas, and descending again to a better knowledge.

agree with the evidence of the Fathers and versions, the preliminary sorting out of the MSS. may be considered satisfactory. The Syro-hexaplar, with its critical marks, and the Old Latin give very material help; and guidance towards the pre-Hexaplar text is the more valuable, because the Septuagint MSS. often differ in character in different books of the Bible. Codd. A and B, for instance, vary, both relatively and absolutely, in the historical books and in the Prophets.

The apparatus of the larger Cambridge LXX. will help this work immensely. At present only the Octateuch has been issued, and it will take time to make use of the improved stores of information. Meantime, independent work has been done upon the text of Kings and Psalms by Rahlfs, and on the Prophets by Ceriani, Cornill, Oesterley, and Procksch. Lagarde's provisional Lucianic text can be more profitably used, now that it can be tested afresh in the earlier books.

At present, a rough classification of the documents we possess will divide them as follows:

Lucianic: For earlier books, N, 19, 82, 93, 108, 118: also, akin to Theodoret's text, 54, 59, 75 (Θ in Deut.?):

For the Prophets, V (=23), 22, 36, 48, 51, (93) (144) 153, 245, 308, etc.: a sub-group, 62, 147:

Slavonic and Gothic versions: John Chrysostom, Theodore of Mopsuestia, Theodoret. The Old Latin represents an ancient element in this composite text, as seen in 62, 147, and others.

Hesychian: earlier books, 44 (*d*), 74, 76, 84, 106, 134:

Prophets, A, Q, (א?) 26, 41 (Isaiah), 49, 68, 87 91, 106, 198, (228) (238) 306. (Perhaps A, 26, 106, 306, form one sub-group; 49, 68, etc., another.)

Bohairic Version: Cyril of Alexandria.

Hexaplar: G, M, 15, 38, 57, 58, 72, 131, and *v* (from Athos). The fragments of copies of the Hexapla. The Gallican Psalter, and Jerome's Septuagint text generally. Parts of the Sahidic Version. The Syro-hexaplar.

For the Prophets, 22, according to critical marks: 86 marg. 88, Q marg.

Pre-hexaplar: The old Latin, Syro-hexaplar, negatively, and according to crit. marks, Sahidic (partly):

Greek and Latin Fathers down to Clement of Alexandria. Especially Epistle of Barnabas, Irenaeus, Justin Martyr, Tertullian, Cyprian, 'Speculum', Tyconius: Philo and Josephus.

Quotations in the New Testament. Elements in the text of the great uncials and some others.

The pre-Hexaplar evidence requires careful sifting. On the Psalms, see Rahlfs, *Septuaginta-Studien*, ii.

Of these, the Hexaplar and Lucianic readings are the easiest to recognise, because the Hexaplar can be checked by the critical marks in the MSS. and by the remains of the later versions, and the Lucianic text is dominent, if not unmixed, in several MSS., and possesses comparatively distinct characteristics. The pre-Hexaplar text is more difficult to recognise, as the evidence for it is mostly fragmentary, and often of a negative character. Rahlfs considers that the Verona Psalter (R) has a 'Western' pre-Hexaplar text. The Hesychian text may be fairly well preserved: the difficulty is to recognise it, because of its rather colourless and therefore elusive character. Hesychius' work, so far as we know it, would seem to have been a slighter and more conservative revision. It is, however, not quite clear whether the ordinary Egyptian text from which he worked was, as most authorities suppose, untouched by the influence of the Hexapla, or not.

Lagarde laid down certain rules for the study of the text of the Greek O.T., which still, on the whole, represent the prevailing views and practice. Briefly, they are to the effect that, firstly, as all our MSS. contain 'mixed' texts, the process of recovering the true text must be 'eclectic'; that is to say, readings must be gathered from various MSS., and the text cannot be based solely on one authority. The critic's 'measuring-rule' must be his knowledge of the particular translator's style, and his chief expedient for resolving difficulties must be his resourcefulness in recognising when the clue is to be found in the Hebrew underlying the Greek, and when it lies in the corruption of the Greek itself. Secondly, a free rendering is to be regarded as more likely to be the true LXX. than a slavishly literal one; thirdly, a translation of a different Hebrew text from the present (Massoretic) one is to be chosen as against one which represents the M.T. The first maxim is probably the most entirely valid of the three; the second and third require great caution in their application; for obviously the LXX. did, frequently at least, agree with the Massoretic text, and their rendering is often closely literal, though not to the same extent as Aquila's.

At a later time, in the introduction to his Lucianic text, Lagarde reiterated the necessity for the 'eclectic' process, but laid more stress on the principle of classifying and grouping the MSS. In the preface to his *Genesis Graece*, published fifteen years before, in 1868, I can find no reference at all to Lucianic MSS., though a good deal to the Hexaplar.

It is hardly possible yet to set straight to work at the reconstruction of the original text. The evidence of the new Cambridge edition will have to be carefully examined and weighed. But as to the preferable reading in many passages, it is already possible to form a judgment. The Old Latin, as Prof. Burkitt has pointed out (*Rules of Tyconius*, pp. cvii–cxviii), serves as a guide to the pre-Hexaplar reading in several places, and even preserves a true reading here and there where all the Greek MSS. have lost it. So also, the true reading is sometimes found in a very few MSS., as in Isa. xxx. 33, where 48 308 are probably right, and in xliii. 14, where 305 is probably right, though alone. Many would add 93's reading *παταχρα* in viii. 21 as pointing to the true text. On the whole, when the true LXX. is reconstructed, it will not be, so far as we can at present judge, anything very different from the resultant of our best MSS., corrected by the versions and occasionally from the Fathers, and with some corruptions removed. There is plenty to be done, but meantime we are not so badly off, especially as in the modern work it may be hoped that few false steps have been taken, even if the progress has not been rapid. If, after all that is possible has been done, some baffling passages and some rival readings remain undecided, this is the case with almost all ancient literature, even with those books upon whose text the greatest labour has been spent.

But, if textual criticism might end here, 'inter-textual' criticism remains; we have yet to balance the LXX. against the Hebrew. We may find, that when textual criticism will do no more for us, when the MSS. are united, or when the evidence strongly favours a given reading, yet that reading may be different from the Hebrew, and, moreover, may be quite unintelligible. To such cases we must return later. Meantime, though it would require a book many times larger than this to deal fully with textual questions, it will be as well to examine a few passages where readings differ. It will be seen that the Hebrew has to be considered before deciding finally upon most of them.

GEN. vi. 2. *ἰδοντες δὲ οἱ ἄγγελοι τοῦ θεοῦ τὰς θυγατέρας τῶν ἀνθρώπων . . .*

The only question here is between *ἄγγελοι* and *υἱοί*, and Heb. has 'sons'. The authorities for *ἄγγελοι* are AE 55* 56* 72 75 121 (B and D are not extant here), the Bohairic, as edited, and the text of another MS., one Ethiopic MS., the margin of Syro-hex., Philo, Josephus, Clement of

Alexandria (apparently), the text of Eusebius, as edited, and the 'Speculum': Cyril of Alexandria also knew of the reading. There is some uncertainty about A, as the word is written over an erasure, and it may not be the original hand of the MS. The asterisk is the usual symbol for the original hand of MSS., as used above.

υἱοί is read by the Hexaplaric uncial M, by correctors 55 and 56, and the rest of the cursives: the margin of the Bohairic MS. mentioned above, an Ethiopic MS., the Armenian, and the text of Syro-hex. by Origen, MSS. of Eusebius, Athanasius, Chrysostom, Theodore of Mopsuestia (Latin trans.), Cyril of Alexandria, Theodoret, and an anonymous chronicler, edited by Lagarde. It is also the reading of Aquila and Symmachus.

ἄγγελοι, then, is read by only a few MSS. But A is the oldest extant, E has ancient elements in its text, and 55 is an important cursive. The versions are divided, the Bohairic and Syro-hex. showing knowledge of both readings. The only Old Latin evidence, the 'Speculum', is for *ἄγγελοι*.

Now as Origen reads *υἱοί*, and Aq. Symm. render so, it is important to notice that all other Patristic evidence for *υἱοί* is later than the Hexapla, while Philo and Josephus are against it. The balance of pre-Hexaplar evidence is thus in favour of *ἄγγελοι*, and Lagarde's maxim also, which recommends us to adopt a free rendering as against a literal one; for *ἄγγελοι* does not represent a different Hebrew text (if it did, Lagarde's third maxim would favour it), but is doubtless an interpretative rendering of 'sons'. For *ἄγγελοι* or *ἄγγελοι τοῦ θεοῦ* is used to represent Heb. 'sons of Elohim' in Job. i. 6, ii. 1, xxxviii. 7. In Deut. xxxii. 8 the Heb. is 'sons of *Israel*'; and in 43 υἱοί θεοῦ and ἄγγελοι θεοῦ are introduced, as parallels, into the expansion of the Hebrew.

We may conclude that ἄγγελοι is more probably the true LXX., and that υἱοί, if not substituted by Origen from Aquila, and perpetuated in the Hexapla, must have been an early correction from the Hebrew. However, the Bohairic MS.'s margin is almost the only evidence for it older than Origen; that is to say, if the version is older than Origen, the MS. is not. Tertullian, indeed (*De virginibus velandis*, 7), has *Conspicati autem filii dei filias hominum*; and though the context shows that he was interpreting the passage of angels, and his textual evidence is regarded as precarious, yet it may be taken to show that υἱοί was not an unknown reading in his time. But for this, we might have classed it as a simple case of a Hexaplaric reading from Aquila; as it is, while deciding for ἄγγελοι, we must make the reservation that the other may have been an alternative reading before Origen's time.

GEN. xxxvii. 24. ὁ δὲ λάκκος ἐκεῖνος ὕδωρ οὐκ εἶχεν.

This is the reading of A 44 75 106 121 and a MS. of Cyril of Alexandria. All other authorities read κενός for ἐκεῖνος, including O.L., Boh., Syro-hex.; except 59, which omits the word altogether. For εἶχεν, Chrysostom, 58 120, and two more cursives have ἔχων, Chrys. and 20 have ἦν κενός, and so O.L. and Boh.

κενός agrees with Hebrew, but is not Hexaplaric, for it is in the O.L. Ἐκεῖνος might at first sight seem an accidental Greek corruption; but more probably the omission of the verb in Greek (naturally supplied in some other versions) led to the alteration, which is neat enough from the purely Greek point of view to suggest Alexandrian work. Now 44 and 106 (and A sometimes) are Hesychian in character; and this is probably the origin of ἐκεῖνος, κενός being the true text.

If this be so, Lagarde's rule would here have been misleading; and an accurate version must frequently coincide with its original.

PSALM lxii. (lxiii.) 6. τὸ ὄνομά σου ℵ*BR*? Boh Sah Aeth O.Lat

τὸ στόμα μου ℵ[ca]T }
στόμα μου R[a vid] } Vulg.

Here ὄνομα seems to be an ancient corruption, corrected from the Hebrew, possibly through the Hexapla. The pronoun was altered to suit the sense.

ISA. v. 26. καὶ συριεῖ αὐτούς] B etc.

αὐτούς] αὐτοῖς ℵAQ* 24 36 41 48 62 90 106 304.
Cyprian, *Testimonia* i. 21, 22 *et adtrahet illos.*
'Speculum' et trahet eas.

The Latin, with its different wordings, is due to a misreading of the Greek, representing συρεῖ αὐτούς. This supports the accusative, and it may be that B and its associates are right, the verb standing for 'hiss them on': cf. another sense in Job xxvii. 23. The dat., cf. vii. 18, may be a change, not so much on account of the Hebrew as for the sake of an easier construction. In xxx. 14, most MSS. read ἀποσυριεῖς, while 109 144 308 read ἀποσυρεῖς, doubtless right (ἀποσύρεις 104 106 198 309).

The corruptions in the two passages go in opposite directions.

ISA. liv. 17. πᾶν σκεῦος σκευαστὸν ἐπὶ σὲ οὐκ εὐοδώσω.

So B, and *e silentio*, 106 109 305.

σκευος του ℵ* σκευος φθαρτον ℵ[ca? cb] AQ* (σκευαστον Q) 22 26 36 48 49 51 62 86 90 93 106 144 147 198 233 308

επι δε σε ουκ ευδοκησω A 233

ευοδωθησεται Q[mg] 22 36 41 48 51 62 87 90 91 93 97 104 144 228 308 309

φθαρτόν, it will be seen, is read by AQ and the greater number of cursives, including some of each class (Luc. Hes. Hex.). Nevertheless, B's reading is almost certainly right; the του of ℵ* is probably from omitting σκευασ after σκεῦος. B, though not at its best in Isaiah, shows its independence here. Its reading is a case of an attempt, rare in LXX., to imitate the Hebrew, which has here an assonance, formed by the words for 'every instrument'. There is a curious parallel to the wrong reading here, in the N.T., 1 Pet. i. 23, where ℵAC read ἐκ φθορᾶς φθαρτῆς for ἐκ σπορᾶς φθαρτῆς. Here φθεῖραι immediately precedes πᾶν σκεῦος.

A's δὲ after ἐπί is an attempt to get sense and connexion. εὐδοκήσω is neither so easy in construction nor so usual in equivalent for the Hebrew as εὐοδώσω, though not impossible. The Luc. and Hes. cursives mostly agree in reading εὐοδωθήσεται: but 26 and 106, generally close associates of A, have left the group, and so has 198, without however giving A's reading. B's reading is probably right throughout, though less certain as to the verb; the third person, however, looks like a modification due to Lucian (if not ancient and preserved by him).

Ezek. xxviii. 7 has been referred to above (p. 53).

At present, textual study is bound to occupy a great deal of the labour spent on the LXX. Those who have no special taste for it are apt to find it dull and difficult, but they ust remcognise that it is needed. If, however, the taste be acquired, the lives of many eminent scholars seem to show that it remains, and often becomes absorbing. The N.T. has probably had more labour expended on its text than any other book; but the Greek O.T. may yet run it hard in this respect. Several excellent books on the textual study of the N.T. have appeared, which form as good an introduction to that of the LXX. as can be desired. But we have seen that in the case of the LXX. we must be prepared at any time to go a step further, and, as we are dealing with a translation, to consider the original also. Our next step therefore must be to examine the LXX., so far as we can, in relation to the Hebrew.

CHAPTER V

THE CHARACTER OF THE TRANSLATION: THE GREEK AND THE HEBREW

The Greek and the Hebrew, as we have them—Their differences: of order, of matter, verbal—Examples—Varying character of the books in LXX.—The task of the translators—Difficulty of reading the Hebrew—The Hebrew verb—'Representation' of tenses—Psalm civ.—The relative—Other points of syntax—Methods of dealing with them—General character of the Greek O.T.

EVEN the question of the relation of the LXX. to the Hebrew has some complications of its own. It is necessary to gain some notion of the capabilities of the translators, and, if possible, of their circumstances; remembering that various hands were employed in the work, ranging perhaps over two centuries, or even more. The character of the Hebrew text before the translators must be realised to the best of our power; and the script in which it was written; and the question has to be kept open, whether the Greek or the Hebrew is to be given the preference, either in general or in certain details. When we say 'the Greek or the Hebrew', this ultimately means, the Hebrew presupposed by the Greek translation, or the Hebrew as now extant, which is substantially the same as that before Origen as he worked. As we have already seen, these points meet us in the textual criticism of the LXX., and may be considered as part of that study; but there is some advantage in considering them also as a separate matter.

At the outset, we may divide the question of this relation of LXX. to Hebrew into three parts; two of these, however, may for our purpose be dealt with together.

(1) The LXX. occasionally gives a passage in a different order from the Hebrew. Prof. Swete (*Introd. to O.T. in Greek*, p. 231) calls the instances of this 'Differences of Sequence'.

(2) The LXX. sometimes gives a different version altogether of a passage, generally a narrative. Instances of this Prof. Swete (*Introd.*, p. 242) calls 'Differences of Subject-Matter'.

(3) There are also differences, greater and less, which still amount only to what may fairly be called *verbal* differences: a word, or words, or their syntax relation, varying in the Greek and the Hebrew.

With each of these three kinds of difference may be associated omissions in either text, or additions in the other, whichever they may appear to be when investigated.

On the whole, the simplest way is to treat (1) and (2), the differences 'of sequence' and 'of subject-matter', together, and apart from the verbal divergences. There may be instances where it is not easy to decide under which head to class a passage; but in general they seem fairly distinct, and moreover to be distinct in kind, not merely in degree. At any rate, this is a convenient working hypothesis, which, if ill-founded, will soon betray itself to be so as we proceed. Dealing then first with the differences of 'sequence' and of 'subject-matter', it will be clear that they cannot, speaking generally, be the result of mere carelessness or accident on the part of the translators, or of copyists of the Greek version. They cannot be dismissed with one general explanation, but need to be examined separately, and judged on their merits; but when considered, in regard to their nature and amount, they certainly seem to point to this, that in some places the Greek translators followed a different and differently arranged Hebrew text from that which we now possess. It is usual to indicate the present (Massoretic) Hebrew by $\mathfrak{M}$, the LXX. text (or, practically, its underlying Hebrew) by $\mathfrak{G}$; sometimes $\mathfrak{G}^{A}$, $\mathfrak{G}^{B}$, $\mathfrak{G}^{Luc}$, etc., for the varieties of the Greek text in MSS. or recensions.

Gen. xxxi. 47–52, xxxv. 16–21.—$\mathfrak{G}$ seems to have rearranged these verses, in the first case to give a more logical sequence, in the second, whether rightly or not, to suit the locality. It would be harder to account for $\mathfrak{M}$ as derived from $\mathfrak{G}$.

Exod. xx. 13–15, Deut. v. 17–18.—The order of the 6th, 7th, and 8th commandments in B, but not in AF, differs from the Hebrew. It is therefore not a simple case of $\mathfrak{G}$ against $\mathfrak{M}$. B's order is in Exodus 7, 8, 6 (this is often misstated), in Deut. 7, 6, 8. The Nash Papyrus of the Commandments (see Prof. Burkitt in *Jewish Quart. Review*, April 1903) has the order 7, 6, 8. In the N.T. Matthew xix. 18,[1] Mark x. 17 ($\aleph^{a}$BCΔ), give 6, 7, 8; while Luke xviii. 19, Rom. xiii. 9, and by implication Jas. ii. 11, put 7 before 6. Philo, twice for B's order, is balanced by Josephus on the other side. The change of order seems to have taken place early: the texts, perhaps, stand naturally in order of age thus: 𝔐 Exodus, 𝔐 Deut. ('wife' before 'house' in 10), 𝔊^{B}. How AF came to agree with 𝔐 is another question; there is no proof that their text was altered to make it agree, but it may be suspected from A's generally regular adherence to 𝔐.

The different order of the latter chapters of Exodus goes beyond all likelihood of accident, all the more because these chapters in a way repeat those preceding, describing the fulfilment of orders previously given. Yet 𝔊 differs considerably, mainly in shifting the description of the 'garments for Aaron and his sons' from the end to the beginning of the passage. It is difficult to detect any intrinsic superiority in 𝔊 here. The passage has been suspected as a later addition to the Hebrew, and it has been remarked that the Greek words used to translate various expressions are not the same as in the earlier chapters; this, however, is not conclusive, because (as Mr. H. J. Thackeray points out) the choice of Greek words varies in xxxv.–xl. taken alone, even in consecutive verses. Some think that 𝔊 was originally made from a text which did not contain these chapters, and that they were supplied later from another text. But this supposition does

[1] But Matthew and Luke have 5 after 9, and Mark after 'Defraud not'.

little to explain the transpositions, or the omissions of 𝔊, which here cannot be separated from the transpositions. There is nothing to show that 𝔊 is better, or the original, as against 𝔐.

In Deut. xxxii. 43, 𝔊 gives an expanded form, probably liturgical, a kind of doxology to the Song. It is not likely to be Christian in origin. The quotation in Heb. i. 6 follows Ps. xcvi. (xcvii.) 7, except the *καί* and tense of the verb, which agree with Deut. In Num. i., xxvi., and at the end of Hannah's song, 1 Sam. ii. 10, there are smaller differences resembling those in Exod. xxxv.–xl. and Deut. xxxii. 43 respectively.

In Joshua there are several differences, some of which are thought to point to 𝔊's having preserved an older text; others seem to be attempts of 𝔊 to rearrange the lists of places and round off the narrative.

Joshua's address to the sun (x. 12), the introduction to David's dirge (2 Sam. i. 18) and Solomon's invocation, transferred in 1 Kings viii. from ver. 12 to ver. 53, have some points in common. The last passage has been examined by Mr. Thackeray in the *Journal of Theol. Studies*, July 1910; he explains the Hebrew underlying the difficult Greek as really a liturgical direction, 𝔊 in this case representing an older form than 𝔐. Verses 12, 13 are supplied in A from Aquila in that place. 𝔊's reference at 53 to the 'Book of the Song' (= Jashar) is not found in 𝔐; in David's dirge it is omitted by N, 64, 71, 92, 106, 119, 242, but is in 𝔐, as it is in Joshua, where it is only a Hexaplar addition to 𝔊. (The reader may be reminded that Hexaplar additions only bring the Greek text, in point of fulness, up to the Hebrew; any true Septuagintal addition gives something not contained in the Hebrew at all: added by one version, or omitted by the other.)

In the books of Samuel and Kings, it has already been said that A and B differ considerably. Here, A is largely a Hexaplar text, whence its general agreement with 𝔐; B seems to represent a different Hebrew text from 𝔐, not very widely different from A with the additions removed. Thus in 1 Sam. xvii., xviii., many verses—xvii. 12–31, 41, 50, 55, xviii. 5, 10, 11, 17–19—are absent from B. Wellhausen thought them purposely omitted, by the translator or an early copyist, to remove what appeared to be difficulties; others have held that they were not found in the text used by the translator, but inserted in 𝔐 after the version was made. Each version, however, is coherent in itself; and the prevailing opinion therefore is that 𝔊 here represents an independent account, as well as in its longer insertions; the shorter ones may be of a different, sometimes inferior, character. B inserts, A with 𝔐 omits 1 Kings ii. 46 *a–l*, xii. 24 *a–z*, xvi. 28 *a–h*; A, however, contains ii. 35 *a–n*, and has xiv. 1–20, which B omits. Lucian's recension stands between A and B. In Kings iv. 20–28, 𝔐's arrangement is considered by some inferior to B's. In chap. vi. the appearances resemble those of Exod. xxxv.–xl. Further information must be sought in the commentaries on Samuel and Kings, and works on the history and literature. Lagarde's 'Lucian' is specially worth attention in these books.

The differences in the Psalms are chiefly those

of division. The LXX. add several titles, some of which are liturgical, and may preserve important information; others, referring to the authors or occasions of Psalms, cannot be accepted without caution and reserve. The 151st Psalm, and the addition to Ps. xiv., have been mentioned already.

In the Book of Proverbs 𝔊 omits some verses found in 𝔐, but adds more than it omits. Some of the insertions are made up from material occurring elsewhere in the O.T.; xxvi. 11 is from Ecclus. iv. 21; some verses appear to be derived from sources outside the O.T. Thackeray (*J. Th. Stud.*, Oct. 1911) has pointed out that many of the Greek lines are more or less metrical, and that there is difficulty in assigning the manufacture of these metrical tags to any other than the translator himself, though models existed for his imitation. It is generally held that some of the Greek insertions may be genuine proverbs, belonging to the time when they were collected, though not preserved in 𝔐. Swete (*Introd.* p. 255) gives a list of those which may be such, and it is to be noticed that they are distributed from chaps. vii. to xxvii. inclusive; and that xxii. 8*a* is quoted, 2 Cor. ix. 7.

In the Book of Job we find a different state of things. From Origen and Jerome we learn that the book was considerably shorter in the LXX. than in the Hebrew; from the critical marks in some MSS. we learn how the gaps, about 200 verses, were filled up. The Old Latin, where extant, gives the older, shorter text; that is to say, the 'African' Latin of Cyprian, Lucifer of Cagliari, and the 'Speculum'; Ambrose has a text equivalent to B's, and Jerome a Hexaplar text (Burkitt, *O.L. and Itala*, p. 8). The shorter text is also found in the Sahidic, though Prof. Burkitt thinks that this was arrived at by working from a Hexaplar text and omitting the passages marked as additions. All four of the great uncials are extant for much of the book, and they and most cursives insert most of the Hexaplar additions, but not all. It is now generally held that the original form of the LXX. is due to the translator, who shortened his original; he treated it with unusual freedom, and seems to have had some acquaintance with the classical Greek writers. The additions at the end of the book are pronounced to be of late date and no value.

The additions to Esther are five in number, amounting to 107 verses (Swete); there is no trace of their having existed in 𝔐, or even at all in Hebrew, though this latter point is less certain. The Greek cursives, both in the parts that are, and those that are not, in 𝔐, give a somewhat different version of the book; these are 19, 93, and 108, generally classed as Lucianic; 93 and 108 give both versions.

In Jeremiah, the difference of order is great, and in a sense systematic, being confined to the latter portion of the book, and consisting there mainly in shifting a group of prophecies from one place to another, and rearranging them within the group. This is explained by some from the standpoint that 𝔊 represents more nearly the original form, and a shorter form, as passages of several verses, appearing in 𝔐, are not found in it, while 𝔊's additions are much slighter and shorter. (See A. W. Streane, *The*

Double Text of Jeremiah, 1896; also G. C. Workman, *The Text of Jeremiah*, 1889.) It may, however, be noticed, that if the rearrangement, in this book and elsewhere, should be due to 𝔊, omissions might take place, through inadvertence, in the course of carrying out the process; but it is true that some omissions occur in the parts of the book where there is no rearrangement.

The Book of Daniel according to the LXX. contains additions which may be compared to those in Esther, and like them form part of our Apocrypha. It also contains smaller additions, and treats the original with some freedom and looseness. This version was early superseded by that of Theodotion, who may, however, have merely revised a second and more accurate version (see above, p. 40). Theodotion's text is on the whole the shorter; it contains Susanna and Bel, and reasons have been given for thinking that these had a late Hebrew or Aramaic original (see the notes in the *Variorum Apocrypha*). It is fuller in a few places: the differences between the versions are marked in chaps. iv. and v.

As to the varying character of the translation, Thackeray (in *J. Th. Stud.* iv. pp. 245, 398, 578, and viii. 262 ff., in the years 1903 and 1907, and *Gramm. of O.T. in Greek*, p. 6 ff.) has classed the books provisionally, according to their style, literalness or freedom, and probable dates. Most of his conclusions would be very generally accepted. For instance, he places the Pentateuch, as a generally good translation in fair Greek of the period, in the third century B.C.: parts of Joshua he classes with it. Isaiah, the first of the Prophets to be translated, he puts near the beginning of the second century B.C.; a poor translation, occasionally falling away into paraphrase, but not in bad Greek. Except for the chapters at the end of Exodus, there are no marked divergences of arrangement between 𝔊 and 𝔐 in these books. In Isaiah, the difficulty of certain passages has caused many verses to suffer strange alteration in the version; but there is nothing to suggest that the translators worked from a text substantially different from 𝔐. So, at least, the present writer holds. Jeremiah and the books of Kingdoms are placed by Thackeray nearer the end of the second century B.C.: Jeremiah i.–xxviii. by a different hand from the rest, and 1 Kingdoms (1 Sam.) apart from the other books, in which more than one hand is distinguished: the Greek is 'indifferent' in Kingdoms, 'unintelligently literal' in the later part of Jeremiah. In Kings there are large differences between 𝔊 and 𝔐, of insertion and omission; in Jeremiah of transposition and omission. In Daniel (LXX.), Esther, Job, and Proverbs, marked by Thackeray as 'paraphrases and free renderings', as well as 1 Esdras, divergences are frequent, though not all of the same kind. The possible connexion between the amount and kind of discrepancy, and the classification of the books, has yet to be worked out.

So far, stress has been laid upon the varying character of the books in 𝔊, in language and in their relation to 𝔐. Yet, in nearly all the translated books, there is, at the same time, some sort of homogeneity. With due caution, therefore, they may be considered together, with a view to observing the problems with which the translators were confronted, and their methods in dealing with them.

First, it is easy to see that they succeed far better in narrative than in lyric and prophetic passages. It is not only that their prosaic style is less suited to these latter, but that they appear to lose the thread of connexion, and the meaning. This happens even in the poetic passages of the Pentateuch, as Gen. xlix., Exod. xv., Numb. xxiii., xxiv., Deut. xxxii., xxxiii. It is conspicuous in the Prophets; but conversely, when a piece of narrative is introduced among prophecies, as in Isa. xxxix., the translation at once becomes closer and clearer. Of course, prophetic and poetic passages are more difficult than narrative; and on looking nearer, we may surmise what one special cause of difficulty was. Greek and Hebrew are very dissimilar languages, though the flexibility of Greek enables it to keep the Hebrew order of words very exactly; but they are naturally remote from one another, and differ greatly, not least in the matter of the verb. The Greek has a rich store of tenses, and Hebrew has but two, or, counting a quasi-finite use of its participle, three. Even these are not so much tenses as *aspects* of the action; which, it is true, applies in some degree to Greek tenses also. Now in historical narrative the context is generally a guide to the necessary tense; in only a small proportion of verbs could there be any doubt. But in lyric and prophetic passages there is often great uncertainty. A comparison of any two modern translations of the Prophets will show this; for instance, many of the future tenses in the A.V. have disappeared in later translations, nor do these always agree. The context gives little or no help; and many of the prophets are given to abrupt transitions, the whole scene changing suddenly. This increases the difficulty. Commentators, indeed, often seem not to appreciate this practice fully; and to their failure in this respect is perhaps due a tendency, which some of them show, to reject many passages as interpolations.

In fact, the task of the translators was hard. When they lived, Hebrew was not exactly a dead language, but in something like the position which Latin occupied in the Romance lands, say about the twelfth and thirteenth centuries. If they understood Hebrew at all well, they were certainly not at home in it as their own language; nor was Aramaic the regular language of the Jews in Egypt. On the other hand, Greek was only an acquired language of two or three generations, and they certainly had not the inheritance of the prime of Attic behind them. They lived, in fact, at one of those periods when language-power, to a Jew at least, was weak: energy in this respect was neither widespread nor concentrated. History seems to show that the use of one language, in its prime, produces better intellectual results than a rough knowledge of two or three for practical needs of intercourse.

There was the further difficulty of script. The rolls of the Old Testament in Hebrew were probably far from easy reading to the translators. The Hebrew alphabet passed through various stages; the old Phoenician characters of the Moabite Stone would be quite unintelligible to one who only knew the later 'square' Hebrew, as seen in printed Bibles to-day; and many minor varieties of script were used at one time or another. What the Greek translators had before them was, as most authorities think, a transitional alphabet, approaching the square Hebrew, and not unlike that of the Nash Papyrus, but in an earlier stage. In this case, besides the usual confusing pairs D and R, V and I, there are possibilities of confusion between B and K, B and M, the two gutturals H and Ḥ, M and S (Samech) and probably Shin with Ayin following Yod. (See the Hebrew alphabet, Appendix.) In case of a bad handwriting even this would not complete the list: and among these letters are some, especially H, V, I, M, which are used for the case-endings of nouns, and the person-endings of verbs. There might thus be great uncertainty as to these endings; the root of the word might be fairly certain, but the syntax would be in danger of being lost. If the MS. were abbreviated, as may have been the case, this would make the matter worse; and the fact that some of these final letters denoted more meanings than one would make it no better. Add the general absence of vowels, and it must be allowed that readers had then some difficulties with which to contend.

And mistakes can be found, often obvious beyond all doubt, in the LXX.'s renderings, which may be easily explained according to one or another of these causes. Years ago, in the preface to his *Hebrew Tenses*, p. xiii, Professor Driver drew attention to the fact that in the Psalms the LXX. go wrong between I and V so often, that their testimony is quite valueless for deciding the original Hebrew. This is the strongest instance, because these letters, affecting the syntax, occur so often; but others are

8

plentiful. When once the translator has been led astray by some such confusion, he may, if not guided back by the context, wander quite off the true track for a verse or two: one mistake leads to another, or to a desperate guess, until scarcely a word tallies with the original. In such straits as this, his attempt is like a schoolboy's exercise; following whatever method promises the easiest way out, he may paraphrase according to what he takes to be the general drift; or, grasping a word here and there, he may preserve the root-meanings, and connect them almost at random in trying to extract some sense; or, it would seem, he may in the last resort guess wildly. Thackeray points out how in the later chapters of Jeremiah, Greek words with some resemblance to the Hebrew are occasionally chosen: a proceeding which we, of course, know to be futile. This is possibly not quite unheard of in other books; but it would be hard to beat *αἶδε* as a rendering for *hedad*, 'shouting', which certainly seems to be intended, Jer. xxxi. (Heb. xlviii.) 33. Yet it may have been at first simply transliterated, and then corrupted.

But let us work through a few verses of a rather difficult passage, such as Isa. xvii. 9–11. Up to this point of the chapter the translators have kept fairly near the original; now, in verse 9, they give 'thy' for 'his', perhaps reading V as final K, not one of the instances given above; and further confuse the letters of 'strength' with similar ones in the next word in the Heb., 'forsaken'. The next words, 'the bough and the uppermost branch', more properly 'the woodland and the (mountain) crest', are in Heb. 'the ḤORESH and the AMIR': which look in some ancient scripts very like 'the ḤIVI and the AMORI', *i.e.*, 'the Hivites and the Amorites'; which Lagarde and others wished to read here, and which LXX. actually has, though in inverse order, and as the subject of the next verb. In verse 10 'abandon' for 'forget' is a slight looseness, which can be paralleled elsewhere with these very verbs. The rest of the verse mostly follows Heb., until the end, where the two parallel verbs are represented by one only, and the adjectives, or rather genitives, 'of pleasantness', 'of a stranger', both by *ἄπιστον*. This seems little better than a guess, if not a corruption; for the Greek word is so rare in LXX. that the concordance gives no Hebrew equivalent for it; Schleusner suggested *πιστόν*, possibly thinking that Aleph had been read for Ayin in the word 'pleasantness'. In verse 11 the Heb. is difficult, and probably means 'In the day of thy planting thou makest a hedge (or, makest it grow), and in the morning thy seed thou makest to bud; a heap of harvest in the day of pain and sorrow grievous'. The Septuagint first reads the verb 'make a hedge' with SH instead of S, and takes it to mean 'err' or 'wander'. Then the syntax of some words is changed, involving the insertion of 'if'. 'Heap' is either omitted, or read with a letter changed, as a preposition. 'Pain', a passive participle, used as a noun, from root ḤLH, with prefix N–, has been read as a verb, 'inherit' or 'obtain', root NḤL. (Vulg. has here *die hereditatis*.) 'Sorrow' is KAB, and has been taken as AB, 'father', with prefixed preposition K–, 'like': 'of a man', ENOSH, is the same, in consonants, as ANOSH, 'grievous'; and 'for the sons' looks like a guess to complete the sentence, induced by the wrong rendering 'as a father'. This passage therefore gives a variety of examples of divergence. In one the Vulgate supports LXX., in another some eminent modern scholars approve their reading, at any rate in part. Elsewhere they have divided words wrongly; read SH for S, not, it would seem, by any good tradition; paraphrased a little, and guessed the rest, endeavouring to make sense on the false track they had followed. Verse 10 emerges in a recognisable form; parts of 9 and 11 have been changed beyond recognition. On the other hand the Hebrew order of words has been so faithfully kept—except, oddly enough, in 'Amorites and Hivites'—that it is easy to see most of the places where they have gone wrong, and to perceive how they came to do so.

Perhaps their habitual tendencies come out most strongly when they are in difficulties; for when all is plain sailing, there is least likelihood of divergence, and least scope for peculiarity. When uncertain as to the meaning, they have apparently some favourite words, which in some books they use as stopgaps. Οὐχ οὕτως, a peculiar but favourite error for Heb. 'Therefore', when uttering correction or reproof, also occurs at times as the result of mere misreading. (Isa. xvi. 6; 1 Kings xxii. 19, etc.: cf. Gen. iv. 15.) In Isaiah, Thackeray has pointed out the recurrence, right or wrong, of μικρὸς καὶ μέγας, and the present writer that of other words, for instance παραδίδωμι and ἐλπίς.

Apart from these mistakes, the way in which the translators treat some aspects of Hebrew requires notice. For those who have no knowledge of Hebrew, a few explanations must be attempted. We have already referred to the Hebrew verb; normally, it is regarded as the foundation of most other words. That is to say, Hebrew, like other Semitic languages, refers almost all its words to roots, which consist regularly of three consonants each, the attendant vowels varying for different (grammatical) meanings; and the standard form for any of these roots is the 3rd pers. sing. of a verb. Take, as an example, the root ZDQ (the first letter is strictly TZ), the meaning of which is 'to be righteous'. Then *zadaq* means, 'he was righteous', *yizdaq*, 'he will be righteous', *zedeq* and *z^edaqah*, 'righteousness', *zaddiq*, 'a righteous one'; the vowels going in and out among the consonants to express different grammatical ideas, but the root-meaning, and the three consonants, in the same order, remaining unaltered. (The doubling of a consonant is a matter of emphasis, marked only by a dot in the letter.) For the persons and tenses of the verb there are terminations and prefixes: thus the Perfect has *zadaq* for 3rd pers. sing. masc., *zad'qah* 3rd pers. sing. fem.; 1st pers. sing. *zadaqti*, 3rd pers. plur. *zad'qu*. The Imperfect makes more use of prefixes: 3rd pers. sing. masc. *yizdaq*, fem. *tizdaq*, 3rd pers. plur. *yizd'qu*; 1st pers. sing. *ezdaq*, plur. *nizdaq*. (The vowels vary in length, but this has been disregarded for simplicity. In the verbs generally given as types in the grammars, the second vowel of the Imperfect is not *a* but *o*.)

There follow the voices or conditions of the verb, which are known by the names of the parts of the old model verb *pa'al* 'do': namely Niphal, a passive originally reflexive: Piel, a causal or intensive: Hiphil, causative, Hithpael, reflexive. Piel has a corresponding passive Pual, and Hiphil one called Hophal: the person-endings and prefixes are the same in each case as those of the simple (Qal) verb. The main object of naming these various forms is to point out how like they are, when the vowels are not written. Without the points, the perf. of Qal, Piel, and Pual are, in the regular verb, indistinguishable: in the imperf., Niphal and Hophal may be added to these three, and Hiphil has only the small letter Yod inserted. Also, on looking on at the prefixes and terminations, it will be seen that the letters I(Y), V, H, T, and N are constantly used in them, and some of these are quite easily confused. Morever, H prefixed is also the sign of the article, and of interrogation; affixed, it indicates that toward which motion takes place. Many nouns are almost identical with participles in form. Thus some idea may be formed of the chances of confusion. The root-meaning may be clear, but the syntax may at the same time be wholly misunderstood; and in fact it often is; but anyone who sees these Hebrew forms for the first time may well wonder how a reader or translator ever distinguished rightly between them. Some have said that the Semitic writing, without vowels, is more a kind of *memoria technica* than complete writing. In those days those who were learned in literature often knew most of it by heart, that they knew at all.

Besides these person-endings, Hebrew has pronoun-endings, which are attached, in somewhat similar (but not always identical) forms, both to verbs and to nouns: *hizdiq*, 'I have justified', *hizdiqka*, 'I have justified thee': *z'daqah*, 'righteousness', *zidqathka*, 'thy righteousness'. Apart from these, and from the sign of the plural, usually masc. *-im.*, fem. *-oth*, there are but few terminations. The cases have practically none; the accusative is made generally by prefixing *eth*, which is also a preposition meaning 'with'; whence Aquila's *σύν* before the accusative of the object. The genitive is formed by a converse process, prefixing the word on which the genitive depends, in a form often shortened or lightened. As adjectives are scarce in Hebrew, this idiom is often used instead: 'a balance of justice' for 'a just balance', 'the hill of my holiness' for 'my holy hill'. This lightened form of the noun preceding the genitive is called the 'construct' state. Other cases are indicated by inseparable prefix-prepositions: b', 'with' or 'in', l', 'to' or 'for', m', 'from', k', 'as', 'like', 'according to'. We still find the same letters doing the bulk of the work as prefixes or affixes; they are, in fact, known as 'servile' letters in the old grammarians' picturesque language, which goes so far as to class the accents (which serve also as stops within the verse) as 'emperors', 'kings', down to 'slaves'; the only modern parallel that I can quote being the masons' names for slates, which are called 'duchesses', 'countesses', etc., according to their size.

It is perhaps this absence of case-endings which enables Hebrew to take up a noun for a fresh clause without much care for the case in which it previously stood. Another vagueness to which the language is prone is that of using a verb in the third person, without a specified subject: as Gen. xlviii. 1; 2 Kings v. 4. The relative is indeclinable, and only marks the character of the clause; the pronoun is afterwards inserted in its proper position. The uneducated use of 'which', most familiar in the mouth of Mrs. Gamp, represents it with fair exactness, as the late Prof. Moulton pointed out. Of the two tenses, the perfect expresses, primarily, action complete, or regarded as a whole; the foreshortened, end view of an action; and the imperfect, incomplete action, regarded as in progress, the extended, side view. For expressing continuous action or continuance in a state, the participle is used. Thus the Perfect may mean 'I have spoken' (over and done with), 'I spoke' (formerly), or previous to another action, whether past or future; in the one case equivalent to a pluperfect, in the other to a future perfect. Also of actions rhetorically regarded as already over and accomplished, either through vividness or certainty: 'unto thy seed I give this land'; 'if not, I take it by force'. This use passes into what is called the prophetic perfect, where future doings are spoken of as already happening or over. The Imperfect (often formerly called the Future) expresses the incomplete action, both in principal and dependent clauses: 'I will make him an help meet for him'; 'a mist (constantly) went up'; 'whatsoever Adam called every living creature'; 'from thence it began to divide', Gen. ii. 10; 'he destroyed their vines', 'he sent upon them his wrath, anger', etc., Ps. lxxviii. 47, 49. In general statements both tenses are used; the perf., perhaps, if a distinction can be drawn, of the obvious statements of experience, 'the grass withereth', Isa. xl. 7; the imperf., of the outcome of reflection, 'Man goeth forth', Ps. civ. 23.

But when either of these tenses are used with a preceding 'and'—u', v', an inseparable prefix of very wide use—it appears almost to take the meaning of the other. The imperfect with this *vav* is the ordinary plain narrative tense; the perf. with *vav* has future, inceptive, frequentative force, when it follows an imperfect. The old idea was, that the *vav* gave one tense the force of the other, and it was hence called *vav* 'conversive'; the later view is, briefly, that it is used to carry on the effect of the preceding tense (almost = Lat. *itaque*); and it is therefore often now called *vav* 'consecutive'. But even this view is not quite free from difficulties, as the imperf. with *vav* has often no perf. preceding; perhaps the last word on the subject has not yet been said. Meantime, the old explanation probably explains as much as the LXX. translators knew; and it is their practice in which we are now interested.

When the context helped them to determine the necessary meaning, they did not hesitate to use any tense from the Greek store that they found suitable. But when this guidance failed them, they resorted, as it seems, to a practice of representation. They took the aorist (and undoubtedly it was the best single tense they could take) to represent the Heb. perf., and the future (which did not so well cover all the range) to represent the Heb. imperf. It is right to state that I had not seen this view expressed before I put it forward in 1904 (*Isaiah acc. to the LXX.*, vol. i. p. 43), and have not seen it either impugned or explicitly supported. A few examples had better be given, to justify and make clearer the statements above. The English versions will not give sure guidance in this matter; the tenses must be noted in the Hebrew. The Variorum Bible (or Parallel or Two-line Bibles) will sometimes show where there is difference of opinion as to the translation of a tense, but that is all.

Let us first look at the tenses in Ps. civ. (ciii. in LXX.). In ver. 1 ἐμεγαλύνθης, ἐνεδύσω, are perfects in the Hebrew; English would naturally use either the perfect with auxiliary 'art' or 'hast', or the present. The next verses translate Heb. literally, with participles. In ver. 5 ἐθεμελίωσεν, Heb. perf., κλιθήσεται, Heb. impf. In 6 a noun takes the place of the first verb; στήσονται, Heb. impf. So far the Greek aorists can be explained in the Greek, on one recognised principle or another; but the constant appearance of aorists alternating with futures is not what we should expect in normal Greek, nor the tenses themselves, in many cases, the most natural. In poetry they would be less surprising; but here there is nothing else poetic in the translators' style. It may further be noticed that the usual participle in the LXX. is the present, and not the aorist. To continue: in ver. 8 the translators have wisely forsaken the future for the present; the aorist ἐθεμελίωσας, Heb. perf., rightly represents action previously completed. From here to the end of 14, every Greek aorist, future, and pres. part. corresponds to Heb. pf., impf., and participle respectively. In ver. 15 two present tenses seem to show that the translators took the Heb. imperfects as expressing general reflections (see above). Modern authorities vary between this view and taking the Heb. impf. here as final (or 'telic'). In the rest of the Psalm it will be enough to specify the exceptions to the regular representation. In ver. 17, *ἡ οἰκία ἡγεῖται αὐτῷ* (v.l. *αὐτῶν*) is the most marked discrepancy from the Hebrew in this psalm; and also a departure from the strict order of the Hebrew words, to match which it would seem that *ἡ οἰκία* should stand after *ἡγεῖται*. This verb is explained as due to reading 'at their head', *i.e.*, as their leader, for 'the fir trees'; a difference in the consonantal text of *yod* and *vav* in the word as against *aleph*. Vulg. has *domus dux est eorum*; for the phrase, cf. Deut. i. 13. There is nothing remarkable about the tense; the only doubt is whether the Greek verb should stand in the true text at all. (Can *ἡγεῖται* be a corruption of *ἡ γειτονία*? and *ἡ οἰκία* of *αἱ πεύκαι*?) In ver. 20 *ἔθου* is an exception, for Heb. has impf.; this may be due to the translators' view of the sense, cf. ver. 9; *ἐγένετο* corresponds to impf. with *vav*, and the verb may have been regarded as parallel to the making of darkness rather than to the moving of the beasts. In ver. 22, the sun-rising is treated similarly. In vers. 27, 28, more idiomatic treatment prevails, with genitives absolute, and one present tense for a future; there is another present in ver. 32. Ἤτω in ver. 31 (note the late form for *ἔστω*) and the pure optatives in 34, 35, are probably right renderings of the Hebrew, as though the translators had gradually warmed to their work. The advantage of working thus through a Psalm of fair length is clear; it avoids the suspicion of selected verses, and shows the proportion of tenses better. It should be carefully gone over, and compared with other Psalms: in which case the strained use of several of these aorists and futures will appear. In cv. and cvi., the narrative character being clear, aorists predominate, and the imperfects, with or without *vav*, are not represented by futures. In cvii., the translators have either taken the Psalm as narrative again, or else done their work exceptionally well as regards tenses; note ver. 26, and compare with civ. 8.

In some books, for instance Job, there is more variety of tenses; but the translation is much more free: here notice indic. after ὡς ἄν, i. 5, εἶτ' ἄν, as xiii. 22 (but itacism is possible). Note also the variety of tenses following εἰ: but εἰ must be looked at carefully, as it is sometimes interrogative, and sometimes (εἰ γάρ) introduces a wish; see vi. 2, xiv. 13, xxxix. 1. In εἶ μήν, both in Job (xxvii. 3) and elsewhere, we have simple asseveration, another way of spelling ἦ μήν; but the MSS. confuse this with εἰ μή, and it will be seen that the negative threat and the positive asseveration often amount to very nearly the same meaning.

In the Prophets, there is a tendency to extend the use of the future, perhaps from its supposed fitness; a probable instance is ἐρεύξεται, Amos iii. 8, with an aorist in the parallel clause. In Zech. x. 1–4, the Heb. tenses are regularly followed, except for two Greek imperfects, probably for euphony; ἐπισκέψεται represents pf. with *vav*. In Isaiah there is some tense-variety; but representation of the Heb. pf. and impf. is fairly common. The future in a comparative clause has a curious effect, as in lxv. 8, cf. vii. 2. The aorist is frequently overworked, as in xiv. 5 ff., and the perf. is used also, with little apparent difference of meaning: compare the perf.

in i. 7 with the aorist in xxiv. 10, and the parallel clauses of liii. 5 (not so in A). We must always remember the varying practice of the translators in the different books of the O.T., and also the varying nature of their task. Representation comes in only when the context does not decide the tense; and even then, looseness, uncertainty of reading, and the occasional desire for variety, may cause exceptions. Most of the aorists could be, singly, justified; but the excess of them demands explanation. Some of the futures are almost more unnatural. With all deductions, there remain enough peculiar uses of these tenses to make the theory of 'representation' worth attention. Here it has been regarded simply from the point of view of the translators' method.

The LXX. frequently render the Hebrew relative clauses in a literal fashion, inserting a relative, necessarily declined, where the Heb. has its indeclinable word, and completing the sentence redundantly with the pronoun in the same construction. The correlative adverbs are similarly used (cf. French *y* and *en*). Sometimes the correspondence is not absolutely, though practically, exact. See Exod. v. 2, Τίς ἐστιν (θεός A) οὗ εἰσακούσομαι τῆς φωνῆς αὐτοῦ; Gen. i. 11, xiii. 4, xxiv. 5, 1 Kings xiii. 31, etc. The construction is also found in the Greek when not actually present in the Hebrew, as Isa. i. 21. So in 1 Esdras vi. 33, Judith v. 19, etc. It is also found in the N.T., *e.g.* Mark vii. 25, and in the Apocalypse. The A.V. of Acts xiii. 25 has it, where the Greek has not: 'whose shoes of his feet . . .' It is found in the Old Latin, *Tyconius*, 32,

33, *in quas ingressi sunt illic*, Ezek. xxxvi. 21; and in the Vulg. (Gallican) Psalter, lxxiv. 2, *in quo habitasti in eo*. The beginner must carefully distinguish it from cases of ordinary relative attraction, such as Gen. ii. 3; here no pronoun follows.

Careful and accurate as Greek syntax is, it generally allows, as a substitute for a construction, what common sense declares to be a fair equivalent. Thus, when the construction *οὐ μή* with aor. subj. or future is used for a future, it can occupy the same place in the apodosis of a conditional sentence; this occurs in classical Greek. An imperative can be similarly used. So again, where the potential force is inherent in the meaning of a verb, as ἔχρην, ἔμελλον, and others, ἀν can be omitted in the apodosis. The construction with *οὐ μή*, originally emphatic, is common in LXX., and often used, at any rate in the later books, where no special emphasis can be discerned; there is a tendency in later stages of a language for exaggerated expressions to be used for ordinary ones, their emphasis being worn out. The N.T. has this use of *οὐ μή*, as in Matt. x. 23. Conversely, the use of the plain future as a command, or with *οὐ* as a prohibition, is extended in LXX.: the Commandments generally are in this form, and see Deut. vi. 5, cf. vii. 3, viii. 1, 2. In classical Greek, we may find such an instance as Eurip. *Med.* 1320, λέγ᾽ εἴτι βούλει, χειρὶ δ᾽ οὐ ψαύσεις ποτέ. But it must be noticed, first, that here the future is only verging on a prohibition, not fully equivalent to it; rather, perhaps, to be described as a threat. Secondly, in Attic this future is generally coupled to a more distinctly imperative construction; thirdly, the negative is more usually *μή*; and fourthly, it is in the translated books a literal rendering of the Hebrew construction. In English, the construction is quite common, but, except in a stately and official style, it savours more of threat or warning than of direct command.

The ease with which Hebrew passes from one case-construction to another has already been remarked; the terminations for cases are almost non-existent. It is not unusual for a noun to be introduced first in the nominative, and then referred to in a different syntax-relation; as Isa. i. 7, 'your land, strangers devour it'. The LXX. often follow the original literally; but the anacoluthon is more obvious in Greek. In Gen. xl. 5, for instance, it is very marked, if the Greek text be right; but perhaps ὁράσεις should be read, or if a substantive verb be supplied, the sentence might possibly be taken as a parenthesis. See also Ps. xviii. 30, and the parallel 2 Sam. xxii. 31, Ps. xc. 10 (note the reading), ciii. 15, Isa. xxviii. 1, xxx. 21, xl. 22.

Verbs in Heb. are often, for emphasis, reinforced by the infinitive ('absolute' form) of the same verb, which regularly precedes; several examples occur in Gen. xliii.; the margin of A.V. draws attention to them. The English version generally renders by an adverb; and LXX. sometimes does the same, as in Exod. xv. 1. More often they use the cognate noun, as Gen. ii. 17, θανάτῳ ἀποθανεῖσθε, cf. xliii. 3; or the participle, as in xliii. 7, while later in the verse the emphatic construction is ignored. Thackeray points out (*Gramm.* pp. 47 ff.) that the cognate noun is used oftener in the Pentateuch, but the participle in the later historical books, and generally elsewhere, except in Isaiah. He notes one instance where B, but not A, has the infinitive quite literally, namely Josh. xvii. 13. The exact force of the Hebrew form of expression can scarcely be expressed in English or Greek; at any rate, not by any fixed method.

Another very common Hebrew idiom is that of expressing a repeated action by the use of the verb ISP[H] 'add', usually almost as an auxiliary, with infin. and a preposition. The regular rendering in LXX. is by *προστίθημι*, either act. or mid., and infinitive, that is, as literally as possible. A coupled verb, or the participle of *προστίθημι*, is rarely found. See the A.V. of Luke xix. 11, 'he added and spake', Acts xii. 3, 'he proceeded further to take . . .'. In English, the word 'again' is generally all that is needed: occasionally rather more emphasis seems to be implied.

The Heb. word for 'between' is usually repeated with the second word, as 'between the light and between the darkness', Gen. i. 4. Sometimes the second word has the prep. l', 'to', as in Gen. i. 6. In LXX. *ἀνὰ μέσον* is sometimes repeated, sometimes not: in the above verses Heb. is literally followed, except that l' is rendered only by the genitive. As a rule, Heb. prepositions are faithfully rendered, though not with complete uniformity. 'Eν most usually stands for b', and consequently is very widely used, often with nearly instrumental meaning. Thus *ἐν μαχαίρᾳ*, *ἐν στόματι μαχαίρας*, and *ἐν φόνῳ μαχαίρας*, are common expressions, though the first is not found (exc. Gen. xlviii. 22) until the later historical books and Prophets. Sometimes in Hebrew a preposition, especially one implying motion, is used with a verb that normally does not suit the motion-idea of the preposition, but suggests a further development according to that idea. Thus Ps. xxii. 21, 'thou hast heard me from the horns of the unicorns', probably means,[1] 'thou hast heard *and rescued* me from . . .' This does not appear in LXX.; but see Hos. iii. 5, 'they shall tremble unto the Lord', *i.e.*, tremble and come to Him; Ps. lxxxix. 39, 'thou hast profaned his crown to the ground'; Isa. ii. 10, 'hide thee into the dust'; Gen. xlii. 28, 'they trembled to one another'. In several cases the Septuagint, following the Heb., uses Greek prepositions beyond their normal force; though hardly going beyond legitimate experiment in language, such as Virgil might have enjoyed. Cf. Horace, *Od.* IV. i. 9:

> Tempestivius in domum
> . . . .
> Comissabere Maximi (you will go revelling),

Or Keats, *Hyperion*:

> . . . On he *flared*
> From stately nave to nave, from vault to vault.

For the present the question is left aside, whether or no these constructions are properly to be termed 'Hebraisms' or 'Semitisms' in the Greek; they are merely noted as specimens of the LXX.'s dealing with certain Hebrew forms of expression. This is advisable, because a Greek scholar coming to the LXX. for the first time would find some of them strange. In another of these idioms, we are able to contrast the usual practice of LXX. with that of Aquila. This is the gerundial use of the infin.

[1] But any translation is apt to over-emphasise what the original idiom implies rather than expresses.

'construct' with l', which is especially common in introducing a speaker's words: 'saying . . .' Aquila, as literally as possible, uses τῷ with infin.; and this has found its way into the text of A, 1 Kings xiii. 26, 2 Kings xix. 10. The true Septuagint commonly uses the participle; this, especially in the Pentateuch, has usually its proper construction, but is also from time to time used in a kind of loose apposition, the nominative participle, sing. or plur., introducing the actual words, though the speaker or speakers have not been mentioned in the nominative for it to agree with. Thus Gen. xxvii. 6 is perfectly regular, the genitive being constantly used after verbs of hearing; but xv. i, xxii. 20, xlviii. 2, 20, have no construction. Notice 1 Kings xii. 9.

The use of ἐγώ εἰμι followed by a finite verb occurs only in certain books, Judges, Ruth, and the later portions of Kings. It seems to be used on the representative principle for the fuller form of the Heb. 1st personal pronoun. Aquila uses it: in Job (xxxiii. 31) it is in a passage supplied from Theodotion, and A's reading differs. In Ezek. xxxvi. 36 it is read by A, but before Κύριος, so that this is not a proper instance. In Isa. xliii. 25, xlv. 19, the phrase ἐγώ εἰμι is itself repeated, but is not followed by a finite verb; the fuller form is not used in xlv. 19, though it is in xliii. 25, and in xliii. 11, where LXX. has ἐγώ simply.

The use of ὃν τρόπον in comparative clauses is very common; in classical Greek it is not known to me, but τίνα τρόπον, 'how'? τοῦτον τὸν τρόπον, 'thus', occur in the best Attic. Conversely, τρόπον with genitive though classical, occurs but once in LXX., Job iv. 19

Πρόσωπον after prepositions, 'from', 'before the face of', etc., is common, almost necessary, to translate the Heb. So χείρ occurs in various phrases; English adopts these in their literal shape too. The phrase λαμβάνειν πρόσωπον is in English 'to accept the person'; elsewhere 'presence' or 'face' is used. In Isa. lxiii. 9 LXX.'s rendering is incomplete. Over some expressions the LXX. avoids being literal, apparently from reverence or delicacy. In particular, they eschew the literal rendering of 'Rock', when applied to the Almighty; this can be seen in Deut. xxxii., in several Psalms, and in Isaiah, even in xxxii. 2. When not thus applied, πέτρα is used freely enough.

The general colouring of the Greek O.T. is thus affected by the presence of various Hebrew ideas and forms of expression, and by the constant matching of Hebrew phrases and constructions. A negative effect in the same direction is produced by the absence of periods, and of the devices employed in classical Greek for connecting the clauses; the sentences are short, and merely coupled together. Even the usual order of article and noun with genitives and other qualifying words between, is rare, and confined as a rule to the shortest phrases, as in Isa. ix. 14, lix. 21. The repeated article, however, in phrases such as οἱ βασιλεῖς οἱ μετ' αὐτοῦ, is common enough. Despite the great use made of the aorist indicative, the aorist of the infinitive and participle is comparatively rare. The cumulative effect of such practices is considerable, and the result is very different from the classical style, and even from the literary work of the period when most of the LXX. was made; though it may, as is asserted, more nearly resemble the vernacular as preserved in papyrus documents concerned with everyday life. But it may be remarked that while the translation distinctly shows knowledge of Egypt—a point on which more emphasis should, perhaps, have been laid throughout this book—this knowledge is chiefly conspicuous in the appropriate parts of Genesis, Exodus, and Isaiah (especially chap. xix.[1]). Now these books are certainly not the nearest in style to the rougher vernacular of the papyri. The Pentateuch, no one denies, is the earliest and best portion of the Version; and Isaiah is very probably among the nearest to it in date, and, as good authorities consider, in Greek style also.[2]

[1] Note *νομός*, ver. 2; *ἄχι*, *βύσσος*, *διώρυγες*, etc., later in the chapter.
[2] Thackeray, *Gramm. of O. T. in Greek*, vol. i. p. 13.

CHAPTER VI

THE APOCRYPHA AND PSEUDEPIGRAPHA

Esdras A—Its relation to Ezra and Nehemiah (Esdras B)—Tobit, Judith—Wisdom—Ecclesiasticus—Its Hebrew text—Problems arisi g—Baruch—The Four Books of Maccabees.

The Psalms of Solomon—Enoch—The Odes of Solomon—The Pseudepigrapha—The Book of Jubilees—The Testaments of the XII Patriarchs—Other books—The Story of Aḥiḳar.

WE proceed to describe briefly the books of which no Hebrew original is extant. It will not be needful to examine these in detail, as the editions of the more important books give plenty of help, and, in the absence of the Hebrew, are based on the text of the LXX., when that includes them. It will be convenient to take first the books which form the English Apocrypha; then any others contained in the principal MSS. of the LXX.; and lastly the works, more remote from the Canonical books, now generally known as the Pseudepigrapha.

It is now generally held that Esdras A of the Septuagint, 1 Esdras of the English Apocrypha, is not, as was sometimes thought, a free working over of Esdras B, the Greek Ezra and Nehemiah; but an independent translation from the Hebrew and Aramaic original. It begins with a version of 2 Chron. xxxv. 1–xxxvi. 21; the rest consists of equivalents for large portions of Ezra, but in somewhat different order, and Neh. viii.; with one passage, Esdras A iii. 1–v. 6, which is independent. Another view is, that it is based upon an earlier Greek version; but this only interposes a stage between it and the Hebrew, and that intermediate stage is at any rate not Esdras B; which latter has been maintained by Sir H. Howorth to be the work of Theodotion. With this view Thackeray has lately come to agree, though not taking the further step of assigning the Greek Chronicles also to Theodotion.

Whether the independent portion be the original kernel of Esdras A or not, it forms an important part of it; and it may be at once recognised that this portion cannot be considered true history. Moreover, it is doubtful whether we have here a translation from a Semitic original, or not; the latter view has generally prevailed, but of late arguments have been urged (by Torrey) in favour of an Aramaic original. Thackeray recognises the same hand in Esdras A as in the LXX. proper of the early chapters, i.–vi. of Daniel. The divisions between Chronicles, Ezra, and Nehemiah are thought not to have existed when Esdras A was compiled; this date is placed by modern authorities shortly after 333 B.C. It would seem hardly possible for the writer to have been ignorant of the time when Zerubbabel really lived, or to have confused Darius with Cyrus (compare iv. 47 with ii. 1–15); and the explanation is therefore more probably freedom of treatment. Many, at any rate, are of opinion that Jewish writers, when not writing definite history, took great liberties when embellishing stories of their great men of the past. This unhistorical portion is inconsistent with the rest of the book, which gives a faithful version, in substance, of the parts of Chronicles-Ezra-Nehemiah included. The style is superior to that of Esdras B; the Greek, if not original, may date from about 100 B.C., and Josephus appears to have used it, though aware of its inaccuracies. It would be difficult to pass without notice the famous and constantly misquoted saying from iv. 38, Μεγάλη ἡ ἀλήθεια καὶ ὑπερισχύει, *Magna est veritas et praevalet.* When the Apocryphal books were admitted by the Council of Trent, Esdras A was rejected; possibly by inadvertence, as the names of the books are easily confused.

[The second book of Esdras in our Apocrypha (=4 Ezra) hardly concerns us, as it is not extant in Greek. The existing Latin was clearly made from Greek, which in its turn may have had a Hebrew original. The Syriac, Arabic, Ethiopic, and Armenian are probably from the Greek. The book is supposed to have been written about A.D. 100. It is apocalyptic, describing a series of visions; a Jewish composition, with Christian additions, which stand at the beginning and end. The Revised Version contains 70 additional verses in chap. vii., discovered by the late Professor Bensly in 1875.]

The Book of Tobit is a tale of the fortunes of a family of Israelite captives in Assyria under Shalmaneser, *i.e.*, about 730 B.C. The story, however, seems to be fiction, and is not strictly historical even in its setting; it may date from 200–170 B.C.; some place it earlier, some as late as 100 B.C. From the part played in the book by the angel Raphael, by the demon Asmodeus, and by magic, some think that it was written in Egypt, not in Palestine; the geography, too, is said to support this view. The description of the exorcism, some say, shows Persian influence; but if so, Professor Moulton (*Hibbert Lectures*, 1912) maintained that non-Zoroastrian Magianism is described. The charm of the story lies in the guileless tone, and the piety and morality of the exiled family. The praise of almsgiving in the book is well known, and iv. 7–9 occur among the offertory sentences in the Communion Service. Jerome's hasty rendering of Tobit is mentioned above (p. 57). The extant Aramaic version is dated about A.D. 300, or even much later. The existing Hebrew texts are also late, and probably go back through Aramaic to the Greek. It is not so easy to say whether the Greek is itself original, or comes from a previous Hebrew or (more probably) Aramaic. Some sentences seem to suggest an underlying Semitic idiom; others could not be literal renderings of such, though they might be paraphrases or corrections. The Greek version itself is, according to Thackeray (*Gramm. O.T.*, p. 28), 'probably the best representative in the Greek Bible of the vernacular as spoken by Jews', and for that reason, among others, deserves attention. It is to be noticed that the MSS. give three different recensions. Two are represented by ℵ and B; A stands between the two, but generally nearer B. The third appears, between vi. 9 and xiii. 18, in the cursives 44 and 106 (with 107); and an Oxyrhynchus fragment (1076) also seems to give a recension distinct from the uncials. Of these, it seems that ℵ's text is the oldest; it is supported on the whole by the Old Latin, and sometimes by 19 and 108, less often 58. Some Aramaic influence is shown in the spelling, Ἀθουρείας, xiv. 15, and the better form Ἀχείχαρος, and even Ἀχειχάρ, xi. 18. B is on the whole inferior, though Prof. Rendel Harris has hinted that it may be nearer to the Alexandrian version; but the belief in א's text has gained ground. The 44–106 text may be an attempt to combine the two. Prof. Harris has pointed out a connexion between Tobit א and the Book of Jubilees, and thinks that whichever borrowed from the other did so in Aramaic. The working in of the Story of Aḥiḳar is interesting, but will be better discussed below, in reference to that book.

The Book of Tobit was widely read and highly esteemed among the Jews at first; later it was popular with the early Christian Church, but then fell out of favour with the Jews, as we learn from Origen. It is thought that St. Paul used the book: compare iv. 7–16 with 1 Cor. xvi. 2, Gal. vi. 10, and 1 Thess. iv. 3, and xii. 10 with Rom. vi. 23. A reference to xi. 9 has been suspected in Luke xv. 20; see also Acts ix. 18, 36, x. 4, xi. 12, 13 (Tob. iii. 16, i. 3, xii. 12). Resemblances have also been noticed in Rev. xix. and xxi. to Tob. viii. 3 and xiii. 16, 18; in some of these passages the verbal coincidences are certainly strong.

Judith is another story on a pseudo-historical basis: telling how Nebuchadnezzar, 'King of the Assyrians', had been warring against Arphaxad, King of the Medes in Ecbatana, but the peoples from Cilicia and Damascus to Jerusalem, Kadesh, the river of Egypt, and the borders of Ethiopia, had not obeyed Nebuchadnezzar's summons to join his army. So, in 'the eighteenth year', he sent Holofernes with a force to punish them; who, after overrunning Cilicia, approached Judaea. The city of Bethulia, overlooking the plain of Esdraelon, resisted his progress; and here the beautiful widow Judith 'put off the garments of her widowhood', and set out to beguile him, pretending to be a traitress, and offering to guide him to Jerusalem. She 'weakened him with the beauty of her countenance', and as he lay in drunken sleep, she cut off his head, and escaped; the 'host of Asshur' was amazed and fled, and Israel hailed Judith as the deliverer of her country.

Clearly this is very far from real history. Some national heroine's deed may have served as the foundation for the story. It has been thought that the names stand throughout for others of a later age, *i.e.*, Nebuchadnezzar for Antiochus Epiphanes, etc. The book probably dates from Maccabean times, and was almost certainly written originally in Hebrew. The Syriac and Old Latin were made from the Greek. The MSS. fall into divisions somewhat as in Tobit, but the differences are not so marked. The uncials form one class, a second is represented by 19 and 108, a third by 58. The pious tone of the book, if strict, is less amiable than that of Tobit; ceremonious observance of the Law, and patriotic hatred carried to any length, and not disdaining craft, seem to be regarded as the ideal.

Little need be said of the Apocryphal additions to Esther. They almost seem to represent another historical romance in process of manufacture. They may date from about 100 B.C., and there is no proof of their having had a Hebrew original. The final note apparently hints at its having been translated;

but the date, the 'fourth year of Ptolemy and Cleopatra', is full of uncertainty, as there were four royal pairs thus named. On the MSS. see above, p. 108.

The Book of Wisdom is of very different character. It was written, probably, originally in Greek (some would say 'certainly', but see below), and at Alexandria, some time between 150 and 50 B.C. It was even attributed by some to the learned Philo, but is not likely to be his, and the author is quite unknown. The language is literary, and by no means devoid of style, as it was regarded in some circles at that date; the writer has some knowledge of Greek philosophy, and of some books of the LXX., notably Isaiah, to which he clearly alludes; cf. ii. 12 with Isa. iii. 10, iv. 19 with Isa. xix. 10, v. 6 with Isa. liii. 6 and lix. 9 ff., and xiii. 11 with Isa. xliv. 12. It is on the whole very much what we should expect that a pious Alexandrian Jew of that time might write; in tone, that is, for the ability is too great to be so dismissed. Whether to make the book more acceptable to curious non-Jewish inquirers, or to give the historic allusions a wider apparent scope, these are all made without naming persons, peoples, or places, except the Red Sea and Pentapolis (xix. 7, x. 6). The book hardly claims to be Solomon's, even if a king's; at any rate, it does not use Solomon's name, nor make references even as definite as those of Ecclesiastes, to which book some have fancied it, to some extent, a rejoinder. 'Wisdom' has steadily risen, of late years, in general esteem. Prof. Margoliouth suggested that there had been a Hebrew original, but Freudenthal urged reasons against this view, and it has met with little support.

Some think that the latter part, from xi., or from xii. 9, onward, is a later edition, belonging to a time between 30 B.C. and A.D. 10; bringing down even the former chapters to a date rather after 50 B.C. than before. Allusions to the LXX. of Proverbs have been found in the book, and points of contact with the Book of Enoch. Thackeray has drawn attention to appearances of rhythm in the Greek, the beginnings and endings of lines having a tendency to fall into similar arrangements of syllables (*J. Th. Stud.*, vi. p. 232).

Books and articles have been produced in great quantity, since 1896, upon Ecclesiasticus, or the Wisdom of Jesus, the son of Sirach. Yet this is not mainly due to interest in the subject-matter. On the contrary, there has apparently been a tendency to disparage the writer as homely and unoriginal, in contrast to the praise that has been lavished on the richness and insight of Wisdom. But Ben-Sira should not be lightly esteemed; there is a four-square soundness about him which might atone for lack of brilliance; but he can rise to considerable heights also. The reason which has led to the writing, if not the reading, of so much matter on the book, is primarily the discovery and publication, from 1896 to 1900, of some two-thirds of the book in Hebrew. There had never been any doubt that a Hebrew original had existed; but the interest of this text, and its relation to the Greek and other versions, accounts for so much having been written about it.

The book, according to prevailing views, was originally written in Hebrew by a Palestinian Jew, about 180 B.C. It aims at setting forth 'Wisdom', and is largely expressed, according to Jewish practice, in maxims or proverbs, such as we have, in diminishing proportion, in Proverbs, Ecclesiastes, and the Wisdom of Solomon. But it approaches practical life in closer and more homely detail than any of these. The maxims are less detached than usually in Proverbs, more woven into sequences, almost into a treatise; at times the maxim-form is set aside, and there takes shape a prayer, as xxiii. 1–6, or an ode, as xxiv. and xlii. 15–xliii. fin. In such passages there is a fine elevation, and rich and telling eloquence. It is usual to deny the writer originality; but though familiar, as it was his duty to be, with the O.T. Scriptures, his expressions of thought have plenty of freshness and power. The Praise of Famous Men, xliv.–l., stands rather apart, and may have been published separately; but there is no need to assign it to a different author. The last chapter, beginning with a prayer, or rather thanksgiving, serves as an epilogue.

Dealing with the book in Greek, two main points of interest arise: that of the Prologue, and that of the text (or texts) preserved. The Translator's Prologue (the other is late, and of inferior interest) is of first-rate importance, for what it has to say about the book, and for light that it may throw on the history of the Septuagint and the O.T. generally. It need not be doubted that the writer is, as he says, the grandson of the original author, and himself the translator of the work. According to the dates usually supported, he came into Egypt in the year 132 B.C., and the necessary allowance of time after that for him to have settled to his studies and made the translation will fix its date. He tells us that he came into Egypt 'in the thirty-eighth year in the time of (ἐπί with genitive) Euergetes the king'. Taking this of Euergetes II., or Physcon, whose reign may be counted from 170–169 B.C., we reach 132 B.C.; and Simon, son of Onias, the 'great priest' referred to in l. 1, will then be the Simon who died 195 B.C., which fits with the date necessary for the grandfather's work. There was, however, another Euergetes, who reigned 246–221 B.C.; also another Simon, son of Onias, high priest 300–292 B.C.; so that, as was long ago perceived, the names which might have seemed sufficient to fix the date, combine to create a doubt. The general verdict of late years has been given for the later bearers of the names. But recently, Mr. J. H. A. Hart (*Ecclesiasticus in Greek*) has revived and urged a plea for the alternative earlier dates. He argues that under the tyrant Euergetes II. a Jew could not have worked peaceably in Egypt; and discusses the phrase 'the 38th year in the time of E. the king', showing that it is not the simplest way of saying 'the 38th year of E.'. In point of fact, Euergetes II.'s 38th year is only obtained by counting from a time when he was proclaimed, but did not rule; this, however, is in accordance with practice. Hart ingeniously notes that the predecessor of Euergetes I. reigned just 38 years; and interprets the crucial phrase, 'in the 38th year, when Euergetes was king'; *i.e.*, in the year which was the 38th of Philadelphus, and in which Euergetes reigned, the last of the one, the opening of the other. This explanation would be very hard to support by an exact parallel; but there is no rendering of the phrase, which is really secure. If Hart's view were to prevail—but, so far, it has not gained much acceptance—it would date the grandson's work about 246, and the grandfather's about 290 B.C. (Compare Pusey's *Lectures on Daniel.*) The point is important, because the Prologue alludes to the Law, Prophets, and other books, and various books of the O.T. are referred to in the body of the work. But on many points in the book there has been disagreement. In the introduction to the late Dean Plumptre's edition of Ecclesiastes (*Camb. Bible for Schools*, chaps. ii. and iv.) there is a list of parallel passages to set out the dependence of Ecclesiasticus upon Ecclesiastes: in that to the *Temple Bible* Ecclesiasticus Dr. N. Schmidt says that 'there is no sign of his acquaintance with Ecclesiastes': and some works do not mention the matter at all.

The Greek MSS. are all derived from a single lost MS., as is shown by a dislocation of the text in them all, in chaps. xxx.–xxxvi.; their order being xxx. 24, xxxiii. 16*b*–xxxvi. 11*a*, xxx. 25–xxxiii. 16*a*, xxxvi. 11*b*. This, of course, means that some leaves of the parent MS. were displaced; the Latin and Syriac have the correct order, which the A.V. obtained from them. The MSS., nevertheless, fall into two classes; one including the uncials, headed by B; the other led by 248, whose text Hart has edited in the work above mentioned. 248 is supported, more or less closely, by 55, 70, 106, 253, 254, the Old Latin, Syriac, and Syro-hexaplar; also by $\aleph^{ca}$ and the quotations of Clem. Alex. and Chrysostom. The A.V. was made from this text, and the Complutensian edition was based on it. The uncials' text is supported by 68,

155, 157, 296, 307, and 308; the Aldine and Sixtine editions followed it, and the R.V. was made from it. The 248-text is a good deal the fuller; hence the number of verses and half-verses which A.V. contains and R.V. omits. The usual opinion is that 248 and its kin represent a later recension, which Hart attributes to a scribe, or scribes, of the Pharisaic school.

Before the portions of Ecclesiasticus in Hebrew were discovered, Prof. Margoliouth had put forward a theory that the original Hebrew was in nine-syllable metre, and could largely be reconstructed. The Hebrew, when discovered, was not in such metre, and early notices of it expressed surprise at the good quality of the Hebrew, as showing a style rather fresh than decadent. Prof. Margoliouth, undaunted, declined to accept the newly-discovered Hebrew as the original text, and declared it to be a late production, translated from a Persian version made from a revised Syriac text. This view has not gained any support in its entirety; but some think that traces of Syriac are to be found in the Hebrew, and it is generally allowed that it is not a very near representative of the original Hebrew, nor of that from which the Greek text (B or 248) is derived. About two-thirds of the Hebrew is now extant, some portions in two MSS., a few verses in three, so that there is material enough to form a judgment. On the other hand, it is declared not to be a retranslation of Greek, nor of the existing Syriac. It is frequently corrupt, but to some extent independent. The Hebrew, Syriac, and Greek appear to represent three fairly distinct recensions; the 248-text comes from a later and fuller Hebrew text than the B-text of the Greek.

There still remains work to be done in comparing and estimating these materials.

The Book of Baruch, according to its title, professes to give the writing of Jeremiah's friend and attendant (Jer. xxxii., xxxvi.), delivered to Jehoiachin and his fellow-captives in Babylon. It contains no genuine history. In the LXX. it was attached to the work of Jeremiah, and Prof. Nestle and Mr. Thackeray, among others, have pointed out the resemblance between the translations; Thackeray, dividing Jeremiah, assigns the second part to the same translator as the first part of Baruch (*J. Th. Stud.*, iv. p. 261). The Book of Baruch is clearly divided into two parts, at the end of iii. 8; the first part, by internal evidence, is translated from a Hebrew original, which is also definitely referred to in the Syro-hexaplar margin. The second part is probably a Greek composition, though Prof. Marshall thought parts of it showed signs of underlying Aramaic. The dates assigned to the first part vary widely, from 320 B.C. to later than A.D. 70; the second part, largely on the strength of reference in it to one of the Psalms of Solomon, is placed at the end of the first century A.D. The problem is complex, because, as Thackeray thinks, the translator of the first part used a Greek version of Daniel; cf. Bar. i. 15 ff., ii. 1–11 with Dan. ix. 10–15. Hence there are several dates to be fitted in. A moderate view is that the Greek of part 1, made by the second translator of Jeremiah, dates from sometime in the first century B.C., its Heb. original about a century earlier; and that part 2 was written, and the two joined together, in the last fifteen years of the first century A.D. Though it is difficult to get away from the evidence alleged for this late date of part 2, Prof. Swete has pointed out (*Introd. O.T. in Gr.*, p. 275) that it was accepted early by the Christian Church; this may have been helped by its connexion with Jeremiah in the LXX.; while, according to Jerome, the Jews paid no attention to it.

(An old Latin version of Baruch, from Monte Cassino, has been published by Dom Amelli.)

The 'Epistle of Jeremy', forming Baruch vi. in the English Apocrypha, is a separate work, standing as such in the LXX. among the works attached to Jeremiah's. It was composed in Greek, and appears to be referred to in 2 Macc. i. (Swete, p. 275).

Whether the additions to the Book of Daniel ever had a Semitic original is doubtful, though Ball thinks that Susanna and Bel were originally composed in late Hebrew or in Aramaic, and the Song of the Three Children and the Prayer of Azarias in Hebrew. Their dates are uncertain, and they cannot be highly rated among the Apocryphal writings.

The Prayer of Manasseh hardly belongs to the LXX., as it is generally found only among the Canticles. The Council of Trent rejected it. Its date is uncertain.

The Books of Maccabees are quite distinct works; the name merely relates to the period with which they are concerned. Cod. B contains none of them.

The First Book of Maccabees is a sound historical work, originally written in Hebrew, as Jerome said in his 'Prologus Galeatus' (introd. to his translation of Samuel). It tells of the Jews' struggles against Antiochus Epiphanes and the following Syrian kings and usurpers, and of the great deeds of Mattathias and his family. It is supposed to have been written near the end of the reign of John Hyrcanus, 105 B.C., whether before or after. The author is accurate in dating events, and in his geography of Palestine. He uses documents, especially letters, and summarises them. The Greek version, from which the O.L. and Syriac must have been made, is probably not much later than the original, perhaps dating about 80 B.C. It is the best of the Apocryphal books in style, and apparently in faithfulness also. The original author was evidently a strong patriot, a supporter of the Asmonaean priest-princes, and probably an adherent of the Sadducees. The book was used by Josephus, perhaps in Hebrew. Its value is fully recognised in modern times.

The Second Book of Maccabees was composed in Greek, and is professedly (ii. 23) an abridgment of a work by Jason of Cyrene. The style aims at being literary Greek, but it is rhetorical, wordy, and uneven; the book may date rather before the middle of the first century B.C. Its historical value, after discounting exaggerations, has been to some extent vindicated by B. Niese (*Kritik der beiden Makkabäerbuch*, Berlin, 1900). The author's tone contrasts strongly with that of 1 Maccabees; some have thought him a Pharisee; but he is a Jew of Alexandria, not of Palestine. With this book we reach the end of the English Apocrypha.

The Third Book of Maccabees is found in several MSS. of the LXX., and is included in most printed editions. Though not regarded as canonical, it was not far from securing a place among the Apocrypha, with which Canon Charles places it in the

Oxford edition. It deals with events earlier than the Maccabean time: the reign of Ptolemy Philopator 221–204 (B.C.) and his profane intentions against the Temple. There is some historical foundation, but a good deal of embellishment, and fabulous details. The style somewhat resembles the more rhetorical parts of 2 Macc., but outdoes them. It has been dated as late as A.D. 40, but is more usually placed in the early part of the first century B.C. It has been suspected that the title *Ptolemaica*, in the Ps.-Athanasian synopsis, stood for 3 Macc.; but as it stands in addition to four books of Maccabees, this can hardly be; Wendland and Thackeray both think it means the Letter of Aristeas.

The Fourth Book of Maccabees has been attributed to Josephus, but doubtless wrongly. It covers some of the same ground as 2 Macc., but with more philosophical rhetoric, a kind of blend of Stoic and Pharisaic doctrines. History is subordinate in it. The book is probably of Alexandrian literary origin, dating from the first century B.C., but before the fall of Jerusalem. The Pharisaic view appears in the belief, strongly expressed, in a future life, with reward, xv. 3, etc., or punishment, ix. 9; *αἰώνιος ζωή . . . αἰώνιος βάσανος*. Also xvii. 12, *τὸ νῖκος ἐν ἀφθαρσίᾳ ἐν ζωῇ πολυχρονίῳ*. It was popular among Christians down to Chrysostom's time.

The uncials A and V (part only of 4 Macc.), and cursives 44, 46, 52, 74, 93, 120, 236, contain all four books; ℵ has 1 and 4, Π fragments of 4; 19, 55, and 106 the first three, 56 and 64 the first two only. See Swete's *Introd.*, pp. 154 ff., 279.

There is also a Fifth Book of Maccabees extant

in Arabic and Syriac. Calmet thought that there had been a Hebrew original and a Greek version. The book was included in Cotton's translation, but is of little value.

The Cambridge *O.T. in Greek* contains eighteen *Psalms of Solomon.* These have been edited also by Bp. Ryle and Dr. James. They are productions of the Pharisees, originally composed in Hebrew, possibly 70–40 B.C. The second appears to refer to the death of Pompey, who profanely entered the Temple. In it there are probable references to the LXX. of Isaiah. The editors assign the Greek version to A.D. 90–100. See above, on Baruch, p. 145. The Psalms of Solomon are not found in any uncial of the LXX., though they are named in the table of contents in A, and may have been lost from it and from ℵ. Among the cursives, 149 and 253 have them.

The Book (or First Book) of *Enoch*, so far as extant in Greek (i.–iii., v.–xxxii., lxxxix.), is also printed in the Cambridge *O.T. in Greek.* Except for small fragments, it was only known in an Ethiopic version until 1886, when the first part, in uncials, was discovered at Akhmîm or Panopolis. The Greek may date from the first century B.C. It is quoted, Jude 14, 15, not exactly according to the text discovered. Canon Charles considers that it was composed partly in Aramaic (vi.–xxxvi., and perhaps lxxxiii.–xc.), partly in Hebrew. The Aramaic portions may date shortly before and after 168 B.C.; xxxvii.–lxxi. and the end of the book before 79 or after 70 B.C. Thus it appears to be rather a series of works, possibly of one school, than a single book. Its influence is traced in Paul's epistles, perhaps in the Gospels, and in the Revelation; and in later apocalyptic works, such as 2 Baruch and 4 Ezra (=2 Esdras). The Epistle of Barnabas (xvi. 4) quotes it with the formula λέγει ἡ γραφή. Early Christian writers (Justin, Cyrian, Minucius Felix, Tertullian) refer to it, but it was never definitely accepted by the Church, and later fell out of use. It is of interest both for its threads of connexion with the canonical Scriptures and as a specimen of Jewish teaching concerning angels, the Last Judgment, and the coming of Messiah.

The *Odes of Solomon* scarcely belong, it would seem, to the O.T. Apocrypha, but may be named here for their connexion, perhaps fortuitous, with the Psalms of Solomon mentioned above. They were discovered by Dr. Rendel Harris, and first published in 1910, in a Syriac text, 42 Odes intermingled with the 18 Psalms. It was at first doubted whether they were the work of a Jewish Christian, or a Jewish composition with Christian interpolations. The view of the Provost of Dublin (Abp. Bernard) is that they are hymns, intended for Eastern Christians to sing at their baptism. In this case their date would be about A.D. 100. If originally Jewish, the groundwork would have to be placed near 100 B.C. See *Cambridge Texts and Studies*, vol. viii. No. 3. Another MS. has since been discovered by Prof. Burkitt in the Nitrian Collection at the British Museum. The question of the original language of the Odes is still being discussed; Dom Conolly (in *J. Th. St.*, xiv. xv.) argues strongly for Greek; Dr. E. Abbott, though allowing the work to be Christian, supports the idea of a Semitic original. References to the LXX. Psalms and Isaiah have been suspected, and even to St. John's Gospel and 1 Peter.

There remain many books which do not appear in printed texts, nor generally in MSS. of the LXX. (or Vulgate); these are generally called Pseudepigrapha, a name which is felt to be rather unsatisfactory, but comes from the fact that, from the third century B.C. onward, many Jewish writings, especially those of apocalyptic character, were pseudonymous. The name is, however, widely used, and the great Oxford edition continues it. It will be consistent to follow the Oxford order.

The *Book of Jubilees*, or 'Little Genesis', is one of a number of books dating from about the time of the prince-priesthood of John Hyrcanus. It seems to be based upon an independent form of the Hebrew text of Genesis and the earlier part of Exodus, and to have been composed in Hebrew, by a Jew of Pharisaic[1] sympathies, probably late in the period 135–105 B.C. The Hebrew, however, is not extant, and only a fragment of the second chapter in the Greek version made from it, besides a few quotations by Justin Martyr, Origen, Isidore of Seville, etc. Appearances have led some to think that the Greek was made from Aramaic and not Hebrew, but the balance of opinion is against this. The Ethiopic version, made from the Greek, is so literal that it goes far to supply its place; it is generally accurate and trustworthy, but somewhat corrupt. Hence the Latin, with differ-

[1] So Canon Charles: others think the author was a Sadducee, or connected with the Hasidaeans.

ent shortcomings, is useful; it is almost as literal, and in places better preserved, but more glossed and corrected. It is uncertain whether the book ever existed in Syriac. It contains an account of the earlier Patriarchs' lives, with a system of chronology reckoned by Jubilees, whence the name. The history is represented as having been given by revelation to Moses on Sinai. The book is said to be based in parts on the 'Book of Noah' and portions of the Book of Enoch, while other parts of Enoch, the Book of Wisdom, and 4 Ezra or 2 Esdras use it in their turn.

The contents of the *Letter of Aristeas* (see above, chap. ii.) need not be further described. Its date has been much discussed, and some opinions place it as early as 200 B.C., others as late as A.D. 33. Wendland, the German editor, puts it between 96 and 63 B.C., and thinks that the writer perhaps assumed the name of the historian Aristeas, of the first, or late second, century B.C. Thackeray, the English editor, seems to favour a date shortly after 50 B.C. Some have suggested that Philo made use of the 'Letter', but Cohn, who with Wendland edits Philo's works, denies this. If the section on the Jewish Law, §§ 128–171, be separated from the rest, and dated near the Christian era, it is felt that the main part of the work could more easily be placed between 130 and 70 B.C. Some cursive MSS. contain the 'Letter' with books of the LXX. It is a purely Greek work.

The Book of *Adam and Eve* is a Jewish compilation of legends, including, or rather running parallel with, an 'Apocalypse of Moses'; this is extant in Greek, the Book of Adam and Eve in late mediaeval Slavonic, in Latin, Syriac, and Ethiopic. The original compilation may have been made from the first to the third century A.D.; with later Christian additions.

The *Ascension of Isaiah* was composed of various materials. Of these the 'Martyrdom of Isaiah' is partly extant in Greek (Amherst Papyri); a different form is represented by the Ethiopic and Latin. Probably it was originally a Jewish work written in Hebrew; but a 'Vision' which follows the 'Martyrdom', and the compilation, are thought to be Christian. The sawing asunder of Isaiah, supposed to be alluded to in Heb. xi. 37, is described in the 'Martyrdom', to which there *may* be allusion. The earlier, Jewish, part of the work may date from the first century A.D.

The *Testaments of the XII. Patriarchs* is a Pharisaic work of the time of John Hyrcanus, written in Hebrew about 109–106 B.C., perhaps earlier. Each Patriarch, before his death, addresses his children, summing up his life, drawing its moral, and urging upon his descendants the virtues of truth, forgiveness, temperance, chastity, and such like. The work exists in Greek, the MSS. apparently representing two recensions of the Hebrew. From one of these the Armenian version was made, before certain interpolations, found in the Greek, and due to Christians, came in. The author was familiar with the O.T., and the books of Sirach and Enoch; his influence is thought to be traceable in the N.T. The work, once popular, fell into oblivion, and when re-introduced into the West, through Robert Grosseteste, in the thirteenth century, it was at first taken to be the authentic work of the Patriarchs. When the New Learning in Reformation times rejected this idea, it relapsed into obscurity, and has only lately emerged again. A few years ago it was generally dated about two centuries later than the date given above.

The *Sibylline Oracles* are partly Jewish, but mostly Christian in origin, a compilation of materials belonging to several centuries, down to about A.D. 500. The earliest may belong to the first, or possibly second century B.C.: one oracle alludes to Rome as not yet ruling over Egypt. The original language seems to have been Greek. The rivalry with the heathen oracles, which found vent in these productions, is curious. But the tone is devout and monotheistic.

The *Assumption of Moses* was known, it would seem, to St. Jude (ver. 9). Composed, shortly after the Christian era, in Hebrew, it was translated into Greek, and later into Latin, of which a sixth century MS. was discovered at Milan by Dr. Ceriani. It is to some extent apocalyptic. If the author was a Pharisee, he was less thoroughgoing than the (earlier) writer of the 'Testaments'. The Assumption now includes a Testament of Moses, originally independent.

The *Book of the Secrets of Enoch* (2 Enoch) was first written in Greek by a Jew of Egypt. Some of the 'Testaments' refer to it; but its present form seems to be later, perhaps near A.D. 50. Only a Slavonic version is extant.

The Syriac Apocalypse of *Baruch* (2 Baruch) is ostensibly a prophecy of Baruch after the fall of Jerusalem. It is really of the first century A.D., apparently an attempt, by a Pharisee, to support declining Judaism against Christianity. The Syriac is from a Greek version of the Hebrew original.

The Greek Apocalypse of *Baruch* (3 Baruch) follows parallel lines with the last named, though independent. It was known only in Slavonic, until a Greek MS. of the sixteenth century in the British Museum was identified by Dom E. C. Butler. The original was Jewish, a blend of Hellenic and Oriental ideas; but it has been worked over by a Christian hand. The extant Greek is apparently a shortened form. In it appears the idea that the Forbidden Tree was the vine.

On 4 Ezra or 2 Esdras, see above, among the Apocrypha. It has affinities with 2 Baruch. The Christian additions, chaps. i., ii., and xv., xvi., are sometimes known as 5 and 6 Ezra. A few verses, xvi. 57–9, are found in Oxyr. Pap. 1010, fourth century A.D.

Pirke Aboth (Sayings of the Fathers) is a collection of maxims, ranging over about 300 B.C.–A.D. 300; part of the Mishna.

The *Story of Aḥiḳar* is a curious and ancient tale, which has enjoyed so wide a popularity that its history would form a chapter of folk-lore in itself. It is heathenish in tone, but has some connexion with the Biblical Apocrypha; and occurs among the supplementary tales of the Thousand and One Nights. Aḥiḳar was, according to the story, vizier to the great Sennacherib, and prosperous in all his ways, except that he was childless. He adopted his sister's son, Nadab or Nadau, who turned out so ill as to plot his uncle's downfall, and to forge documents to this end. Aḥiḳar was imprisoned and condemned, but escaped death by the substitution (as in *Measure for Measure*) of a criminal in his place, and remained hidden until Sennacherib, missing his counsels, regretted his loss, when his friendly executioner ventured to bring him forth. The restored vizier revenged himself on his nephew, casting him in his turn into bonds, and upbraiding him with a remarkable store of proverbial similitudes. The nephew finally succumbed, miraculously (?) smitten.

The Story was first edited by Prof. F. C. Conybeare, Dr. Rendel Harris, and Mrs. Lewis, in 1898, from various incomplete versions, Syriac, Arabic, Armenian, Ethiopic, Greek, and Slavonic. In Greek, Aḥiḳar appears as Æsop; according to Clement of Alexandria, Democritus borrowed from the work. In the Book of Tobit, allusion is made to Aḥiḳar, who is mentioned as Tobit's nephew. This seemed at first to require a late date, at least for those portions of Tobit where the allusions occur. But the Story is older than was thought. A fragment of it, in Aramaic, was discovered at Elephantine; the actual papyrus fragment is assigned to the fifth century B.C., which makes it the oldest extant document among Biblical or Apocryphal texts. The Aramaic is believed to be the original form, and the story may date from about 500 B.C. Parallels to it have been traced in the Book of Jubilees, the Testaments of the XII. Patriarchs, Sirach, Daniel, Proverbs, and some Psalms; and allusions in the New Testament, the clearest of which is the 'sow that returned to her wallowing', 2 Pet. ii. 22; where, if the proverbial tale is originally as in Aḥiḳar of a 'swine which went to the bath with people of quality', Prof. Moulton is surely right (*Gramm. of N.T. Greek*, p. 238) in allowing λουσαμένη reflexive force. Of the various versions, the Armenian, of the fifth century A.D., is as important as any.

The *Fragment of a Zadokite Work*, which Canon Charles has edited, is to be dated somewhere near 100 B.C. It represents the tenets of a priestly reforming body of that period, who preached penitence, and believed in a future life, yet were not altogether out of sympathy with the Sadducee party. Part only is extant, in two Cambridge MSS. It is written in Hebrew, on the whole, in the editor's opinion, good, with a few Aramaisms and late Hebrew expressions. With this the Oxford volumes end, but the list of Pseudepigraphic writings is far from being exhausted. There are many more 'Testaments' and 'Apocalypses,' whole or fragmentary, extant in various languages; the 'Paralipomena' of Jeremiah, the 'Book of Eldad and Medad', 'Joseph and Asenath', and many more works of varying merit. But they have no pretensions to admission into any canon, and for our present purpose the limits of the Oxford collection will be amply sufficient. Among these books we find great variety in date, character, and value. Probably a modern student will find most interest, among the Apocrypha, in Wisdom, Ecclesiasticus, and 1 Maccabees; of the rest, in Enoch, the Book of Jubilees, and the Testaments of the XII. Patriarchs. From a different point of view, the Story of Aḥiḳar is good reading, and its history deserves attention. It is important to study some of the books which were originally composed in Greek, and to compare their style with the translated books; and the fortunes of the versions of many of the Pseudepigrapha may prove instructive. But the student whose business is chiefly with the O.T. had better devote himself at first, with the above exceptions, mainly to the contents of the Greek Bible.

CHAPTER VII

THE LANGUAGE AND STYLE OF THE SEPTUAGINT

Translated and Original Books—Question of Semitic idioms in the Greek—Parallel idioms in the papyri—Arguments that Semitic influence is slight, and 'Biblical Greek' simply the vernacular of the time, apart from 'translation-Greek' (Deissmann and Moulton)—Arguments in favour of Semitic influence—What causes these idioms? Examples—The history of languages—The points at issue not very weighty—The difficulty of translating from the LXX.—The intention of the LXX. translators—Remarks on the literary style of the LXX.

IT has already been necessary to refer more than once to the character of the Greek in which the Septuagint is written. The books vary much in this respect; one distinction is between those which were translated from a Semitic language, usually Hebrew, and those which were originally composed in Greek. There is not often much room for doubt on this point; Esdras A, Tobit, and the additions to Daniel may be considered uncertain; Judith, Sirach, 1 Maccabees, and Enoch had Semitic originals, Baruch is probably composite, the other books of the Apocrypha, excepting 2 Esdras, are original Greek works, and so are 3 and 4 Maccabees. The canonical books of the O.T. are all translated; but not all at the same time, nor by one hand, nor exactly in the same style. The question now to be discussed is, how far the Greek is affected by the idiom of the Semitic languages; a question which has already been seen to concern the subject somewhat nearly. It has become prominent in recent years, in connexion with the papyrus documents which have been discovered by Drs. Grenfell and Hunt and other searchers, and the examination of their language which has been made. The results of this examination, so far as it has gone, have been to some extent popularised, chiefly by Prof. Deissmann in Germany, and Prof. Moulton in England; and a new aspect of the language of the O.T. and N.T. in Greek is strongly suggested by them.

The New Testament would not directly concern us, if it were not that Moulton and Deissmann have discussed it almost more than the Old, and their opponents on this question, Wellhausen and Dalman, have pointed to Semitic constructions in the Gospels as an argument that there were underlying documents in Aramaic, on which they were based. From the point of view of the LXX., it is not necessary to magnify the difference in views, if Deissmann and Moulton are thoroughgoing in making an exception of 'translation-Greek,' for the greater part of the LXX. is translated; and it would be easy to assent generally to a view of the subject such as this (from Deissmann's *Philology of the Greek Bible*, p. 63, Eng. Trans.): "Not one of the recent investigators has dreamt of denying the existence of Semiticisms. They are more numerous in the Septuagint than in those parts of the New Testament that were translated from the Aramaic; but in the original Greek texts they are very rare". It becomes rather a question of what is to be considered a Semitism, and how far the total of the Semitic influence affects the language. Deissmann (p. 37, and Lecture II. generally) derides the term 'Biblical Greek', and he and Moulton claim to show that it is not an 'isolated' language at all. 'When a grammarian of balanced judgment like G. B. Winer came to sum up the bygone controversy, he was found admitting enough Semitisms to make the Biblical Greek essentially an isolated language still. It is just this isolation which the new evidence comes in to destroy' (Moulton, *Gramm. N.T. Greek*, p. 3). And again (p. 1), 'the disappearance of that word "Hebraic" from its prominent place in our delineation of N.T. language marks a change in our conceptions of the subject nothing less than revolutionary'. But whereas Dr. Moulton dates this change as late as 1895, there is earlier evidence to show that, except in the matter of ideas, the language of the Greek Bible was not regarded as specially isolated; and there are still some people to-day who are not quite satisfied with all his instances of cancelled Hebraisms. On the first point, a few sentences may be quoted from a work published in 1875 (A. Carr, *Notes on the Gospel acc. to St. Luke*): 'The book that was intended for the people was written in the language of the people. . . . Hellenistic Greek has a further interest. It is the stepping-stone between the Greek language in its perfection and the Greek that is being spoken in the streets of Athens to-day. . . . The Greek language in the New Testament is strongly influenced by Aramaic forms of expression. It is, indeed, often simply Aramaic thinly disguised by a Greek dress. But, on the others hand, there has been, perhaps, too great a tendency to set down every idiom that offends the scholar's ear as a Hebrew mode of expression. . . . Sometimes the idiom will be found to be Greek as well as Hebrew, but Greek of a kind that had been heretofore confined to the speech of the vulgar.' This, though written before the papyri had been much studied, hardly asserts that 'isolation' of the language of the Greek Bible which the 'new evidence' is supposed to 'destroy'. The second point, the separate consideration of various expressions, now claimed as Greek and not Semitic, shall be treated presently. Meanwhile, some surprise may be expressed, when philologists object to its being said that Hellenistic Greek, the κοινή, is inferior to the Greek of the 'classical' period. Deissmann (p. 55) says: 'Qualitative judgments describing it as "bad" Greek, and so on, are either uttered by doctrinaires regardless of history, or echoed from the grammarians who fancied themselves able by their authority to prevent the changes and chances of things.' And Moulton (p. 22) similarly, 'Classical scholars have studied the Hellenistic literature for the sake of its matter; its language was seldom considered worth noticing except to chronicle contemptuously its deviations from "good Greek".' This is astonishing; surely philology has, since it came into being, studied the historical development, and the 'changes and chances' of things as shown in language. If things change it must surely be either for the better or for the worse; and languages have their rise, their prime and their decay, followed, it may be, by a remaking. Is the prime of Greek not to be placed in the fourth and fifth centuries B.C.? or was it at Alexandria, in the days of the librarians, and not in the days of the dramatists and orators at Athens, that it reached its best? Other languages give us similar results; Prakrit was not the equal of Sanskrit, nor is English to-day what it was in the days of Elizabeth, though still capable of much. Tastes will differ, of course; but there are many who find taste and philology still at one.

But to come to specific instances of expressions, which were formerly termed Hebraisms, but which are claimed as Greek by Prof. Moulton and others, because they occur in papyri or non-Biblical documents. There are some, to which reference has been already made, from a different view-point (p. 127 ff.), such as the use of the relative with redundant pronoun following, of *προστιθέναι* as a quasi-auxiliary to express repeated action, and of the verb reinforced with cognate noun, or participle, where Hebrew has the verb and infinitive: also the extended use of *ἐν*, and *πᾶς* with a following negative for 'none'; and such phrases as *εἰς συνάντησιν*, Isa. vii. 3, and its variations, or as *υἱὸς θανάτου οὗτος*, 1 Sam. xx. 31. These, one might have thought, could at least have been conceded under the head of 'translation-Greek'. The list, moreover, might easily be increased. Some lay stress on phrases like *δύο δύο*, *ἑπτὰ ἑπτά*, Gen. vii. 2; but it is perhaps reasonable to give this up, as a kind of primitively simple expression which might occur in almost any language; only the asyndeton distinguishes it from our familiar 'two and two'. And though Prof. Nestle is quoted by Moulton (*Camb. Bib. Essays*, p. 473) as saying of *ἕως πότε* that it 'is for me a Hebraism', it is as well to abandon this, in face of ἕως ὅτε, Xenoph. *Cyr.* V. i. 25, and ἕως ὀψέ, Thucyd. III. 108. It may be that to all the phrases quoted above, and to many more, parallels may be found in papyri of dates approximately coinciding with the composition of the LXX. and N.T.; and surely this is as full a concession as can be desired. But, as Moulton readily allows (*Gramm. N.T. Gr., Prol.*, p. 72: cf. Thackeray, *Gr. O.T.*, p. 29), the LXX. use these expressions constantly: he speaks of 'the over-doing of a correct locution in passages based on a Semitic original, simply because it has the advantage of being a literal rendering'. With this it is easy to agree, except in so far as the word 'correct' begs the question. In regard to the defence of this or that expression as Greek, because it occurs in the papyri, it is necessary to consider whether the writers of the papyri were themselves free from all Semitic influence; and some are clearly illiterate. But when an O.T. translator, or a writer in the Apocrypha or N.T., uses such phrases as those given above, the real question is not, 'Does this phrase occur in papyri or non-Biblical documents?' but, 'Does the writer use this phrase *because* it was familiar in the Greek of his time, or *because* it was familiar in Semitic idiom? Which circumstance accounts for its appearing, and that frequently, in the Greek Bible?' To the question so put, the only possible answer seems to be, that it was because of the Semitic usage.[1] The mere

[1] It may be possible to argue the question, how far the phrase 'That goes without saying' has become naturalised as vernacular English; it is familiar to all, and its meaning well understood. But if it should occur in a translation from French, or in a passage where any

occurrence of an expression in papyri does not abolish its Semitic affinities. If it occurs regularly in them, the case would be stronger; but then comes in the point, already raised by Prof. Swete (*Apocalypse*, p. cxxiv, note 1): the existence of a really large Jewish population in Egypt, the main source of our stock of papyri. Their speech might influence their neighbours; and some of the papyri may have been actually written by Jews; this, considering their numbers, is but natural to suppose; and some of the names that actually occur point to the probability in individual cases. The general influence of Jewish speech is not easy to prove as a fact; but (*a*) there is analogy for it; the Persian and Indian languages furnish examples of mixture of Semitic and non-Semitic tongues, and Syriac and New-Hebrew show slight signs of Greek counter-influence; (*b*) the argument that the *κοινή* was practically homogeneous throughout its extent is balanced by the use of Aramaic for centuries as a language of general intercourse over much of the East; Pahlavi, for instance, was perceptibly influenced by it. Indeed, as the Jewish Dispersion and the Hellenic extension covered so large a space in common, linked, moreover, by the pursuit of trade, and by Phoenician associations, it would be strange if no effect were produced by one upon the other. The belief must still be held, that according to philology itself, languages have their life, their vicissitudes, their

connexion with French thought or literature is traceable, none would hesitate to attribute its occurrence to the French usage; it is, in fact, a Gallicism; and such authority as can be found in this country pronounces it to be 'bad English'.

prime, and their decay. It is in their decay that they are weakened, and less able to resist outside influences. The decay is most likely to coincide with some breaking up of the nations themselves; and it is clear that certain periods of history show such breaking up; boundaries shifted, populations displaced and on the move, the nations in a state of flux. Thus the Romance languages arise from the remodelling, after the Barbarians' inroads, of the weakened Latin; the later Persian is a blend with the conquerors' Arabic, and itself, thus blended, an ingredient in further mixtures. It is inconsistent to suppose that Alexander's conquests, which spread the Greek language far and wide, could do so without its purity being to some extent impaired. Therefore it must not be taken for granted that the κοινή was entirely free from Semitic influence; and when close parallels to Semitic forms of speech appear in translations from Hebrew, and in the writings of Jews and close associates of Jews, it requires the strongest of proofs to fortify the assertion that such parallels are due to natural development of the Greek itself, and not to imitation, or influence of the Semitic idiom.

However, except for a few statements in the writings of Deissmann and Moulton, which may after all be taken as *obiter dicta*, or set off against other remarks of theirs, the difference between their position and the older estimate of Semitisms is not, for a student of the LXX., very important. It seems, on examination, to be rather a matter of emphasis on the one aspect or the other, and of the use of terms. And with much that is said by Deissmann and Moulton (as, for instance, in the latter's most readable

Prolegomena to his *Gramm. of N.T. Greek*) it is possible to agree almost without reserve; though there seems to be a recurring tendency to minimise the influence of Aramaic and Hebrew, and to insist on the resemblance of the Greek Bible to an ordinary specimen of the κοινή.

A difficulty, which is not unconnected with this subject, often arises in translating from the LXX. It sometimes happens that they have rendered a Hebrew word by a Greek one which, according to its derivation or established use, is rather a substitute for the Hebrew than the exact equivalent for it. In such a case, it is possible to ignore the Hebrew, and translate the Greek strictly as Greek, which will present the difference between original and version as more marked; or to assume that the LXX. intended to give, as nearly as they could, the meaning of the Hebrew, and to translate their rendering as nearly in accordance with the Hebrew as the Greek will permit, on this assumption. The reader may very likely think that between these alternatives, so put, the former is the only right and proper course. And he will find it weightily supported by Deissmann (*Philology of the Greek Bible*, pp. 89 ff.), who holds that 'the meaning of a Septuagint word cannot be deduced from the original which it translates or replaces, but only from other remains of the Greek language, especially from those Egyptian sources that have lately flowed so abundantly'. This position, he continues, 'unfortunately, is not conceded at once, but has to be slowly won by combat with an unmethodical school'. But a case is not proved by attributing want of method to those who take a different view.[1] The examples which he gives of this 'mechanical equating process' (pp. 91, 93) are, it may be supposed, such as he considers to present a strong case, and we shall return to them shortly. It may be granted that the principle for which he contends gives us *a* right way of translating, and if the correct rendering of the Greek on this principle can be ascertained with accuracy and security, a translation of the LXX. on these lines is highly desirable. But it may be doubted whether it is the only way; and if it be not, then, unless two translations can be furnished, it may be advisable to admit, meantime at any rate, some compromise in rendering. The position of the Greek translators must be remembered; they were translating from a language and a literature full of a peculiar, nay, unique range of ideas into another language, philologically remote, and completely strange to these ideas. It was not possible for them, perhaps it was not possible at all, to find clear and intelligible Greek renderings for every Hebrew idea. As Deissmann (p. 89) says, 'All translation, in fact, implies some, if only a slight, alteration of the sense of the original'. It is, indeed, probable, that when the translation was made, many of its readers understood its renderings as in the light of Greek; and this increasingly, as time went on. But it is no less probable, that the translators understood or intended their own renderings in the sense of the Hebrew as they understood

[1] For a contrary statement see Herriot, *Philon le Juif*, p. 83, on the LXX.: 'Ils donnent, et ceci est très important, à des mots grecs les acceptions des mots hébreux correspondants . . . transportent dans la syntaxe grecque des constructions hébraiques.'

it; they can scarcely have intended anything else. Translation on the one principle, therefore, will really be aiming at the meaning which later readers, including generally the makers of the secondary versions, attached to the Greek; on the other principle it will aim at expressing the intention of the translators. In the one case we translate according to what they seemed to say, in the other, what they meant. Both ways may be valuable; if we can have only one, which is to be preferred?

To come to Prof. Deissmann's examples; the case of trees changing their species in translation need not detain us long. There is always a chance that the identity of natural species may be lost, in transmission from one language to another, or even without this, in the course of a long period of time. In some cases, if lost, it may be recovered, with at least a high degree of probability; and it is doubtless right to restore a more correct term, if dealing with the original, and to preserve the different rendering of the version. Yet it is possible that in some cases, even the Greek term is not certain; and in the matter of the Hebrew, we must face the fact that the meaning of some words may be irrecoverably lost; natural species, of trees, animals, plants, stones; some artificial objects, as tools or musical instruments; and a few others. It is not safe to assume that identity of name means identity of species; the familiar example of *φηγός* and *fagus* shows the contrary.

But in the more important case of *ἱλαστήριον*, what are we to say? Deissmann (p. 92) says, 'You will read of this word in many respectable books on theology that in Septuagint Greek or in "Biblical"

Greek it "means" "the lid of the ark of the covenant", because the corresponding Hebrew word "kapporeth" is in most cases so translated by modern scholars. Now the etymology of the word, confirmed by certain inscriptions, shows that ἱλαστήριον means "object of expiation or propitiation" . . . the Septuagint has not translated the concept of "lid" but has replaced it by another concept which brings out the sacred purpose of the ark. The lid of the ark of the covenant *is* an ἱλαστήριον, but it does not follow that ἱλαστήριον means "lid" either in the Septuagint, in St. Paul, or anywhere else; it can only mean "expiatory or propitiatory object".'

Very well; but a commentary on a word cannot always be packed into a translation, though 'mercy-seat' is a beautiful attempt to do so. More than this; though no one can ever have seriously supposed that ἱλαστήριον in itself means 'lid', it actually occurs first in Ex. xxv. 17 as an adjective, the substantive being ἐπίθεμα, which does mean something put on, a 'lid' or 'cover'. When it is used without a substantive after this, it must necessarily carry the same meaning; for it is spoken of as a material object, with dimensions and ends, which is placed (ἐπιθήσεις, Ex. xxv. 20) upon the ark from above. Now as a rule, whereas Greek can suppress the substantive in such phrases, English has a tendency to keep the substantive, and finds some difficulty in using the adjective alone, though instances do exist. If anyone prefers to render 'propitiatory', after the Vulgate, the rendering, applied to the LXX., must carry with it the meaning of 'lid' at the first occurrence, and this will be inherent in it thereafter. This rendering, 'propitiatory', is suggested by Prof. Driver on the passage in Exodus (*Cambridge Bible*) to translate the *Hebrew*; and his note throws doubt on 'cover' in a literal sense, as the primary meaning of the Heb. word, which he renders 'a propitiatory thing' or 'means of propitiation'. The result seems to be that some word or phrase which includes the 'covering' idea is, if anything, more to be justified in translating from the LXX. than from the Hebrew. After the first mention of the subject, no one can fail to know that the mercy-seat was a propitiatory object on the one hand, in its spiritual aspect, and a material 'lid' or 'cover', on the other hand, in its outward visible form and position. To suggest another example, which happens to occur in the N.T. (Acts xvi. 20) and in secular Greek, as Polybius, and later. The word στρατηγός, in ordinary Greek, would usually be rendered 'commander' or 'general'. But when it occurs with clear reference to the Roman officials, whether in a translation from a Latin original or not, it is surely reasonable to render it by 'praetor'; and this without any reference to the original position of the Praetor at Rome, or to the derivation of the word, or to the bearing of these upon the choice of στρατηγός to represent the Roman title. In the same way, had it been customary to translate the Heb. *shophet* 'leader' or 'chief' instead of 'judge',[1] it would have been advisable to render κριτής in the same way when representing *shophet*: for the Greek translators meant whatever *shophet* meant.

[1] Our English word 'judge' is in fact clearly bearing a special sense in this connexion. See Judg. ii. 18.

The problems, therefore, of translating from the Septuagint are not entirely simple, nor quite like those of translation in general; and something can be said on behalf of more than one method. The question has some analogy with that of 'representation', which has already been mentioned as a feature of the LXX.'s treatment of the Hebrew. This, of course, appears in the other Greek translators' work; strongly in Aquila, and perceptibly in Theodotion. In Symmachus it is less recognisable. Latin translations from the Greek Bible show the same practice at work. The difficulty was often felt, of transferring the Hebrew meaning, and forms of expression, into another language; and then the translators preferred to put down something which should stand for the original in such a way, that they could, as it were, point to the original phrase or word, and say, 'This is what we mean': both in cases where they did not feel sure of the meaning, and in cases where they knew it, but found a difficulty in expressing it intelligibly. Later on, the position of readers using the translation, as many generations, ignorant of the Semitic original, did, was different, and in some respects unfortunate, as history shows that it was felt to be. The clues were lost, and the Septuagint, taken as a purely Greek work, is sometimes difficult or impossible to understand; so much so, that they seem at times to have put down the best they could, though consciously out of their depth, and scarcely forming a distinct notion as to what they themselves intended to convey. A translator dealing with such passages has so hard a task that he may well seek for some method of compromise.[1]

In these remarks on translating the Septuagint, on the character of its Greek, and on Hebraisms, the reader must understand that I cannot claim to be representing any opinion but my own. Those who are convinced by the advocacy of Professors Deissmann and Moulton, whose views I have tried to represent fairly, will be, at any rate, in good company. There are still several who hold the opposite view; but, while I find it easy to agree with nearly all that they say, I cannot guarantee that they would endorse what is said here, or support this presentment of the case. The balance is very fairly held by Mr. Thackeray in his *Grammar of O.T. Greek*, vol. i. pp. 29 ff.; and there is a review of Moulton's Prolegomena, by Mr. G. C. Richards, in the *Journal of Theol. Studies*, vol. x. No. 38, p. 283, which is well worth attention. The study of the Septuagint comes into contact with so many branches of learning, and has been the principal labour of so few men, that what is written upon it proceeds from scholars whose training and main interests differ widely. Some are Semitic students or Orientalists; some are primarily classical scholars; some, theologians; some, philologists; some specially interested in the papyri and Modern Greek; some come to the LXX. from the New Testament, some from the Old. On questions, therefore, of Semitisms in the Greek of the

[1] On the difficulty of translating where one thing is meant, and another thing, to the best of our modern knowledge, is written, see J. T. Sheppard, *Greek Tragedy* (Camb. Manuals), p. 39, and Prof. Gilbert Murray's *Anc. Greek Literature*, Pref. p. xvii.

Septuagint, and of the value of the text it represents, as compared with the M.T., it is as well, at least, to notice what has been the main line of study pursued by each writer on the subject.

There remains one point, on which opinions might easily differ, but on which so little has been said, that I am not aware that any controversy has as yet arisen. I mean the style of the LXX., from a purely literary point of view, as it is calculated to affect a reader. The difficulty in making an estimate is to find any standard of comparison. It is, as we know, possible, if a rare thing, for translations, including those of the Scriptures, to achieve literary merit of a very high order. But to attain this result, some fortunate combination of circumstances is required. In the case of the English Authorised Version, the language employed was in its prime; the earlier renderings of which the translators took account imparted a slightly archaic tinge to the Jacobean English; and the terse sentences and divisions of the original saved the version from the chief fault of its time, the tendency to loose expansion and overloaded richness. Thus the effect of the limitations imposed was felicitous, and the translators' language peculiarly well suited to their task. But the Septuagint, generally so literal as to preserve the very order of the words, and in prose, whereas the matter translated is often poetical, is at a disadvantage when compared with a version so happy as the 'Authorised', or with original works which, finding their own ideas, have liberty in the expansion, emphasis, and arrangement of them. Also, the language at their command was a somewhat blunted instrument. Not much can be gathered from the fortunes of the LXX. in ancient times; the later rival versions were doubtless made in the hope of improving upon its accuracy, and not upon its style, in which latter respect they can claim (perhaps excepting Symmachus) no superiority; and conversely, the faithful adherence of the secondary versions to their quasi-original was due rather to reverence for the written word, and to difficulties like those felt by the LXX. themselves, than to any appreciation of the literary merits of the Greek. The modern critic can hardly presume to lay down the law, and pronounce whether a reader is to admire or to contemn. Individual judgment, feeling, and taste must have their way, subject to the duty of laying aside prejudice and bringing to bear as much unbiased fairness of consideration as possible. It may be added, that it ought to be regarded as necessary, for forming an estimate, to read at least some fairly long passages continuously, and without allowing oneself to be distracted by the problems which have to be noticed when making a detailed study. My own feeling, after endeavouring to read the LXX. thus, is that an impression of ugliness, which may make itself felt at first, soon wears off, and does not return. In some ways, the style is uneven; we have seen that the work must be assigned to different translators, and to somewhat different dates; and there is no sign of any attempt to revise the whole to any uniform standard. We can also see that many sentences are not well-balanced; the translators were almost debarred from making them so, and even those that are originally admirable in this respect are apt to lose their character in the version.

Especially is this the case in poetical passages. The terseness of the original loses its effect, not merely in spite of, but because of, the literalness of the rendering; the free movement which we find in the Authorised Version is completely lacking. Though what is said here refers chiefly to the translated books, I must confess that I perceive no marked superiority in the others; Job and Proverbs, with some literary affinities, are curiously diffuse in effect, even when not really lengthy; but Wisdom, if rich, is often heavy and cumbrous. Generally, there seems little power to maintain either elaboration or simplicity. Awkward, lumbering words (like *παρασιωπάω, προσαναπαύω, ὑπερασπιστής, κληρονομία*) block and load the sentences, all the more because they are mingled with short pronouns and particles, of which a small stock is used again and again with monotonous frequency. Finally, there is either no ability, or no attempt, to shape a telling sentence, which may strike the ear and linger in the memory. Anyone who cherishes the sounds and cadences of a favourite text, either in the Hebrew or in the more familiar English, is liable to meet with disappointment on turning to the Septuagint. If anyone is to be stirred, terrified, cheered, or consoled by it, it must be by the underlying thought, and not by the music or word-power of the language. There is scarcely a trace to be perceived of the thundering force of the third chapter of Amos, the richness of Isa. xi. 9 and xl. 1–12, or the searching pathos of Hos. vi., upon the flat bald surface of the Greek.

The New Testament seems to me to suffer less than the LXX. from this lack of power and grace in language; though even there the assertion has been made, that the English version is a greater literary work than the Greek. It is curious, at the same time, that the quotations from the LXX. in the N.T. do not seem, generally, unworthy of their surroundings in point of style. This may be due to the felicity of their choice and introduction. The Epistle to the Hebrews shows many excellent examples. In isolated texts, some might put in a word for the Vulgate; it might well be thought that *Si in viridi ligno haec faciunt, in arido quid fiet?* is more telling than the Greek which it translates; and the testimony to the power of *Dies irae dies illa* is probably more widely spread than the knowledge of its original home.

The merit of the LXX. is likely to be felt most easily in narrative, not only for reasons which can be supplied from other passages in this book, but because it is in continuous reading that the charm of the faithful, artless Greek emerges. The Book of Jonah is excellent reading for a first taste; the whole of Genesis, Exod. i.–xx., a good deal of Deuteronomy, parts of Joshua, and much of Samuel and Kings, will repay him who reads them through. In the Prophets, besides any narrative portions, Isa. xxxii., xxxv., and much of xlvi.–lv., Hosea xiii., xiv., Zechariah, and Malachi may be recommended: in the Apocrypha, a good deal of Ecclesiasticus, and certainly 1 Maccabees. This selection is not meant in any way to prejudice the reader against books or passages that are not named. It has been made without much reference to the accuracy of the translation, though of course it is less advantageous, especially for beginners, to read where discrepancies and mistakes abound. For simple *reading* it is seldom worth while to linger over such passages, which demand careful and detailed scrutiny; and the more the Septuagint is read continuously, by chapters and by books, the more pleasure is likely to be gained from it.

CHAPTER VIII

SOME PASSAGES EXAMINED—REMARKS ON GRAMMAR

Genesis iv.—Num. xxiv. 15 ff.—1 Kings xviii. 10, etc.—Grammar—Asseverations—Comparative and conditional sentences—Absence of the devices of classical Greek.

IT is now possible to turn to the Greek text again, with more general knowledge of what is to be expected there, and to examine a few passages of it somewhat closely. Some points may now be passed rapidly over, as by this time familiar; but it is better to aim at leaving no difficulty, or discrepancy with the Hebrew, untouched. Let us first remind ourselves of the LXX.'s general practice of preserving the Hebrew order of the words; which is extremely convenient for the student, enabling him to trace correspondences and discrepancies with greater ease; while conversely, in most books, any departure from the Hebrew order may be taken as a warning to put him on the watch at once for difficulties. A good passage to begin upon is Gen. iv., of which we will examine the first part carefully.

In ver. 1, the verbs συνέλαβεν καὶ ἔτεκεν, co-ordinate, follow the Heb. exactly; but we see that the uncials DE (the reading of D, destroyed by fire, is negatively inferred, because no note of its reading otherwise is preserved) read συλλαβοῦσα ἔτεκεν, which is more natural Greek, and is found in vers. 17 and 25 below; in 17, Heb. is the same as here; in 25, Heb. omits the former verb altogether, and LXX. inserts it. The aorist ἐκτησάμην answers to a 'perfect' in Heb. It is easily explained here as an 'aorist of the immediate past', and is at least as natural a tense for Greek to employ as the perfect would be. The Heb. verb is from a root which resembles the name Cain in letters and sound; modern critics tell us that we must not take this, in such cases, as showing the true *derivation* of the name; anyhow, the translation does not attempt to mark this resemblance. διὰ τοῦ θεοῦ, 'through', 'by the help of', Vulg. *per Deum.* Here Heb. has the word ETH, which may be either a preposition, meaning 'with', or the sign of the accus. case, which Aquila so often represents by σύν. If we take this latter meaning, Eve is made to say, 'I have gotten (or, produced) a man, the Lord': i.e., *the* promised seed. This is a perfectly possible rendering of the Hebrew; Luther and others have taken it so; but it may be doubted whether the announcement in ii. 15 is in itself enough to make it likely that Eve meant this. And as LXX. and Vulgate both have a preposition, we see that neither the Alexandrian translators, nor Jerome, were aware of, or at any rate saw reason to favour, any traditional interpretation to this effect. If we then take ETH as a preposition, διά is not an exact translation of it; ETH means 'with', possibly with less implication of help or association than another preposition 'IM (as in *Immanuel*), but not very different in use. However, it is in this very sense of 'with the help of' that the

Greek comes nearest to the possible meaning of the Hebrew. The A.V. 'from the Lord' can hardly be got fairly from Heb. as it stands; it might render, if Heb. had one letter more, the compound preposition METH, lit. 'from with', almost 'from'; very like the common use of *παρά* with genitive (and translated by it in LXX., Gen. xix. 24, xxiii. 20, etc.). The Targum attributed to Onkelos paraphrases in this sense, 'from before the Lord'; so that there is a tradition of some age in its favour, whether as an interpretation, or as evidence of an ancient reading METH. The R.V. renders in the way that LXX. apparently intended.

In ver. 2, *προσέθηκεν τεκεῖν* has already been noticed as a literal way of rendering the Heb. idiom: cf. the A.V. of Acts xii. 3. We may notice in passing, that *ἐγένετο* answers to a Heb. imperf. with *vav*, *ἦν* to a Heb. perfect; *ποιμήν* and *ἐργαζόμενος* both represent participles, but the former is perhaps more on its way to be regarded as a simple substantive in Heb. than the latter.

In ver. 3, *ἐγένετο . . . . ἤνεγκεν* is a construction which is common in Heb. as a way of introducing a subject; the second and main verb more usually, as here, has the copula *vav*. In the LXX. there are several instances without *καί*, but it is generally inserted in the later books, especially Judg. Sam. Kings; according to Thackeray's estimate (*Gramm. O.T.*, p. 51) it is in the majority in all historical books after the Exodus, but not in the Prophets. This construction occurs in the N.T., in St. Luke's Gospel; he also uses the infin. following *ἐγένετο*, and this is the regular practice in the Acts. If anything is to be called a Hebraism, the construction here is; it may of course strike some as a natural, primitive form of expression; but in this case we may be influenced by familiarity with phrases from the A.V.

μεθ' ἡμέρας is quite a fair translation of the Heb., which is literally 'from the end of days', almost equivalent to a compound preposition, and exactly = 'after'. The rest of the sentence is perfectly accurate and literal, the plural στεάτων included; the Heb. of this word is written 'defectively', and the unpointed text does not show the number; but it is generally agreed that it is a plural. In the next sentence LXX. gives two different verbs, ἔπιδεν . . . προσέσχεν, Heb. repeating the same verb. The Greek verbs represent it fairly well, though not used for it elsewhere; but the motive for the variety is not clear; possibly the translators could not find a verb that satisfied them in both clauses. Προσέχειν is usually followed by νοῦν in classical Greek, in the sense of 'notice', 'attend to'; but Aristophanes uses it alone (a colloquialism?) and so do Xenophon and later writers; LXX. use it with following dat., and as a simple verb with accusative (cf. Lat. *animum advertere*): also with εἰς, ἐπί, and even ἀπό, as in 2 Chron. xxxv. 21, following Heb. in the extended use of the preposition; 'beware, and retreat from . . .' The rest of ver. 5 is not so close a rendering; Heb. is literally 'And it was hot' (or, 'it was angry', quasi-impersonal verb) 'to Cain, greatly, and his face fell'. The same phrases are differently treated in ver. 6, and the second clause is literal. ἵνα τί, clearly originally with a verb to be supplied (γένηται, see Liddell and Scott), has become in colloquial Attic, as Aristophanes, practically an adverb = 'Why?' This is common in LXX., and is matched by *Ut quid* . . . ? in Latin. So εἰ has had its use extended from indirect questions,[1] and becomes a simple interrogative particle perhaps with some remnant of hesitation in asking the question, though this tends naturally to disappear; see Gen. xliii. 7, 27, etc.

The reader has already been reminded of the value of the English versions, and of the importance of the use of italics, especially in the Authorised Version. Here, in ver. 7, the margin gives warning that the Heb. is difficult, and the English less literal than usual. And we shall find difference enough between Heb. and Greek to make it advisable to set out the two in literal renderings, side by side, for comparison:

HEB.	LXX.
7. [Is there] not,	[Hast thou] not,
if thou doest well,	if rightly
uplifting?	thou bringest,
and if thou doest not well,	but not rightly
at the door	dividest,
sin coucheth :	sinned? be quiet :
And unto thee [is] his desire,	To thee [is] his turning,
And thou shalt rule over him.	And thou shalt rule over him.
8. And Cain said to Abel his brother.	And Cain said to Abel his brother,
. . . . .	Let us go out into the field,
And it came to pass,	And it came to pass,
in their being in the field,	in their being in the field,
etc. etc.	etc. etc.

Arranging the texts thus, it can be seen what are the corresponding expressions in the two. In ver. 7, a vague general resemblance can be traced, but the parts of speech constantly differ. LXX. represent 'thou doest well' and 'thou doest not well' by ὀρθῶς

[1] This seems the easiest explanation; but the analogy of εἰ μὴν suggests the possibility of its arising from ἦ.

and ὀρθῶς . . . μή: not that they took the Heb. expressions for adverbs, but because they felt themselves obliged to render the next word, which they took to be an infinitive in each case, by a verb; 'to do well in carrying' = 'to carry rightly'; they have attempted to render idiomatically. So they render 'up lifting' by 'thou bringest', a possible but not usual equivalent for the root-idea of the Heb. verb, to 'raise' or 'carry'; and 'at the door' by the idea of 'opening', 'cleaving asunder'; the word is used of the rock, Ps. cv. 41, and of the earth, Ps. cvi. 17. Apparently their interpretation is that Cain committed some fault in presenting his offering; he did not divide with proper ceremonies; cf. Abraham's proceedings in chap. xv. 9, 10. 'Sin' they take as 2nd pers. sing. of a verb, instead of a noun with fem. termination (same consonants); and the imperative, 'be quiet', has the same letters as the 3rd pers. sing. of the perfect of the verb, which is used of animals lying down, and of resting; LXX. render it by ἡσυχάζειν in one other place, 'thou shalt lie down, and none shall make thee afraid' Job xi. 19. The rest of the verse is identical in language, except ἀποστροφή for 'desire', and πρός without the copula, where ἐπί might be more usual; the Vulgate has *sed sub te erit appetitus eius*, but in his *Quaestiones Hebraicae* Jerome renders *et ad te societas eius*. The general meaning of Heb., by the parallel clause, seems to be that of subjection, and LXX. apparently aimed at conveying the same idea: the root-meaning of the Heb. word appears to be 'flowing' or welling over'; besides this passage and Gen. iii. 16, a similar phrase occurs in the Song of Sol. vii. 10 (LXX. ἐπιστροφή). It is suggested (by G. J. Spurrell,

Notes on Heb. Text of Genesis, on iii. 16) that LXX. read the word in Genesis from the root S^HUB for S^HUQ; this might reasonably be translated 'turning', see 1 Sam. vii. 17 (ἀποστροφή, perhaps='return' or 'resort').

It should be noticed that some commentators (as Jerome) translate the Heb., 'and unto thee is its desire, but thou shouldst rule over it': *i.e.* over sin, the beast which crouches ready to attack. But the other rendering is equally possible, and there is no certain clue. If sin is referred to, as the pronouns are masc., it must be regarded as personified.

Ver. 8 has only one point of difference, but that an important one. The clause 'Let us go out into the field' is not in the Heb., which has simply 'And Cain said to Abel his brother': the A.V. 'talked with' is not the proper meaning of the word, and 'told', as R.V., is still straining it; Exod. xix. 25, perhaps the nearest parallel, is hardly enough to build upon. Besides, so far as anyone is entitled to judge, the last thing which Cain would do would be to 'tell' Abel. The LXX.'s insertion, at any rate, gives an intelligible sense. More than this, the insertion is also found in the Vulgate, the Samaritan, the Syriac (Peshiṭta), and the Jerusalem Targum. Gesenius, who for the time demolished the textual authority of the Samaritan recension in general, approved its reading in four passages of Genesis, of which this is one: the others are xiv. 14, xxii. 13, xlix. 14. The Heb. is certainly difficult to render satisfactorily; other attempts have been made to emend it. It is supported by Aquila; but the general opinion is in favour of LXX.'s reading.

To sum up, it can be seen from this analysis of the

eight verses, that, as a rule, the LXX. follow the Heb. closely. Even in ver. 7, the differences in the final result may be seen to arise from variety in the possible renderings of the unpointed Hebrew, or from a very slightly different text. But generally, even the turns of expression are followed, and are still recognisable in the Greek. On the other hand, the insertion in ver. 8 is quite clearly marked, and is exceptional; it makes the sense easier—a double-edged argument—and is supported by much ancient and independent testimony. Most interesting of all is the way in which LXX., while keeping the root-meanings of the words, can be seen going off the track in ver. 7: each word in order can be traced to its corresponding Hebrew; yet they have lost the syntax, missed the meaning, apparently, at προσενέγκῃς, and produced a sentence which, if not unintelligible, is quite divergent from the Hebrew, and so far inferior to the Hebrew that few will think it worth treating as a possible rendering. (Of course, if the explanation as here given be right, it is not a serious rival to the Hebrew as we have it, but a case of downright error.) The variants in the Greek text here are not of importance enough to make it worth while to complicate the matter by discussing them.

We cannot afford space to examine the rest of the chapter so fully. It may have been noticed already that the LXX., according to the leading uncials, is not rigid in rendering JHVH by Κύριος; see ver. 9, and above, ver. 4. This need not, perhaps, surprise us in a translation; it is rather from the point of view of criticism that it may prove to be important. In ver. 11 E's ἀπό is rather better supported than ἐπί, and renders the Heb. better. In ver. 12 the order of words varies from Heb., δοῦναι not following προσθήσει immediately; perhaps an attempt at dropping the Semitic idiom and improving the Greek. The Greek MSS. are all but unanimous, but several versions have the Heb. order. In the same verse, στένων καὶ τρέμων is not quite exact; had the participles been reversed in order, the second Heb. word might conceivably be rendered by στένων (τίς στενάξει αὐτήν, Nah. iii. 7), and τρέμων is *possible* for the first, or might result from reading Z for N. This method of explanation, however, would have been more suitable in a later, worse translated book; and as the phrase is repeated in ver. 14, it is better to take it as a loose rendering; there is perhaps an attempt to imitate the similarity in the two short Hebrew participles. In ver. 13 the genitive infinitive is literal, Greek not needing a preposition as Heb. does; the rendering of the verb is quite possible, see margin of R.V.; the inserted pronoun is by way of touching up the translation. In 14 εἰ is a possible rendering of the Heb. particle 'behold', but probably not right here. In 15 οὐχ οὕτως, a favourite phrase of LXX., is used by mistake for 'therefore', which requires an additional letter; this mistake is not uncommon, see 1 Kings xxii. 19, Isa. x. 15, xvi. 6; and consult the concordance. Notice the use of 'all' in Heb., copied by the Greek, where we should say 'any', with and without the negative. In 16 *Naid* for *Nod* shows the LXX.'s uncertainty as to vowels, and ver. 18 gives us Γαιδάδ for '*Irad*. The statement commonly made that LXX. read *Maleleel* (cf. chap.

v. 15–17) for *Mehujael* must be corrected, if we follow the uncials; but these do not distinguish *Methushael* from Methuselah, ver. 21. Ver. 20*b* is slightly but correctly paraphrased. In 21 καταδείξας is a word peculiarly used in LXX., cf. Isa. xl. 26, xli. 20, xliii. 15, xlv. 18; in all which passages it stands for Heb. words meaning 'create'. Here it seems equivalent to 'invent', a paraphrase (Heb. 'handle'). 'Father of all' is omitted; a few versions and MSS. insert simply 'father'. The instruments are uncertain; if LXX. are right in Ps. cl. 4, they are wrong here with κιθάρα. They seem to have read the name of Zillah's son simply as *Thobel* or *Thubal*; paraphrasing his description. In the rest of the chapter the difficulties are mainly unconnected with LXX.'s rendering; οὗτος ἤλπισεν in the last verse perhaps points to a slightly different reading.

Let us now try Num. xxiv. 15 ff., the final utterance of Balaam. These poetical passages are generally imperfectly translated, and full of difficulties in the LXX. Indeed, they are by no means free from difficulty in the Heb., where attempts are often made to emend the text. The present specimen is fairly easy in LXX.; difficulties belonging to the Heb. must be left alone here, and the reader must consult the commentaries for them. Space will only allow us to treat briefly of the LXX.'s rendering.

At the beginning, LXX. omit an 'and', and the third 'saith' or 'hath said' (the Heb. is of solemn utterance). ἄνθρωπος might have been expected to be ἀνήρ, as the Heb. root is GBR, generally implying 'mighty man' or 'hero'. ὁ ἀληθινῶς ὁρῶν, probably the right reading, see ver. 3, might be taken for a mere paraphrase, and in favour of this view is the use of ὁρῶν, as the word for 'eyes' is so familiar, and no verb is found in use from this root. The Heb. construction of 'eyes' is what a classical scholar would call an accusative of 'respect' or 'part affected'. The word for 'open', however, is peculiar, occurring only here and ver. 3; and this rendering 'open', though quite possibly right, and supported by Jewish tradition, is little more than a guess; some prefer the directly opposite meaning, 'closed'. LXX. would seem to have taken this word, S^{H}T^{H}M, as made up of S^{H}, a form of the relative, and T^{H}M (Thummim), which they render by ἀληθεία in Exod. xxviii. 30, Lev. viii. 8; in Deut. xxxiii. 8 the Heb. order of words is varied, and LXX. most likely kept the customary order, in which case ἀληθεία is again their rendering. Ver. 16 renders Heb. straightforwardly, except for omitting 'saith', and giving ἐν ὕπνῳ as an explanatory rendering of 'falling'. Ver. 17: δείξω, taking the verb as causal, a matter of vowel-points; μακαρίζω, taking the Aleph of 1st pers. sing. imperf. as part of the root (AS^{H}R, 'happy'). 'Near' is rendered by a verb, which properly requires V to be inserted; but LXX. are quite uncertain on these points, perhaps from the way in which their Heb. MSS. were written. Ἄνθρωπος for 'sceptre' is weak; the Heb. word also means 'tribe', but in any case the rendering is inadequate; cf. ver. 7, above. For 'corners', ἀρχηγούς looks like a guess at the interpretation, which is uncertain, possibly 'corners of the forehead'; προνομεύσει is a rather vague attempt; the Heb. verb is rare, and means to 'dig down' or 'out'; in Isa. xxii. 5 of undermining. 'The sons of Sheth' (or Seth) is on the surface the meaning of the Heb.; so A.V., and R.V. marg. This rendering is of old date, and obvious; on the other hand, the sense is not easy; why should any 'sons of Sheth' be marked for destruction? The word 'Sheth' is now generally taken to mean 'tumult', in the light of Jer. xlviii. 45, where the word is S^HON; some also emend the word 'dig down', QRQR, to QDQD, 'crown of the head', as in Jeremiah. Ver. 18: Ἠσαύ is explanatory for *Seir*, and ὁ ἐχθρός is possibly right, except for the singular, which may have been put to suit Ἠσαύ, or used collectively; in any case it is only the difference of the small letter *yod*. F's reading ἀδελφός is peculiar; it may be due to reading AHIV for AIBIV, or to reading ABIV, 'his father', and altering this as being the wrong relation. Ἐποίησεν, which breaks the sequence of futures, is most likely intended to represent a supposed Heb. perfect; the present Heb. text points the word as a participle. Ver. 19: ἐξεγερθήσεται, Heb. 'one shall rule out of Jacob': *i.e.* come out of Jacob and rule. Even if LXX. took the verb as from another root, IRD for RDH, the translation would not be exact. If taken as 'him that escapes', σωζόμενον is as good a rendering as 'remnant'; σώζεσθαι and διασώζεσθαι in Josh. viii. and x. are repeatedly used for the present Hebrew root. Ver. 20: σπέρμα, as in xxiii. 10, is an attempt to interpret Heb., lit. 'after-part'; it is wrong in xxiii. 10, and probably here also; another form from this root occasionally has nearly this sense. In ver. 21 LXX., with νοσσία, cannot preserve the play on words which the Hebrew has between QINI 'Kenite' and QIN 'a nest'; then LXX. repeat 'nest', instead of the proper name.

The first ἐάν is wrongly supplied; the second is a slight misinterpretation of 'But surely', of which the second part constantly means 'if'. Τῷ Βεώρ, 'for Beor', happens to be the same letters as 'for destruction'; but Balaam's father has no business here. Πανουργίας is due to confusion of D and R; 'AD-MH, 'till what', 'how long?' has been read 'ARMH, 'cunning', 'subtlety', which is commonly translated by πανουργία. In Job v. 13, although LXX. render otherwise, the word is used in St. Paul's quotation, 1 Cor. iii. 19. In ver. 23, LXX. insert 'and looking on Og', which is not in Heb., and is hardly appropriate, because Og, unlike the others referred to, is already destroyed, xxi. 33[1]; θῇ is literal; the LXX., Vulg., and English versions agree, but some doubt the Heb. text nevertheless. In 24, ἐξελεύσεται is due to misreading ᵀZIM 'ships' as IᵀZAU, 'they shall go forth'. (Vulg. is curious, *venient in trieribus de Italia.*) On the whole, considering the character of this passage, LXX. have kept fairly close, and it is not hard to trace the cause of their divergences. Before leaving it, it may be worth while to point out ἐτελέσθη in xxv. 3, cf. 5; the word is also used in Ps. cvi. 28, and Vulg. has *initiari*; which shows the interpretation that was placed on Heb. 'joined'.

An interesting case of misreading, or rather misinterpretation of the Hebrew, coupled with corruption in the Greek, is in 1 Kings xviii. 10, 'he took an oath of . . .' LXX. have ἐνέπρησεν, 'he burnt up'. If we emend to ἐνέπλησεν, 'he filled', 'satiated', there is no satisfactory sense, which is probably the reason why it was changed; for the clue is here, as 'he filled'

[1] Cf. the appearance of Γώγ in Ecclus. xlviii. 17.

represents the Heb. letters exactly, only that the S at the beginning would be dotted (in later times) on the left, S, instead of on the right, S[H]. In this chapter, note also the curious version of ver. 21, 'How long halt ye on your two branches', *i.e.*, 'parties', where LXX. have 'upon both knees'. This seems to be a paraphrase, perhaps to cover the translators' ignorance. See Heb. of Ps. cxix. 113. There is a more disappointing paraphrase in 1 Kings xx. (LXX. xxi.) 11, where Ahab's famous reply to Benhadad is flattened into 'Let not the crooked boast as the straight'. Here Aquila's literal version is preferable.

There are few more incomprehensible phrases in the LXX. than that in Isa. li. 20, where the Greek gives, 'Thy sons lie at the head of every way of escape, like half-cooked beet-root'! When translating this passage some years ago I took refuge in softening the phrase down to 'sodden herbs', but this is quite unsatisfying. Jerome knew the passage as an awkward and difficult one, and made attempts to get at the source of the mischief. The Heb. is literally 'like an antelope of a net'; assuming that the word here is a different spelling of one in Deut. xiv. 5. Vulg. has *sicut oryx illaqueatus.* Jerome can only suggest that the LXX. thought of a Syriac word, which appears as THORETH; but there is nothing to show that it means 'beet', in fact it is not known even to exist. Prof. Burkitt has suggested in its place THOMECH, a herb used at the Passover, which with M[A]R, 'bitter', gives the Hebrew letters. But however good this may be as an emendation of Jerome, agreeing with the consonants of the M.T., it does not help us to account for LXX.'s ὡς σευτλίον ἡμίεφθον. The last word is probably a corruption of some participle, a compound beginning with ἠμφι-; for Aquila has ὡς ὄρυξ ἠμφιβληστρευμένος, and Symmachus ὡς ὄ. ἐν ἀμφιβλήστρῳ. Even more puzzling is σευτλίον; nothing better has yet occurred to me than σιτευτός, 'fatted', used of cattle; cf. Jer. xlvi. (LXX. xxvi.) 21, a rather similar passage. But this word appears not to be used in LXX. except as an attribute. So the passage remains obscure; the reader will perceive that, other remedies having failed, the corruption has been supposed to lie in the Greek. As a rule, however, it will be found simpler to look first for a difference between the Heb. as now found, and as read by the LXX. For instance, in Eccles. v. 17 (16), καὶ ἐν πένθει is clearly due to reading VABL for IAKL, 'he shall eat'; when this is seen, the merits of the two readings can be argued, if there is any temptation to do so. In the last verse of the same chapter, ἄλλα, instead of 'much', is due to reading an *Ayin* for a *Beth*; and περισπᾷ, for 'answereth', to the existence of two similar roots in Hebrew. So many divergences arise from causes such as these, that it is generally better to search for them before suspecting corruptions in the Greek; though sometimes the latter are obvious.

In Song of Sol. vii. 9, ἱκανούμενος is a case of R read for D, καὶ ὀδοῦσιν of V for I(Y); this I is part of the root of thc word for 'sleep'. There is hardly a chapter of the O.T. in which some such difference of reading may not be found. Here the reader may be inclined to say, 'But if the Septuagint is so incorrect, what is the use of studying it?' The answer to this will be given later; meantime let us remind ourselves that, besides other independent reasons for valuing and studying the LXX., many of these divergences represent readings which critics often approve, wholly or in part; so that the Septuagint may not be always incorrect, though undoubtedly it often is.

We have now surveyed the Septuagint from various points of view, if superficially; its language, its history, its position as the parent of other versions, and its relation to the Hebrew. Further, we have examined a few passages in detail, as specimens of the work in general, noticing the treatment of the original, and occasionally the Greek text itself. Textual criticism, apart from the 'inter-textual' treatment of version and original, must not take up more space here, because, after what has been said about it, the student can use his general knowledge of the subject, and more especially of New Testament textual criticism, and study the matter for himself in the Cambridge editions, and in Holmes and Parsons, if available. For the LXX. text considered by itself, the N.T. handbooks are excellent aids in many ways.

The grammar of the Greek O.T. is not systematically dealt with in this book. It is the less necessary, because the first part of a grammar likely to become the standard work in England has already appeared, and there are some slighter sketches in existence. Several points have been noticed incidentally, and a few more may be alluded to now. As a rule, the danger is, not that a reader may find himself perplexed, but that he may glide over unusual passages without discovering their peculiarity: the general ɔurport is usually easy enough from the grammatical ɔoint of view, though a few amorphous sentences nay be found; but in these grammar gives but ittle help.

We may now look at a few passages and con- tructions. First, Num. xiv. 23, εἶ μὴν οὐκ ὄψονται. t is perhaps better to write εἶ μήν, with a circumflex ccent, as it appears to be merely a way of writing ɔr spelling ἦ μήν. This instance is one of the learest; but often the MSS., besides ἦ μήν, have lso the variant εἰ μή, as in Isa. xlv. 2; this, as it appens, gives as nearly as possible the same meaning, or in Hebrew 'if not' is an ordinary way of assever- ting, and 'if' of denying. Thus Ps. xcv. 11 is ranslated into English 'they shall not enter,' or, as n Heb. iv. 5 (cf. iii. 11) 'if they shall enter.' In Gen. xlii. 16 εἰ μή is not actually found, so far as know, in a Greek MS., but the Armenian version as the equivalent of it, and a glance at the context hows how easy it would be. Num. xiv. 28 gives nother instance, and whereas in ver. 23 the Heb. vas 'if they shall see', here it is 'if I will not do'. Εἰ μή was hardly possible in 23; and though read ere by A, the other is preferable. In this verse ῶ ἐγώ, a constant formula, common in the Books f Kings, is indicative, not subjunctive; when such phrase as ζήτω ὁ βασιλεύς occurs, the meaning is ifferent. The Vulgate gives *Vivo ego* regularly, and is an assertion; the 'as' of the English version italics in A.V.) expresses the general meaning, but he original has nothing corresponding to it.

Ezek. xxxviii. 9, ὡς νεφέλη κατακαλύψαι γῆν, ver. 16 he same with simple verb καλύψαι (some MSS. read *καὶ καλύψεις*, and one *τοῦ καλύψαι*). Is the verb infinitive or optative? Probably most people, seeing the passage for the first time, would answer with little hesitation, infinitive. So, perhaps, it may be; but the case is by no means so simple as might be thought. The Heb. is infin. with prefixed prepos. l'-. The Old Latin has (9) *sicut nubs operire terram*, (16) *operiet*. Vulg. has *ut operias*. In Ezek. xx. 32 the infin., but with *τοῦ*, is unmistakable. So Num. xxiii. 19, infin. without article, while Heb. has a finite verb, the 'jussive' form of imperfect; but in Num. xxii. 4, Heb. has infin. with k'-, and B reads *ὡς ἐκλίξαι*, AF *ὡσεὶ ἐκλίξει*, cf. Deut. xxxii. 11. It is clear that some of these are comparative sentences. Further, there seems to be little necessary difference in the meaning of these constructions; for in Hab. ii. 14 and Isa. xi. 9, Heb. has different forms, imperf. in Hab., participle in Isaiah; the Greek has Hab. *καλύψει*, Isa. *κατακαλύψαι*. So far we have some ambiguous cases, and some certainly infinitive; but an unmistakable optative is found in Isa. xxi. 1, and a probable one, unless the reading of the future be preferred, with *ὡσεί* in Ps. lxxxiii. 14. (In Ps. lxiii. 5, xc. 6, the construction is different.) In Isa. xviii. 3, the best reading appears to be the *subjunctive*; Jerome in his commentary translates *sicut elevetur*.

The conclusion is, that either infin. or opt. is possible, as are the nearest corresponding forms in Heb. Ambiguous forms must be decided, if decision be possible, each on the merits of the case. On the whole, while the infin. appears to predominate, the clearest cases of it are best taken as epexegetic the *ὡς* going with the noun. The Heb. finite verb can bear very nearly this meaning. The comparative clauses, on the other hand, are best regarded as optatives, though Isa. xi. 9 is open to some doubt; and the verses first quoted from Ezekiel show how hard it is to draw a certain distinction. Nor is the future out of the question altogether; though seldom the best reading, it is not infrequent as a variant. It also occurs in passages of another cast, as Isa. xxx. 30, xxxii. 6. I cannot recall an instance of an undoubted future of this kind after ὡς; but after ὃν τρόπον it is not infrequent in comparisons, general or imaginary, in Isaiah; v. 24, xiv. 19, lii. 14, lxii. 5, lxv. 8; occasionally the subjunctive is found, as 2 Sam. xvi. 23, Isa. vii. 2, xxxi. 4 B. The use of ὃν τρόπον in comparative clauses generally is common in the translated books of the LXX.; in the others it is practically unknown, so that two instances in Judith are almost worth counting as evidence for the Semitic original of the book; only one instance (2 Macc. xv. 39, at the very close of the book) appears quite clear in the four books of Maccabees.

From whatever cause, the distinction between indicative and subjunctive is by no means so clear-cut in the LXX. as in classical Greek. It may be that error or looseness on the part of copyists is to some extent responsible for this. But this is not a very safe ground to take up; in point of fact the MSS. often show signs of faithfulness in such matters, and some instances give no reasonable ground for doubt. Moreover, the tendency of scribes would naturally be to alter, if at all, towards the more regular construction. We find such instances as the subjunctive ὃς οὐκ ἐπαισχυνθῇ, Job xxxiv. 19; as the indicative ὅταν ἀπέκτεννεν, Ps. lxxviii. 34, cf. Gen. xxxviii. 9, Num. xi. 9, etc.; and what is not less striking, the two moods coupled, as in Ex. viii. 8, Lev. vi. 2, while in Job xviii. 11 ff. we find a sequence of pure optatives and futures. The subjunctive with ἕως, as in Ps. cxii. 8, Ecclus. l. 19, is less remarkable. In Eccles. ix. 14, 15, the subjunctives are quite independent; it is almost as if the Greek meant, 'Suppose there come a great king. . . .'

It is difficult to find a clear case of εἰ, conditional, with subjunctive in LXX. (The instances in the concordance must be carefully scrutinised.) Job xxxiv. 16 may be indicative; in Judg. xi. 9 the construction drifts into the subj. παραδῷ, but the first verb is indicative. In Deut. xxii. 26, perhaps the clearest case, εἴ τις [1] may be compared with ὅς in Job xxxiv. 19 quoted above. There seems to be a tendency to shift the mood, with the intention of marking a modification of the time or circumstances, and perhaps of expressing the force of the Hebrew as the translators understood it. Thus in Isa. vi. 10, so often quoted in the N.T. (Matt. xiii. 14, Mark iv. 12, Luke viii. 10, John xii. 40, Acts xxviii. 26), the indic. ἰάσομαι, following subjunctives after μή, is found in the uncials and most cursives, and has been maintained in the best MSS. of the N.T. quotations generally. This may be primarily due to following the Hebrew; but it cannot be denied that a certain force is given by the change to the simple future, as though equivalent to 'in which case I will heal them'.

[1] Probably the indefinite pronoun supplies the force of ἄν to some extent; see Soph. *O.T.* 198, *Ant.* 710.

See the remarks on the passage in the Acts in T. E. Page's edition; comparing Jebb on Sophocles, *O.T.* 1389.

It must be remembered that εἰ is constantly used as an interrogative particle. Also, μή is frequently interrogative, in the sense of Lat. *num*. It is therefore conceivable that εἰ μή might be interrogative, with the meaning of Lat. *nonne*. But Gen. iii. 11 is more than doubtful; and Isa. xl. 28 is difficult, in any case, but more difficult to take as conditional. It might be thought that the negative should be οὐ: but a fusion of μὴ ἤκουσας and εἰ οὐκ ἤκουσας does not seem impossible here. Similarly, it is tempting to take εἰ as interrogative in Isa. xl. 15. There are 'deliberative' subjunctives to be found after εἰ interrog., as in Judg. xx. 23, 28, 2 Sam. v. 19.

Conditional sentences are certainly at times very irregular in LXX., but more so in appearance than in logic. Thus in Job xxxi. 5 ff., the conditional indicatives following εἰ are rhetorical, 'if it was the fact that . . .'; culminating at ver. 40 with the pure optative, for a solemn imprecation. Cf. Job xi. 13, 14. So in Isa. xlix. 15, even if the future in the apodosis is due to the disuse of opt. with ἄν in potential sense, yet it seems to give an added assurance; at any rate, if ἐάν with subj. would have been possible in the protasis, it would have been less forcible. There are enough perfectly regular conditional sentences in the LXX. to make it seem reasonable to suppose that they mean something when they depart from rule; but as the use of ἄν in apodosis is all but extinct, some regular forms are no longer possible. The cases of opt. with ἄν are almost restricted to Genesis and Job, and nearly always potential clauses with interrogative pronouns or particles. The past indic. with ἄν is also scarce; Gen. xxx. 27, xxxi. 27, 42, xliii. 10 are regular, xliv. 8 a mixed conditional sentence (with opt.), Deut. xxxiii. 7 a respectful quasi-imperative. In Ezekiel there is one comparative and one interrogative optative (i. 16, xv. 2), and the remaining optatives with ἄν are in 4 Maccabees, which is on a different plane. But here too the strict use in conditional clauses, free from irregularity, is rare; vi. 32 (unaugmented pluperf. in protasis), viii. 16 (imperf. of εἰμί otherwise regular), ix. 6 (irreg., like Gen. xliv. 8), xvi. 5 and xvii. 7 (regular, past indic.), are, I think, all the instances that concern us.

Owing to the Hebrew use of *vav* to introduce the main clause of an apodosis, it is sometimes difficult to tell whether καί has not this intention here and there in the Greek. In Isa. lviii. 13, 14, it is not even easy to see where the apodosis begins, though the beginning of ver. 14 is the most likely point. The use of δέ has become, comparatively, so rare, that we can hardly expect to find it thus used. Unfortunately, the Oxford Concordance does not give the occurrences of δέ; this is hardly surprising, but it would have added much less to the editors' labour than might have been expected. Μέν is also rare, so that the familiar antithesis is conspicuous chiefly by its absence; and when it does occur, something in the arrangement of words often robs it of its wonted force. In Wisdom, Job, and 2–4 Maccabees it is fairly common; in Proverbs, where one might have thought it would occur freely, it stands in vi. 10, xi. 31, xxiii. 14. There are a few instances in Genesis,

xviii. 12, xxxviii. 23, xliii. 14, xliv. 8, 26; and Exodus i. 16 is one of the best balanced and most natural antitheses in the O.T. There are also some in Daniel, especially in chap. ii., both LXX. and Theod. The reader can search out more, if he can command the use of the concordance.

This absence, or comparative absence, of many of the familiar devices of classical Greek, is very marked in the LXX.; for instance, genitives absolute are rare and comparatively pointless; the arrangement of the article is seldom neat or elegant; the distinctions of direct and indirect interrogatives, and relatives, are blurred; participles, especially aorists, are little used; the dependent optative is obsolete, and pure optatives are occasionally piled up heavily. In almost every book the student will find plenty to mark and consider; and it is as well to keep in mind the difference between the translated books, early and late, and the original Greek of Wisdom and 2–4 Maccabees.

CHAPTER IX

THE VALUE OF THE SEPTUAGINT: HOW TO WORK AT IT

The LXX. aids us in approaching the original—No other version does as much—LXX. and N.T.; wide range of Greek at that time—The Bible of the Apostolic Age, and of the Fathers—Theological and ecclesiastical terms—Merits of the Greek and Hebrew texts—Questions to be answered—Verdict in favour, generally, of the Hebrew—Mistakes of the LXX. on minor points numerous and demonstrable—Its 'authority' often a misnomer—Its value in confirming the Hebrew—Its claim to consideration—Often represents the Heb. more closely than English can—More divergent than other versions—Evidence of N.T. quotations—Advantage of learning Hebrew—Methods for general and special work at the LXX.—The working copy and private note-book—Read the LXX. itself, not merely about it.

IT is to be regretted that comparatively few English literary men in modern times appear to have been readers of the Septuagint. Ruskin is an honourable exception; but so far as can be detected, he read it without any special regard to the peculiar position it holds, simply on the sensible ground, as it would appear, that he could read Greek more easily than Hebrew. But many who could do likewise have, it must be feared, neglected their opportunities.[1] Yet most intelligent readers of the

[1] The plain truth is, that except among professed scholars, the classical tradition in England, especially in the seventeenth and eighteenth centuries, meant Latin, and hardly included Greek. In Parliament, probably not one Greek quotation has been made for a thousand Latin. Cf. Shakespeare, *Julius Cæsar*, Act I. Sc. ii. l. 282.

English version of the Old Testament must, at some time or other, have felt a wish to approach nearer to the original. Now it is scarcely too much to say that, except by the direct study of that original itself, the only road to this goal is by the Septuagint. The modern versions can, from the nature of the case, do nothing for us here. Even in the few places where some of them may render more correctly than the English, the correction can be reached more easily and safely by other means. The ancient versions, with one principal exception, are either based upon the Septuagint itself, or are in languages familiar only to a few specialists, and less accessible than Greek, or even than Hebrew. The later Greek versions are fragmentary, are later in date than the Septuagint, and have not exerted any comparable influence on thought and language generally. There remains the Vulgate. Here, alone, is a really powerful competitor; but its character as a translation, intermediate between an ancient and a modern version, somewhat diminishes the importance of its renderings; the fact that it was made from the Hebrew, and from a Hebrew text substantially the same as that we possess, warns us not to expect much instruction from any divergences we may find; and its date, nearly six centuries later than the LXX., makes it impossible that it should have affected the thoughts and diction of the *early* Church as the LXX. has done. Finally, the Vulgate, in its current form, owes a great deal to the LXX., both directly and indirectly; for it may be doubted, whether Jerome would have accomplished his great work at all, without the existing examples in Greek, and the Latin taken from them, and without the stimulus and experience gained from his own early exercises upon the LXX. If we work upon historical lines, we should at any rate make some study of the Septuagint before proceeding to the Vulgate.

Again, it is not mere accident that has given us the Greek Old Testament in our great uncial Bibles, side by side with the Greek New Testament. It is clear that the two Testaments in Greek were, in the fourth century, making their appeal together, and as a whole, to the same readers. These readers, as we have seen, were numerous, and widely diffused. For the Septuagint had at least begun to make its way, before the coming of Christ, wherever Greek wanderings and conquest and the Jewish Dispersion had gone together. The N.T. writers practically all use it; only in St. John's Epistles are no quotations found from it; and some N.T. writers use it exclusively. This, of course, is important, not only for the study of the N.T. writers, but because they cannot have stood alone in this respect. So we find Josephus, their contemporary, and Philo, their predecessor, enlarging the circle of representative witnesses. Now what is true of the N.T. writers with regard to the LXX., is broadly true of the early Church writers, from the second century onward, with regard to the LXX. and the N.T. combined. Here the central position of the Greek Bible is seen to be prominent; its language reigns over the whole space between the smaller, more isolated regions where Semitic, Eastern Aryan, and Coptic tongues prevailed, and the Western and African lands where Latin was the principal speech. Even in these, Greek had many speakers, and some writers. If a man had had to traverse the whole Roman Empire, and the border countries beyond it, with only one language at command, he would unquestionably have found Greek, at any time during the first four centuries of the Christian era, far more capable of serving his needs than any other language, and almost adequate. Along the beaten tracks, Greek would have been more useful to him through Italy from Rome southward, and even along the coasts of Gaul and Spain, than Latin would have been in Egypt, Asia Minor, or Syria. Paul preaches in Asia and writes to the 'Romans' in Greek; Arrian, the Roman Consul of A.D. 146, an Asiatic, Appian of Alexandria, the historian, and Aelian, of Italian birth, write in Greek also. The Christian Fathers, at first excepting only those of Africa, and the compilers of early liturgies, write in Greek, and use the Greek Bible exclusively, with no knowledge, and hardly a thought, of the original Old Testament behind it. The great African writers, in using the Old Latin, are still no less dependent on the LXX., bound by its language, and by any traditions of interpretation which it carried with it. The LXX. contains the keys to their allusions, their thoughts, and their reasoning; the Hebrew, until Origen's work has produced its effect, has only slight and occasional influence upon them.

Consequently, the technical terms and phrases of the early Church are Greek; that is, when they are not based solely on the New Testament, they are Septuagintal. And those based solely on the New Testament are few, owing to the wide and deep influence of the LXX. on the language of the N.T.

The Sacraments were 'ordained by Christ Himself'; and *baptism* and *κοινωνία* in its Latin dress *communion* may be regarded as ideas pertaining to the New Testament; but even here a glance at the Septuagint concordance may not be amiss. But for *Ecclesia*, *Lay*, *Priest*, *Deacon*, as well as for terms that are religious rather than ecclesiastical, such as *Parable*, *Apostle*, *Prophet*, *Angel*, *Alms*, we must first seek the Septuagint. One might almost hazard a guess that indirectly the Greek Bible has helped to secure the prevalence of Greek words beyond its own range; 'cathedral' and 'cemetery' are curious words to be so much at home in English as they are. Curiously, some of the Church's Latin terms have suffered from misunderstanding or depreciation. 'Testament,' 'Charity,' 'Person,' and 'Substance,' for instance, have not always fulfilled their intention with complete success.

These mere hints must suffice, as to the influence of the LXX. upon our religious thought and language, and its consequent importance for the historical tracing of ideas. But there are other ways in which it can be used and studied. As a version of the O.T., it may be considered as a means of gaining light upon the Hebrew, by studying the two side by side; and, owing to its age, it may, as we have seen, at any rate here and there, give us traces of an older Hebrew text, and arrangement of the text, than that contained in the Hebrew MSS., and now used (the M.T.). There is also its use, as mentioned above, as a means for approaching nearer to the original than can be otherwise done without systematically studying the Hebrew itself. Though in practice these methods of study may be blended together, we will endeavour to discuss them separately. We are by now familiar with the fact that the MSS. of the Septuagint, and still more the version itself, date back to a time long before the MSS. of the O.T. in Hebrew. There is, therefore, a theoretical possibility, which in the case of most ancient literature would amount to a fair working hypothesis, that the text of the ancient version will represent an earlier form of the Hebrew than the existing MSS. of the Hebrew itself. There are, however, three questions to be asked: (i) is the text of the LXX. trustworthy? (ii) is the text of the existing Hebrew MSS. corrupted, or is it substantially the ancient original? (iii) in comparing the LXX. with the present Hebrew, does either show clear signs of intrinsic superiority?

These questions can be answered, to some extent, from the previous discussions in this book. (i) The text of the LXX. has passed through many vicissitudes, which have left their marks upon it. There are many rival readings, and there are distinct recensions; and the original text has not yet been completely and satisfactorily determined. But there is good ground for hope that much may yet be done in this matter, and that, eventually, a text of the Greek O.T. may be secured, which shall be not much inferior to that of the N.T. Nor is the text, even now, of large portions, in a really bad state; while evidence accumulates, if slowly, to show that the MSS. have preserved a great deal of very ancient material. The utmost care is needed, but the material, at any rate, for much of the text is there, to be sifted and examined further. (ii) As to our present Hebrew text, there is some variety of opinion. The variants in the MSS. are *comparatively* few and slight; but this, in itself, does not count as an argument in favour of the text, but merely points to relatively slight divergence from an archetype, whose own character must be weighed. The consonantal text may be judged by the evidence of Jerome's Vulgate, of Origen's Hexapla, and of Aquila's version, which last carries us back to a point probably rather earlier than the middle of the second century A.D. In all these we find witness to a consonantal text closely resembling that which we now have. The *scriptio plena*, or writing of the long vowels I and U with the consonants *Yod* and *Vav*, was probably established half a century before the death of Rabbi 'Aqiba in A.D. 135, from which time the spelling now used is said to date, being probably based on a MS. of that date. The text had been studied during the years that followed the fall of Jerusalem, and R. 'Aqiba had strongly insisted on the importance of preserving it unaltered. On the whole, the Massoretes in their turn succeeded wonderfully well in preserving the consonants of this second-century text: and they did their best to preserve also the tradition of the vowel sounds, a more precarious matter. Then comes the question, how far this second-century text itself preserved the traditional text of the previous ages. Here external evidence is very scanty. The witness of the Samaritan Pentateuch still lies under some suspicion; Gesenius only allowed four passages in Genesis, namely, iv. 8, xiv. 14, xxii. 13, xlix. 14, to be preferable to the M.T.; three of these, as being readings of the LXX. also, have already been discussed. The existence of some intentional alterations in the Samaritan has shaken confidence in it; and though it is now regarded by some more favourably than by Gesenius, there is no general desire to press its claims. The N.T., though its quotations are largely from the LXX., has yet a few which agree more nearly with the M.T.; but unfortunately their quantity is scarcely enough to serve as a principal basis for argument. Still, from such quotations as Matt. xi. 29 from Jer. vi. 16, John xix. 37 from Zech. xii. 10, and Rom. xii. 19 from Deut. xxxii. 35, we may gather at least this much: that in the time of the N.T. writers there was a text current which was not that used by the LXX., and which was nearer to the M.T. The importance of this fact may be far-reaching.

There is, too, a consistency about the M.T. which points to its having preserved early traditions with success. Passages occur in duplicate; chapters of Kings, for instance, recurring in Chronicles, Isaiah, Jeremiah; Jer. xxvi. 18 quotes Mic. iii. 12; genealogies arc found in Genesis and again in Chronicles; the Ten Commandments are given in Ex. xx. and Deut. v. These passages are not all exactly identical in both places where they occur. There are differences between D and R, as between Gen. x. 4 and 1 Chron. i. 7; final and initial letters differ, and words are varied here and there; compare Isa. xxxvii. with 2 Kings xix. 1, 12, 27, etc.; the Ten Commandments have certain quite marked variations, as in the reason given for the observance of the Sabbath. But in very few points do these differences give any ground for thinking that the writer of one passage knew the other in a form materially different from that in which we know it; still less that he knew it in a form approximately that which the LXX., if it differs, appears to represent. In Isa. xxxvi.–xxxix., and the corresponding portions of Kings, it happens that the LXX. of Kings (a late portion of the version) is more literal than that of Isaiah; and the Greek of Kings is not only a more exact rendering of the Heb. Kings, but in many, probably in most places, a more literal version of the Heb. Isaiah than the Greek Isaiah is. In Jeremiah, quoting Micah, one final letter in the Heb. differs, after the quotation is fairly started; the LXX., but for one quite different word, is here identical in the two passages. When, in Hab. iii. 9, Thackeray discovers liturgical directions embedded in the text, it seems to follow that the consonants, although misunderstood at an early time (perhaps the third century B.C.), and subsequently a puzzle to all who have tried to render them, have nevertheless been faithfully preserved to this day, while the Greek, amid its mistranslations (there are here two versions) has retained traces enough to be recognised as giving a clue. Here both the M.T. and the LXX. bear witness to the Heb. consonantal text as genuine; though no one understood it, it remained; the Alexandrian translators found the same difficulties as those that followed them.

On the whole, therefore, the M.T. deserves the most respectful treatment, and substantially, it appears to have preserved a very ancient consonantal text, while its traditions in the matter of vowels are at least as good as any others available; the greater age of the LXX. is counter balanced by its numerous and obvious mistakes in this respect.

(iii) On the question of the intrinsic merits of the readings of the M.T. and the LXX., where they differ, it is clearly impossible to discuss separate passages here; we have no room for lengthy disquisitions on the subject-matter, and questions of taste hardly admit of final determination. Fortunately, the general verdict emerges fairly clear, however opinions on separate points and preferences in method may differ. On the whole, it is agreed, that here and there the LXX. may represent, or may give help towards recovering, a better text than the M.T.; but in the majority of passages, the M.T. holds its own. From this view only extremists on either side are likely to dissent.

As to the proportion of passages where the LXX. deserve the preference, there is, naturally, more divergence of opinion; and on any given passage, there may be much disagreement. For though there is, in textual criticism, a constant and growing endeavour to get rid of personal prepossessions, and determine the text on rigidly scientific principles, yet the consideration of intrinsic merits of readings has to be admitted at one stage or another, and when it comes in, personal judgment is, because it must be, employed. It may seem needless to state, that no one will finally admit a reading the character of which is, on the face of it, absurd, or repugnant to the general spirit of the writing. But, in point of fact—besides the possibility of opinions differing even on these points—there are a few exceptions even to this general statement; in the case of the LXX., as a translation made under difficulties, there is sometimes a chance that the absurd reading is what they actually wrote, or is the wreck of their actual words. Again, personal judgment enters into the estimate of documents. Thus, in Hort's summary of his and Bp. Westcott's attempt to proceed on the most scientific method possible, we find that to 'the rudimentary criticism founded on Internal Evidence of Readings' has succeeded 'a threefold process . . . (1) provisional decision or suspense on readings; (2) estimate of documents by this standard; and (3) final decision (or suspense) on readings on comparison of all evidence' (*Introd. to N.T. in Greek*, pp. viii, ix). Only from (2), it will be observed, can personal judgment possibly be abolished, if at all. Now in estimating the merits of the M.T. and the LXX. we need an analogous process. But most scholars approach the subject, not, perhaps, with minds made up, but with certain prepossessions, possibly unconscious, induced by the line of their previous studies. The M.T. is most likely to be followed, through thick and thin, by Hebrew students who have no thorough acquaintance with the LXX., and no disposition towards free handling of their text; on the other hand a tendency to favour the text indicated by the LXX. is apt to manifest itself in those who have accustomed themselves, as Hebraists, to treat the M.T. with freedom, and in some of those who are familiar with the LXX. from considerable use of it; more, however, among the former than the latter. On the surface, the weakest point in the procedure of these emenders of the M.T. is its inconsistency. They produce the impression that they turn to the LXX. only when they are dissatisfied with the Hebrew; which, though a natural course to follow from one point of view, impairs the value of their judgment as an impartial estimate of the relative merits of the LXX. generally, because they leave out all mention of it except when they think it contains something to their purpose. Suppose, for a moment, that anyone tried to construct a text on the converse principle: to start with the LXX., as it stands, for a basis, consulting the Hebrew only when something quite unsatisfactory was found in the Greek. We can easily see—a very short experience in any book outside the Pentateuch will convince anyone who needs to be convinced—that one of two results will follow. Either a text will be produced which must utterly fail to stand criticism; or the corrections from the Hebrew will be so numerous that the resulting text will be, after all, more M.T. than LXX.; more than half of the LXX.'s peculiarities will have disappeared. In the Pentateuch the result will differ only in degree; but as the general resemblance between the two texts is much closer, both being on the whole at their best, the effect is less marked. In other words, a text which is at least fairly good exists in the M.T., and it can be used, as it was in making most modern versions, with practically no reference to the LXX. But the LXX. as it stands is hardly to be regarded as a possible text; even if certain obvious mistakes and misreadings are corrected, it is still impracticable; if we go a step further, and reconstruct a Hebrew text from it, giving its readings the benefit of every doubt, it is still, on the whole, markedly inferior to the M.T.

Mr. W. W. Cannon, in his recent edition of the *Song of Songs* (Cambridge, 1913), collects the principal divergences in the book, and endeavours to judge between the two texts on their merits, in these cases. The result is, that out of between 30 and 40 passages, he pronounces in favour of some half-dozen of the LXX.'s readings, or for readings mainly based upon them; in the remainder the M.T. is preferred, generally with little or no hesitation. Against his decisions, which are apparently unbiased, the present writer, at least, has little or nothing to say. In this short book, therefore, something like onc-sixth of the LXX.'s principal divergences are approved; over a longer space the proportion would perhaps be less, hardly more than ten per cent, if so much. Among the slighter divergences the balance in favour of the Heb. would be immensely greater. Of course opinions will differ: for instance, Cornill in his edition of Ezekiel makes great use of the LXX., and in most people's view goes rather too far; but, according to G. Jahn, he does not go far enough. In any case, it must be remembered that beside the more marked divergences, there are generally numerous small points (of number, person, etc.) in which there is, as a rule, no reason to think that the LXX. are right, or indeed anything but simply mistaken. We have seen, in the examination of various passages, how they misread and misinterpreted, losing the clue, and straying farther and farther from the right track, until an easier sentence gave them a fresh start. Let the reader examine such a place as Isa. xxviii.–xxx., and he will not, I think, remain in any doubt as to this. We may remember the frequent mistakes between D and R, and between I (Y) and U (V); with Driver's remark, already quoted, p. 113. On the smaller points, which after all form the great majority, the LXX.'s evidence is really of no importance; and to appeal to it as 'authority' is an absolute misnomer. Yet it is far too frequent an experience, to find commentators proposing to alter the Hebrew and read 'with the LXX.' on some such point, while close by in the very same verse, it may be, the LXX. are obviously wrong on a similar or more important point. What is really true is, that the LXX. read something decidedly like the M.T., and within the range of probable confusion with it; the critic may approve the reading which the LXX. suggests, and may have taken the hint from the Greek; but he might equally have devised the reading for himself, and the LXX. no more impugns the correctness of the M.T. than it confirms it.

It may be thought that this goes too far, and that, if admitted, it proves too much; that it reduces the value of the LXX. almost to nothing. It is not so, however, for two reasons. First, it leaves the confirmatory value of the LXX.'s evidence almost unimpaired. For if the M.T. and LXX. agree, then only in two cases can the reading be wrong: (*a*) where there is a corruption earlier in date than the point where the two texts parted company, and therefore perpetuated by them both; (*b*) where one text has gone wrong, and the other has, later, been altered to agree with it, or stumbled accidentally into the same mistake. Neither of these cases is likely to be very common; in instances of (*a*) we are exactly in the position in which we should be if we had one text, somewhat older than either of our two, and the other did not exist; if, for instance, we had a Hebrew text of about 300 B.C., and no LXX. at all. Instances of (*b*) are probably few, are not unlikely to betray themselves, and if not recognised for what they are, leave us again in the same position as those of (*a*), dependent practically upon a single text.

Second, there remain some readings of the LXX., which for one reason or another are sure to attract attention, and to be dealt with on their merits; as, for instance, the insertion, backed by the Samaritan recension and other witnesses, in Gen. iv. 8, which has been discussed. The omission of 1 Sam. xiii. 1 is another case, and the fact that LXX. have preserved the connecting particle at the beginning of ver. 2 is evidence of their care. Side by side with their numerous errors, there are, no doubt, some faithfully recorded portions of the truth, beyond what might have been expected. Therefore, while refusing to follow the LXX. blindly, or to attribute fictitious 'authority' to its readings, the student should never dismiss it without consideration; even its apparent absurdities may conceal a fragment of truth, or a hint, or clue. Above all, it should be consulted continuously; and by this means both its value and its shortcomings will be more fairly judged.

Something has already been said about the differences between the two texts in contents on the larger scale, and in arrangement ('subject-matter' and 'sequence'). Here the LXX. is on stronger ground, as it cannot be supposed that differences of this kind are due to accidental mistakes; and the Greek text, even if not always perfectly logical and coherent, generally shows these qualities at least in fair degree. Opinions differ, moreover, on such points; for instance, what some critics (Robertson Smith and others) regard as an interpolation in the M.T. of 1 Sam. xvii., Kuenen calls a harmonistic omission on the part of the LXX. There is a general disposition to allow full weight to the LXX. in such cases.

We may now return to the point raised at the opening of this chapter, that the Septuagint has a value of its own, as enabling us to approach the original more nearly than by any other way, excepting the direct study of the Hebrew. It is, indeed, astonishing that so little attention has been drawn to this aspect of the case. The proportion of English readers who can read the Old Testament in Hebrew is, at the best, very small. Even among the clergy, probably more than half, including many who are highly educated in other respects, know practically no Hebrew at all; and the Semitic attainments of the remainder are, on the average, only on a par with what would be considered a very moderate knowledge of Greek. A far larger number can read the N.T. in the original than the O.T.; among laymen the proportion is doubtless still greater; and for these the step to the LXX. is comparatively a short one. [As Hebrew is not generally taught in our schools,[1] those who take up its study are, for the most part, already grown up, and some are self-taught. Consequently, their special knowledge of Hebrew hardly corresponds to their general education and intelligence; and,

[1] Merchant Taylors, and Pocklington, Yorkshire, have long been honourable exceptions; but it is hardly to be expected that in these crowded days the number can be increased.

especially as many clues may be for ever lost, it may be doubted whether even Semitic specialists really possess so thorough and penetrating a knowledge of Hebrew, such ingrained familiarity, almost as a matter of second nature, with the language, as the best classical scholars do of Greek.[1]] A fair Greek scholar, used to reading the N.T., will find in the LXX., at the outset, a good deal of simple narrative, in which the Hebrew order and idioms are rendered very closely, and the phrases reproduced in bald but straightforward fashion. His knowledge of the English version, if he knows no Hebrew, or a commentary, should be enough to tell him when the LXX. are diverging; so that the Greek and the English can be made at every turn to play into each other's hands, and combine to enlighten him; what one does not tell him, the other will. Even from the modern point of view, the LXX. sometimes attains accuracy better than the English version; as in the account of the plagues of Egypt, where the 'hardenings' of Pharaoh's heart are differentiated very nearly with exactness, as according to the Hebrew.

The additional width of view gained by reading the LXX. is another point worth considering. Whatever the worth of its divergent readings, they are at any rate the most independent that we can obtain from any source. For it stands, of all versions and texts, at the greatest distance from the M.T.;

[1] See D. S. Margoliouth, *Lines of Defence*, pp. 84, 134; E. Reich, *The Failure of the Higher Criticism*, p. 37, quoting Spinoza, *Tractatus theologico-politicus*: 'Significatio . . . multorum nominum et verborum, quae in Bibliis occurrunt, vel prorsus ignoratur, vel de eadem disputatur.'

not, of course, here counting the secondary versions, which, having been made from the LXX., have rendered its divergences, and introduced some fresh corruptions; for our present argument these are simply texts of the Septuagint. As we know, the MSS. of the LXX. vary a good deal, and some of them, especially in certain books, as (A) F in parts of the Pentateuch, and A in Samuel and Kings, give us a Greek text much closer to the Hebrew than B in those books. The general principle, as laid down by Lagarde (see p. 93), is to prefer, as the true Septuagint, the text which is furthest from the M.T. There must be some exceptions to this rule, but in general it is a sound one; for there are obvious reasons why a divergent text should have been, eventually, liable to alteration to conform to the Hebrew; while accidental corruption would very seldom have this effect; the Greek text, if originally in agreement, would not be likely to be altered to disagree; and corruption, if it occurred in such passages, would probably be comparatively easy to detect. Intentional alteration, *e.g.*, by Christian hands, has probably affected the text very little; it is clear that, if it had been systematically attempted, many passages would not now stand as they do; and it may be observed that the famous insertion *a ligno* in Ps. xcvi. 10 (ἀπὸ τοῦ ξύλου in Justin Martyr) is practically without support in the Greek MSS. (See Swete, *Introd. to O.T. in Greek*, pp. 424–5, and Kenyon, *Our Bible and the Ancient MSS.*, pp. 89 ff.)

Later, when Aquila's closer version, Theodotion's revision, and Symmachus's improved paraphrase-revision had, through Origen's Hexapla, intruded at various points upon the LXX.'s text, the Greek came to present much more resemblance to the Hebrew. We have lately said that the LXX. stands, of all versions, furthest from the M.T.; and, as has been said by O. Procksch, in his work on the text of the LXX. in the Prophets, its history is the story of its removal from the maximum to the minimum distance from it. This remark sums up the case; or, conversely, we may say, that in so far as we can reach the original LXX., we reach the text between which and the M.T. is the greatest amount of divergence of which we have knowledge.

But can we, from this, deduce anything as to the relative age and merit of the two texts? Directly, from the mere fact that they differ, little or nothing; indirectly, something which leads to a reasonable presumption, perhaps almost a working hypothesis. If we find, that before the time of Aquila, when the LXX. had as yet no Greek rival, there are signs that another text, nearer to the M.T., was known, this may point to the conclusion that the aberrant text was the LXX., and not the M.T. Now we find in the N.T. quotations, signs of such a text. Most of them follow the LXX. more or less closely; but there are some which do not. A few, indeed, from Daniel, agree with what we know as Theodotion's version; but, as Theodotion's reputed date is later than that of the N.T. writers, we are forced to the provisional conclusion that he was revising a text already in existence at the earlier date. The range of these quotations, however, is small, and the question, though otherwise of interest, is not directly important to us now. But there are other quotations, which appear to be made from a text (whether Hebrew or a Greek version matters not) quite distinct from the LXX., and closer, sometimes quite close, to the M.T. It is necessary to sift the quotations carefully. Thus, it is best not to accept unheedingly all the instances where Westcott and Hort's list has 'Heb.' appended, or even those given by Bp. Lightfoot, *Biblical Essays*, pp. 136 ff. The student had better eliminate Matt. xiii. 41, John ii. 17, vi. 45, Jas. ii. 23, Heb. xii. 2, xiii. 15, or at least examine them afresh and satisfy himself. In Jas. v. 20, 1 Pet. iv. 20, let him compare the LXX. of Ps. lxxxv. 2, in Rom. ix. 22, that of Jer. l. (xxvii.) 25, before deciding that they are from the Heb. But in John xii. 13, 15, 40, xiii. 18, xix. 37; in Matt. ii. 15, viii. 17, xi. 29, xii. 18, xxvii. 9; in Rom. xii. 19, 1 Cor. ii. 9, Rev. ii. 8, iii. 7, 9, and some other passages, will be found quotations from the O.T., which differ widely from LXX., and approximate, sometimes closely, to the M.T. If even a small number of such quotations can be found, it is enough to prove that when the N.T. writers lived, there was another text in existence, and the LXX. did not hold the field entirely.

It can be seen that these non-Septuagintal quotations occur principally in Matthew and John, with an occasional variation in Paul's Epistles from his usual adhesion to the LXX. This is precisely what might be expected, from a general point of view; and it tends to show that in the less Hellenised circles, a text nearer to the M.T. was current; therefore, it is evidence that the M.T. represents, more or less closely, a text as old as the days of the Apostles, and then existing side by side with the LXX. This is decidedly of importance; for evidence earlier than Aquila's time is exactly what is wanted, and if the M.T., or something substantially near to it, is brought so far back in time, the main difficulty in assigning it an earlier, even pre-Septuagint date, is greatly lessened. The argument from the duplicated passages in the O.T. (p. 209) points the same way, and carries us further back in time; so that we can fairly say that the text apparently represented by the LXX. was not the only Hebrew text current between 200 B.C. and A.D. 135, nor the text which was generally regarded, outside Hellenist circles, as preferable. And the Hellenists, on the whole, were not well acquainted with Hebrew. Add to this the results of the analysis of passages, such as those that have been made in this book, and the balance of evidence again favours the M.T. on the whole; the more, because the earliest, and earliest translated books, show generally less divergence between the two texts. We may repeat what has been said before: that where marked differences of matter and arrangement exist, the LXX. may generally be credited with reason for what they have done, and may possibly, in one place or another, have preserved the older form of the text, or traces of it. Where, however, the difference is one of a small point, a sentence, a word, or the form of the word, though the LXX. may occasionally be right, there is, in the majority of cases, little or no ground for thinking that they are. More than this, there is constantly good reason to think that they have simply misread or misinterpreted their original; and all that their reading proves is, that they thought they had before them words, such as might be confused with what the M.T. contains. Often, indeed, it is as though their reading might have come from mere mistakes in dealing with the very M.T. itself. But the study of the LXX. is not in reality any the less desirable and important. Besides the other reasons for it, which still hold, it remains a valuable auxiliary, sometimes a support to the M.T., even if its authority cannot be rated consistently high as a rival to it.

A few words may not be amiss, before parting with this ancient version, on the way to work at it to the best advantage. There is an old story of Ferdinand Hitzig, Biblical critic and Hebraist, to the effect that he used to say to his class, 'Gentlemen, have you a Septuagint? If not, sell all that you have, and buy a Septuagint.' Hardly any better advice could be given to anyone wishing to study the Septuagint than a return of the compliment: 'Do you know any Hebrew? If not, before anything else, learn at least a little Hebrew.' Despite the proverbial warning against the danger of a little knowledge, every step, from the very beginning onward, repays the learner of Hebrew. (It may be assumed that it is his first attempt at a Semitic language.) From the first, he is learning facts which bear in one way or other upon the Bible, and which are often novel and striking. The mere knowledge of the alphabet throws light on familiar Biblical words and names; the simplest constructions and root-connexions are full of interest and instruction. As soon as the principle of the 'triliteral root' is mastered, innumerable word-relations are made plain.

Every page of the grammar, every verse of the Hebrew Bible spelt out, helps towards the understanding of the standard commentaries, as well as towards independent knowledge of the text. It also helps to make clear the intentions of the Greek translators, and their comparative success or failure.

But the student of the LXX., whether he knows any Hebrew or not, must of necessity be equipped with a fair knowledge of Greek, and be accustomed to read the N.T. in the original. He should also be closely familiar with the English Bible in the Authorised Version. As to the Revised Version, opinions will differ; but the writer's conviction is that it is best used simply as a companion to the A.V., keeping the actual words of the latter fixed in the memory. In this way the literary masterpiece is treated with justice, the great difficulty of remembering two versions is escaped, and the wrong or doubtful renderings of the A.V. are mentally corrected as easily as in any other way, perhaps more easily. One can hardly forget, for instance, the 'linen yarn' of 1 Kings x. 28, 2 Chron. i. 16; and the corrected rendering occurs instantly to the mind in connexion with it. The *Variorum Bible* of the King's Printers is invaluable, and if intelligently used, gives an enormous amount of help, precisely of the kind that is needed; it is a great advantage, moreover, to have so much guidance for the whole Bible together. Its references to the Septuagint are not enough in themselves; but to anyone who is working at the Septuagint itself, it gives, perhaps more than any one other book, the needful supplement.

A list of the most necessary books will be given below. Anyone who means serious work will provide himself, as a matter of course, with the Cambridge 'manual' text, in three volumes, adding to it Prof. Swete's *Introduction* and Mr. Thackeray's *Grammar*. A small edition in one volume, even if it does not contain the Apocrypha, is also useful for rapid looking up of references, and for following the lessons in church. At least one part of the Cambridge 'Larger' Septuagint should be at hand, to study the apparatus. Holmes and Parsons' great book can only be seen, as a rule, in large libraries, and is cumbrous and sometimes not altogether trustworthy; but for some work, and in the later books, it is indispensable. The Oxford concordance is also invaluable; if the student cannot procure it, he may note down the points on which he wants to consult it, and keep them till he can visit a library; meanwhile it will be useful practice to search the LXX. (and the Hebrew as well) for instances of the required word or use. An ordinary English concordance to the Bible, if intelligently used, will often give considerable help in this kind of search.

It is necessary to aim at gaining both general and special knowledge. For the first, some of the more familiar narrative books should be read continuously. Any peculiar words or constructions should be noted; as much light as possible should be got from the lexicon and grammar, and parallels found in the LXX. itself, in the N.T., in classical and later Greek writers, and in any available papyri; of these there are a few small volumes of selections. If this makes progress slow, then keep these details mostly for a special portion, and work out only the most important. But in any case, underline any words that differ markedly from the Hebrew or the English Version; and try to account for the difference. Mark in the margin any clear or likely instance of confusion between D and R, or other similar letters. If this is done carefully and neatly, it will long remain useful. The Cambridge edition has margin enough to be used in this way, and the paper will stand ink, though it is better not to write too large or too heavily. A note of the Hebrew root as it is in the M.T., and as apparently read by the LXX., should be concise, and is best made on some one fixed principle; the simplest is to put LXX.'s reading first; underline the Greek word, and put in the margin (say) AHD for AHR (in Heb. letters for choice); or, when the Hebrew is well enough known, the one letter that differs will often be enough. Mark as many of these points as possible in a working copy, and the references to parallels. If, after trial, this is too difficult, leave it for a time, and try again later; for it is important to gain some familiarity with the version in bulk, and in various books. But always, as far as possible, underline the Greek where it differs from the Hebrew. Read some of the Pentateuch, of the Historical books, and the Prophets; then try the Poetical books, at least to some extent. Keep a look out for differences in style. Read also some of the Apocryphal books, with an eye to their characteristics, whether original Greek or translated. In Wisdom, for instance, where you need not expect to find translation errors or effects, look for parallels with other parts of the Bible. In

Ecclesiasticus, be cautious about the Hebrew, and work with a recent commentary. In Job, look out for possible allusions to the classics. Follow Psalms and lessons in church with the LXX.; to some, it is a specially easy way of learning, to hear one version read, while following another with the eye.

For the special portion, be prepared to go slowly, attending to as many details as possible. In easy passages, the marginal noting may be enough, at any rate if occasionally supplemented with a note-book. But in dealing with difficult passages, it will often—at first, generally—be useful to copy out Hebrew and Greek, or, failing Hebrew, the best English rendering and Greek, in parallel columns, only a word or two in each line. For this the Hebrew is by far to be preferred, as the order of the words generally agrees, or if it does not, the fact is worth noting, and the passage usually demands extra care; such places, indeed, are frequently beyond the beginner's powers. Note every point of difference between the Hebrew and the Greek: every substitution of one part of speech for another, every change of number and person in the verbs; and especially every place where the LXX. appear to have read a word from a different Hebrew root, but one not very far different in lettering. The different voices or aspects of the Hebrew verb (generally indicated in the Oxford concordance) are to be noticed, but are generally of less pressing importance for the purpose in hand. The beginner must be careful when dealing with roots belonging to the 'weak' classes; especially verbs beginning with N, or containing Aleph, V, Y, or H, as these letters may either be part of the root or belong to the prefix or suffix, and LXX. may have read these, rightly or wrongly, in a different way from the M.T. tradition. Commentaries will sometimes show that the text represented by LXX. has supporters at the present day. These cases and every point of difference or of interest should be noted. The margin and the notebook will gradually become fuller, and will be found of lasting value.

Unless the work is being done with a view to examinations, the student may to a great extent please himself in the choice of passages. He may as well begin with those books which he knows best and enjoys most. The Poetical books, however, other than the Psalms, are the least suited to the beginner, and should not be attempted at first. Among the Prophets, Amos is short, most interesting, and provided with a fair amount of help at a low price (see list of books below); Isaiah has been edited by the present writer, with the intention of providing guidance for the student. Mozley's *Psalter of the Church* is more advanced and condensed. The treatment of the LXX. in general commentaries is often incomplete, uneven, and out of date; much help can be gained from them, but the reader has generally to sift it carefully. Moore's *Judges* is more Septuagintal than most in its treatment, but the double text makes the book difficult. The Notes on the Hebrew text of Genesis (Spurrell), Samuel (Driver), and Kings (Burney) are often of value in regard to the LXX.

There is little fear but that the learner will soon find means to read *about* the Septuagint; it is more necessary to urge him to explore, and to read, the text itself. It is well to work through some chapters at least with Lagarde's Lucianic text, and with Field's Hexapla; and sooner or later some particular branch of the study will be likely to attract special attention and interest. But the best foundation, in any case, is as much general and detailed acquaintance with the Greek Version itself as can be attained; and eventually, the reader's own annotated copy should become his most practical help towards further knowledge. The greater the familiarity with the LXX., the more the good that can be derived from its use.

CHAPTER X

BOOKS FOR STUDY. MANUSCRIPTS OF THE SEPTUAGINT

A. Texts—B. Editions of Books—C. Lexicons, Grammars, Concordances—D. Ancient Versions and Recensions—E. Language—F. Apocrypha and Pseudepigrapha—G. Commentaries—H. Miscellaneous. MSS.: I. Uncials—II. Some Cursives.

LIST OF BOOKS

A. TEXTS

THE Old Testament in Greek, edited by H. B. Swete, Cambridge, 3 vols. Vol. i., Genesis–4 Kings; vol. ii., 1 Chronicles–Tobit; vol. iii., Hosea–4 Maccabees, with Ps. Sol., Enoch, Canticles. First edition, 1887–94; fourth ed. now in progress. [By far the best for general use.]

Vetus Test. Graecum, Oxford, 3 vols. 1848, 1875. Sixtine Text, variants of Cod. Alex. Smaller size, and convenient for some purposes.

Vet. Test. Gr., 1 vol., Bagster. (Sixtine Text, with variants of Grabe's text at beginning or end of book; therefore containing Hexaplaric matter, but not marked as such.) Small print, but exceedingly portable, and handy for comparison. Does not contain Apocrypha. Canonical books in order of English Version.

The Old Testament in Greek, edited by Alan E. Brooke and N. M'Lean. Vol. i., part 1, Genesis, 1906; part 2, Exod., Levit., 1909; part 3, Num., Deut., 1911; part 4, Josh.–Ruth, 1918. Cambridge, Univ. Press. [The critical apparatus is a very full, representative, and accurate selection of materials.]

Dr. F. Field's edition, published by the S.P.C.K., 1859, reprints Grabe's text, without the critical marks, but to some extent corrected. Hexaplar matter is thus included in the text, as the object is to give a Greek version from ancient sources corresponding as nearly as possible with the Hebrew. It must therefore be used with a clear understanding that it is not a true LXX. text; but for comparison it is still valuable. The type is large and clear. This book can generally be procured second-hand.

On Holmes and Parsons' great edition, see p. 67; on Grabe's, p. 66; on Lagarde's *Librorum V. T. Canonicorum pars prior Graece*, ed. P. A. de Lagarde (Göttingen, 1883), p. 72.

The *text* of the Cambridge manual edition of the Pentateuch and the Psalter is now issued by the British and Foreign Bible Society.

B. Editions of Particular Books

Genesis Graece, P. A. de Lagarde, Leipzig, 1868. (Sixtine text, with variants of several MSS., and introduction.)

Judges, the Book of, acc. to Cod. Alexandrinus, ed. A. E. Brooke and N. M'Lean, Cambridge, 1897. For comparison with the Camb. text (B).

Psalms. *The Psalter of the Church*, by F. W. Mozley. Notes on the Septuagint Psalter, to be used with Camb. edition. The Psalms are numbered as in English Version. Text not given.

Ecclesiasticus in Greek, ed. J. H. A. Hart, Cambridge, 1909. (Text of Cod. 248, apparatus referred to Cod. B. Full treatment of Hebrew and Syriac readings, and discussions of text and date.)

Amos, *Studies in the Gr. and Lat. Versions of the Book of Amos*, by W. O. E. Oesterley, Cambridge, 1902. (Texts of Codd. Q and 22 in parallel columns, with variants of Hesychian and Lucianic MSS. The later versions and the Latin texts are also discussed, and the principal Greek MSS. described.)

Amos the Prophet, ed. J. Meinhold and H. Lietzmann, Cambridge, 1906. Nos. 15, 16 of *Materials for Use of Theol. Lecturers and Students*, Deighton, Bell & Co., Cambridge, 1907. Emended Heb. text and LXX. (Cod. Q) on opposite pages; certain selected variants. Small, cheap, and handy; somewhat advanced, and free in treatment of text.

Isaiah according to the Septuagint, ed. R. R. Ottley, Cambridge, vol. i. 1904, 1909, parallel translations from Heb. and LXX., with introduction and brief notes; vol. ii. 1906. Greek Text (Cod. A) with select apparatus, introd., and fuller notes. (Text with app. also published separately.)

Selections from the Septuagint, by F. C. Conybeare and St. G. Stock. Passages according to the Cambridge text, with notes and explanations.

C. Lexicons, Grammars, Concordances

There is as yet no Lexicon for the LXX. J. F. Schleusner's *Novus Thesaurus* (1820), though still useful, does not serve this purpose. E. A. Sophocles, *Greek Lexicon for the Roman and Byzantine Periods*, New York, 2nd edition, 1888, is the nearest thing to what is needed, but in no way specially applied to the LXX. It is, however, a mistake to suppose that Liddell and Scott's lexicon is useless for the LXX., though its main field of operation is, of course, remote.

A Grammar of the O.T. in Greek, acc. to the Septuagint, by H. St. J. Thackeray, vol. i., Cambridge, 1909. This contains Introduction, Orthography, and Accidence, all sound, useful, and interesting. The Syntax, when it appears, can hardly fail to supply a great want.

Grammatik der Septuaginta, by R. Helbing, Göttingen, part 1, 1907, covers about the same extent of ground.

Some of the N.T. grammars will be found useful at times; in particular, the Prolegomena, vol. i. of *A Grammar of N.T. Greek*, by Prof. J. H. Moulton, ed. 3, 1908, will be found most stimulating reading.

A Concordance to the Septuagint, by E. Hatch and H. A. Redpath, Oxford, 1897–1906, should, but for its price and size, be in every student's hands. The nature of the work hardly admits the hope of a smaller edition that could be of any comparable service. See p. 76.

D. The Later Greek Versions, the Hexapla, Recensions of the LXX., Latin Versions

On Field's great work (*Origenis Hexaplorum quae supersunt*, ed. F. Field, Oxford, 1875) see p. 72. A course of study of this is advisable. The larger

Camb. LXX. gives the available material that has since come to light, but of course not treated according to Field's methods.

Dr. G. Mercati is understood to be engaged upon the recently discovered fragments of copies of the Hexapla, but the work has not yet appeared.

AQUILA. *Fragments of the Books of Kings*, according to the translation of Aquila, ed. F. C. Burkitt, Cambridge, 1897. Text, with introd., critical notes, and facsimile complete. A cheaper edition, without facsimile, has since been issued.

Portions of the Psalms (xci.–civ.) in Aquila's version are also to be found in *Hebrew-Greek Cairo Genizah Palimpsests*, ed. C. Taylor, Cambridge, 1900.

Extracts can be seen in Prof. Swete's *Introduction*, and in the art. *Septuagint* in Hastings' *Dictionary of the Bible.*

For THEODOTION and SYMMACHUS there is little to be found, except in Field, Swete's *Introd.*, and fragments of their actual work in the apparatus of the Larger Camb. edition for the Pentateuch, and of the manual edition (under Q^{mg}) for the Prophets.

The *Old Latin* version, apart from articles in Biblical dictionaries and encyclopaedias, is discussed by Prof. Burkitt in his edition of *The Rules of Tyconius*, and in *The Old Latin and the Itala* (*Camb. Texts and Studies*, vol. iii. No. 1, vol. iv. No. 3). The text of Tyconius gives considerable fragments, chiefly from the Prophets. See also *The O.L. Text of the Minor Prophets*, by W. O. E. Oesterley, in *Journ. of Theol. Studies*, vols. v. vi.; and E. Ranke, *Par palimpsestorum Wirceburgensium*, Vienna, 1871. The main collection of quotations from the O.L.

version in the Fathers is that of the Benedictine P. Sabatier, 1743, consequently in need of revision. MSS. of the O.T. in this version are comparatively scarce and incomplete. The principal one is the Lyons Codex of the Pentateuch and early historical books, edited by U. Robert, Paris, 1881, and Lyons, 1900.

For the *Vulgate*, S. Berger's *Histoire de la Vulgate*, 1893, is the standard work. Enough for immediate needs will probably be found in Sir F. G. Kenyon's *Our Bible and the Ancient MSS.*, which has passed through several editions. The article in Smith's *Bib. Dict.* is by the late Bp. Westcott.

On other versions see Swete's *Introduction.*

E. THE LANGUAGE OF THE SEPTUAGINT, HELLENISTIC GREEK, THE PAPYRI

Besides the grammars, see G. A. Deissmann, *Philology of the Greek Bible*, tr. by L. M. Strachan, London, 1908; J. Psichari, *Essai sur le Grec de la Septante*, in *Études Juives*, Paris, 1908. The art. by Prof. A. Thumb on *Hellenistic and Biblical Greek* in the *American Standard Bib. Dictionary* I have not seen, but it cannot fail to be valuable. A review of Prof. Moulton's *Prolegomena*, by G. C. Richards in *Journ. of Theol. Studies*, x. p. 283 (1909) is worth consulting.

Among the collections of papyri and fragments recently published, first place must be given to the *Oxyrhynchus Papyri*, edited by Drs. B. P. Grenfell and A. S. Hunt; nine volumes so far, which can be seen in libraries. There are many other series, as the *Amherst* and *Rylands* collections. A useful

The Song of Songs, W. W. Cannon, Camb., 1913.

Jeremiah, the Double Text of, A. W. Streane, 1896.
The Text of, C. H. Workman, 1889.

Ezekiel. Das Buch des Proph. Ezechiel, C. H. Cornill, 1886.

H. MISCELLANEOUS

Articles in Hastings' *Dictionary of the Bible* and Cheyne and Black's *Encyclop. Biblica* should be consulted on all points with which they deal. Especially, Dr. Nestle's art. *Septuagint* in the former, and Prof. Burkitt's *Text and Versions* in the latter, should be studied. Dr. Nestle has written a full account of the Septuagint in the *Real-Encyklopaedie* (Hauck-Herzog) *für prot. Theol. u. Kirche*, 3rd ed.; and a concise one in the American Schaff-Herzog, under the heading *Bible-Versions*. The former, in German, has been published separately (*Urtext und Uebersetzungen der Bibel*, 1897). The *Septuaginta-Studien* of Prof. Alfred Rahlfs, Göttingen, i. 1904, ii. 1907, iii. 1911, are important, dealing mainly with the LXX. text of Kings and Psalms.

Essays in Biblical Greek, by E. Hatch, Oxford, 1889, is interesting; but his views have been much criticised, and should be received with an open mind. Prof. D. S. Margoliouth's *Lines of Defence of the Biblical Revelation*, 1904, deals incidentally with the LXX., and represents forcibly, if with somewhat strained logic, the 'other side' of several questions.

Prof. K. Lake's small book on the *Text of the New Testament* (Oxford Church Textbooks) is very clearly put, and should be useful to all beginners and many others, as the subject is closely akin to part of the textual criticism of the LXX.

Dr. J. Rendel Harris's *Stichometry* is the most convenient English book on its special subject. On *Catenae*, see an art. in the *Church Quarterly Review*, April 1900.

The *Letter of Aristeas* has been edited by P. Wendland in the Teubner series, and by H. St. J. Thackeray as an appendix to Swete's *Introduction*. A translation of the *Letter* by Thackeray appeared in the *Jewish Quarterly Review*, April 1903, and was reprinted for the Jewish Hist. Society, 1904. An article on the *Letter*, by I. Abrahams, *J.Q.R.*, Jan. 1902, is independent and interesting.

Articles in the *Journal of Theological Studies* bearing in any way on the LXX., should be read if possible; note especially those by Messrs. A. E. Brooke, F. C. Burkitt, W. E. Barnes, G. B. Gray, N. M'Lean, and H. St. J. Thackeray. The last-named has written on the division of various books of the LXX.; also his art. on *The Psalm of Habakkuk*, Jan. 1911, should not be left unread. The alternative text of this *Psalm* is given by E. Klostermann in his valuable *Analecta*, 1895.

This list of books might be almost indefinitely extended; the object here has been to give those most useful to the beginner, and easiest of access. A few which hardly come under this head are included, as representing the highest work on the subject, being standard works of reference. The drawback to work at the Septuagint used to be that the aids and materials were widely scattered, difficult to obtain, and even to find. Prof. Swete's *Introduction* has done more than any single work to gather up the threads. The difficulty is now much lessened, and the text available is so much improved that it may be hoped that the Septuagint is coming to its own, not only as a hunting-ground for specialists, but as a source of profit and interest to ordinary Biblical students. It may now be comfortably read by all Hellenists, and need no longer be a sealed book to that interesting but rare person, the general reader.

MANUSCRIPTS OF THE SEPTUAGINT

I. UNCIALS

For א (or S), A, B, C, see, in the first place, p. 6.

א. Codex Sinaiticus. Part of this MS., 43 leaves, containing parts of Chronicles, Esdras B, Esther (entire), Tobit, and Jeremiah, was found by Tischendorf in 1844 at St. Catharine's Convent on Mount Sinai. These, at Leipzig, were known as Cod. Frederico-Augustanus. The remainder of the O.T. portions, and the N.T. entire, were secured by Tischendorf in 1859, and are at Petrograd. Each page, in ordinary prose passages, contains four columns. Tischendorf thought that one of the four scribes whose hands he distinguished in the MS. was the writer also of Cod. B. Prof. Lake, who has lately examined the MS., thinks not. The original hand passes straight from the middle of 1 Chron. to Esdras B ix. 9: the mistake, noticed by one of the numerous later hands, is most easily explained by supposing the MS. from which he copied to have had its leaves out of order.

A. Cod. Alexandrinus. It was generally thought, without trusting the note in the MS. declaring it to be written by an Egyptian martyr named Thecla that Alexandria, if not its actual birthplace, had long been its home. Prof. Burkitt has lately suggested that the Athanasius, who makes a note in the MS., was not, by his signature, an Alexandrian Patriarch of that name; and that it did not necessarily arrive in Egypt before 1616, shortly before the then Patriarch offered it to James I. It arrived in England after Charles I.'s accession. The writing is in two wide columns on each page. In Holmes and Parsons it is quoted as III; 'Alex.' standing for Grabe's text.

B. Cod. Vaticanus. Its history before it reached the Vatican is unknown. It has been thought that this and Cod. א were two of the fifty copies which Constantine deputed Eusebius to have prepared at Caesarea; but its place of origin is still doubtful. It has three columns of clear and regular writing to the page. Quoted by H.-P. as II; but their text being the Sixtine, references to it are less frequent.

C. Cod. Ephraemi rescriptus. Tischendorf thought it Egyptian in origin. In the O.T. nothing has survived except parts of Ecclesiastes (nearly complete), Job, and Sirach, and smaller fragments of Wisdom, Proverbs, and Song of Songs. One wide column on each page. Not quoted by H.-P.

D. Cod. Cottonianus. The Cotton Genesis belonged to Henry VIII., and came from Philippi in his reign; it passed into the Cotton collection, having been given by Queen Elizabeth to Sir J. Fortescue. Practically destroyed by fire at Ashburnham House, 1731. The charred fragments remain mostly at the British Museum. The MS. was collated for Walton's Polyglot and for Grabe, so that its readings are fairly well known. Illustrated with miniature paintings. Fifth or sixth century. I in H.-P.

E. Cod. Bodleianus. At Oxford. Ninth or tenth century; the text is valuable. Contains part of Genesis, in uncials. A leaf, at Cambridge, has cursive writing on one side. A Petrograd MS., lxii., carries on Genesis, and continues, with gaps, to 1 Kings xvi. One missing portion, from the end of Joshua to Ruth, proves to be in a Brit. Museum MS., 20002; all these, therefore, seem to have been parts of one MS.

F. Cod. Ambrosianus. At Milan. Fifth century. Contains from Gen. xxxi. 15, with gaps, to Josh. xii. 12. Accents, breathings, and stops by original hand. Often agrees with A against B. VII in H.-P.

G. Cod. Sarravianus. 130 leaves at Leyden, 22 at Paris, one at Petrograd. Parts of each book from Genesis (begins xxxi. 53) to Judges. Fifth (possibly fourth) century. A Hexaplar text, with many of Origen's critical marks. Photograph published 1897. Two columns to the page; an excellent hand of early style. IV and V in H.-P.

H. Cod. Petropolitanus. Palimpsest, at Petrograd. Parts of Numbers. Cent. vi.

I. Cod. Bodleianus. At Oxford. Psalter and O.T. hymns. Cent. ix. H.-P. number it 13.

K. Fragments, at Leipzig, of Numbers–Judges. Palimpsest. Cent. vii.

L. Cod. Purpureus Vindobonensis. Portions of Genesis, in silver letters on purple-stained vellum, with miniatures. Photograph published 1895. Cent v. or vi. VI in H.-P.

M. Cod. Coislinianus. At Paris. Most of the Octateuch, part of 1 Sam., all 2 Sam., 1 Kings

viii. 40. Hexaplaric notes in margin. Cent. vii. X in H.-P.

N. Cod. Basiliano-Vaticanus (see p. 7). 132 leaves at Rome, H.-P.'s XI. Another portion, V, Cod. Venetus, 164 leaves, is H.-P.'s 23. Its text in the Prophets is akin to the Lucianic MSS. In Hab. iii., with 62, 86, 147, it gives, in addition, a distinct text. It is important for Sirach, and a leading authority for the Books of Maccabees Cents. viii.–ix.

O. Fragments, at Dublin: eight leaves, parts of Isa. xxx., xxxi., xxxvi.–xxxviii. Text considered Hesychian, said to have been written in Egypt. Cent. vi. VIII in H.-P.

P. At Emmanuel Coll. Camb. Fragments of a Psalter. H.-P. 294. Cent. xiii.

Q. Cod. Marchalianus. At Rome, in Vatican Library. Contains the Prophets, complete. Written in Egypt. Text considered Hesychian; readings in margin from later Greek versions, and from Origen's Hexaplaric text. There are critical marks in margin and text, but sometimes hard to read. Photograph published 1890, with introduction by Dr. Ceriani of Milan. One of the most important uncials for the Prophets. XII in H.-P. Cent. vi.

R. Cod. Veronensis. At Verona. A Psalter, in Greek (Roman letters) and Latin. In Ps. xcvi. 10, the Latin page has the remarkable reading *a ligno*, familiar from its adoption in mediaeval hymns. The only MS. reading thus in Greek is 156 (at Basle, written in uncials). See however Justin, *Trypho* 73; Swete, *Introd.*, pp. 424, 425. Cent. vi.

S=Cod. Sinaiticus, see above.

T. Cod. Turicensis. At Zurich. A Psalter, in silver and gold letters on purple vellum. Often agrees with A. Considerable portions missing; it now begins at Ps. xxvii. 262 in H.-P. Cent. vii.

U. At British Museum. Fragments of Psalter on papyrus. Probably cent. vii.

V. See N, above.

W. Cod. Parisiensis. At Paris. Part of a Psalter, xci. 14 onward, with gaps. H.-P. 43. Cent. ix. (or x.).

X. Cod. Vaticanus Jobi. At Rome. The greater part of Job, with gaps, and last chapters missing. Hexaplaric notes. H.-P. 258. Cent. ix.

Y. Cod. Taurinensis. At Turin. The Minor Prophets, with several gaps. Transcriptions by W. O. E. Oesterley (*J. Theol. Stud.*, vols. vi.–viii.; reprinted separately, H. Frowde, 1908 (now H. Milford)). This MS. has been twice exposed to damage by fire, in 1666 and 1904. Whereas V, W, X were wrongly classed by H.-P. as cursives, this is really a cursive, with uncial headings only. Cent. ix. or x.

Z. This capital, with small index letters, is assigned to various fragments collected by Tischendorf, belonging to cents. v.–ix., generally palimpsest.

A few uncial MSS. are denoted by Greek capitals.

Γ. Cod. Cryptoferratensis. At Grotta Ferrata. Portions of the Prophets. Palimpsest, and in many places illegible. Cent. viii. or ix.

Δ. At Oxford. About 20 verses of Bel and the Dragon, in Theod.'s version. Cent. v.?

Θ. The Washington MS., a recent addition to the uncials of the LXX. Bought at Gizeh in Egypt, 19th December 1906, by Mr. C. L. Freer, with three other

MSS., of the Psalms, Pauline Epistles, and Gospels. It is to be housed in the Smithsonian Institute at Washington, U.S. Contains Deuteronomy and Joshua, nearly complete. The text in Deuteronomy has resemblances to that found in K, 54 and 75, and 59; in Joshua there is some affinity to A. Written in a good bold uncial hand. Photographed and published with introduction by Prof. H. A. Sanders (Univ. of Michigan Studies, Humanistic Series, vol. viii.), 1910.

Π. At Petrograd. Small fragments of 4 Maccabees viii., ix. Cent. ix.

A great number of smaller fragments have been discovered of late years, and many of them have been published or described. In the larger Cambridge LXX. the readings of several are given. Some are on papyrus, dating back to cent. iii. or even ii. The various publications of papyri include several of importance; e.g., *Oxyrh.* 656, 1007, 1073, *Rylands* 1 and 2, *Amherst* 1, 4, 6, 191, 192, Strassburg Pap. 748.

II. Cursive MSS

The cursives cannot be separately named here; a list is to be found in Swete's *Introd.* For the larger Camb. LXX., a selection of thirty is made. These are, for Genesis, Nos. 15, 19 (with 108), 29, 38, 44, 52–59, 61, 72, 75, 82, 85, 106, 120, 121, 129, 131, 134, 135, with a few not used by H.-P., namely, the two that are recognised as continuations of E, and four others, from Jerusalem (Holy Sepulchre, 2), Athos (Pantocr. 24), Athens (Bibl. Nat. 44), and the Brit. Museum (Curzon 66).

(Students should at least examine a few passages

in the photographs of such uncials as A, B, G, Q, and try to read some portions in a cursive or two.)

The cursives vary widely in contents, age, and value. Only a few remarks on them can be made here. Those quoted in the larger Cambridge LXX. have, naturally, been chosen for their importance and representative character. But there are many more. Not less than 128 are known, as containing the Octateuch, or parts of it; some few contain the entire O.T., or both Testaments, as 68 and 106; and others appear to have once belonged to whole Bibles. We may note 15, 38, and 72 as Hexaplaric, 19, 82, 108, 118 as Lucianic, 106 and 134 as Hesychian. Most of the numbers from 14 to 136 contain at least part of the Octateuch, some continuing further. The Historical books are found, more or less complete, in some sixty cursives, including 240–248, and several of the Octateuch MSS. The Brit. Museum MS., 93, begins with Ruth. Lagarde used it to construct his text of 'Lucian', with the Lucianic MSS. named above.

The Poetical books, or parts of them, are reckoned to be in about 180 cursives; but about 130 are Psalters, or contain little else, unless sometimes the 'canticles' or hymns. Nos. 140–146, 162–227, 263–294, are nearly all Psalters. We may note 55, as having a text somewhat akin to B, in the Psalter and some earlier books; also 115, 141, 269, 272; see Rahlfs, *Sept. Stud.*, ii. pp. 40–55.

In Ecclesiasticus, 248 is considered the leader of a group which gives a fuller text (see p. 143). From this text the A.V. was made, but not the R.V. 106 belongs to this group; also 23, 55, 70, 157, 253. In

Judith, 19, 58, 108 seem to be important; in Tobit, 44 and 106; in 1 Maccabees, 19, 44, 55, 62, 64, 106.

In the Prophets, the characteristics of the MSS. are sometimes fairly clear. Here 22, a Brit. Museum MS., is important among the Lucianic class, and with it 36, 48, 51. Q, generally taken as the chief Hesychian MS., is supported in Isaiah by 41, and generally by 49, 68, 87, 91; A most closely by 26 and 106: these two groups standing near together. B is often followed by 109, 305. The Lucianic text is again represented in 93 to some extent, while 62 and 147 form a kindred sub-group, agreeing in several readings witnessed by the Old Latin; *i.e.*, the O.L. preserves a text with ancient materials which Lucian used (Burkitt, *Tyconius*, pp. cviii, cxvii). In Isaiah, 86 gives the Hesychian text, with Hexaplaric readings in the margin.

There still remains much interesting work to be done in examining the cursives throughout the O.T., and in proceeding, on the result of this examination, towards the establishment of a satisfactory text.

CHAPTER XI

A GLOSSARY FOR REFERENCE

THE reader will by now have realised that the range of LXX. study is wide, and has many large subjects on its borders. A student may thus find himself suddenly facing a branch of study, a name, or a term, of which he has never heard before. Many of these could not be treated in this book; and a kind of glossary is therefore added, in which he may find, alphabetically arranged, an explanation of those he is most likely to meet. Under some heads are summaries of what has been already said; under others, matters often referred to in other books on the LXX. The result is a curious mixture; but practical usefulness has been the object. References are sometimes given to pages of this book; but it is not intended to serve as an index.

ABBREVIATIONS.—The Heb. MSS. from which the Greek translators worked perhaps had some words incompletely written. Lagarde thought that final -h, -th, -m, were omitted; and as these form endings for number and person, their absence would cause difficulty in determining the syntax. The *a.* in uncial MSS. of the LXX. consist chiefly in writing a dash over a vowel at the end of a line for final N; and in what are more strictly called *contractions*, when letters in the middle of the word were omitted, as ΘC̄ for *θεός*, ΥC̄ for *υἱός*, ΔΑΔ̄ for *Δαυείδ*. Also *κ*, for *καί*, *τ*, for the verbal ending *-ται*, and a few more. In marginal notes to MSS., *a.* are more often used, and may cause confusion. Aq., Theod., Symm., are referred to as *α'*, *θ'*, *σ'*: the three together as *οἱ γ'*. Lucian is Λ̥, but *οἱ λ̥* means *οἱ λοιποί*, 'the rest' of the authorities concerned. It is just possible that this *a.*, being a note of a variant, has found its way into the text of Isa. ix. 1, and carried its variant with it, forming a 'doublet' or duplicate rendering. The usual *a.* for the LXX. itself is *οἱ ο'*, *i.e.* 'the seventy'.

ACROSTIC.—A composition in which the initial letters of verses or divisions form words, or a definite (usually alphabetical) arrangement. In the Hebrew O.T. they are not uncommon; the best known is Ps. cxix., of which eight verses begin with Aleph, eight with Beth, and so on; other acrostic Psalms are ix.–x., xxv., xxxiv., xxxvii., cxi., cxii., cxlv. (not all exact or perfect). Also Lam. i.–iv., Prov. xxxi. 10–31, and Ecclus. li. 13–30, where Bickell suspected an *a.* before the Heb. text was discovered; it is, however, corrupt and incomplete. The arrangement may have been intended to help the memory; in Ps. cxix. the poem is long, and the logical sequence by no means obvious; it may also have served, as in some non-Biblical cases, to preserve the text from corruption or misplacement. In Lam. and Prov. the Pe-verse stands in some texts, Heb. and Gr., before the Ayin-verse, doubtless the original order.

AKHMIMIC, a dialect of Coptic; not very well

defined, but Middle Egyptian, inclining to the Southern rather than the Northern division.

ALCUIN, A.D. 735–804.—An Englishman from Northumberland; taught at York, and later invited to join Charlemagne's court circle of learned men; became Abbot of Tours. *A.* produced for Charles a revised text of the Vulgate, good for its time, but soon in its turn corrupted.

ALDINE EDITION OF LXX.—See above, p. 64.

APOCRYPHA.—Books not belonging to the Hebrew canon, and so called either as being kept 'hidden' because esteemed inferior in value, or because their origin was obscure. The name is first expressly applied to a group of these books in a Frankfort Bible of 1534. It is now generally used for a collection of them, attached to the English Bible. They stand in date mostly between the Old and New Testaments; the majority are contained in MSS. of the LXX.; but the LXX. and the English *A.* each contains some works not found in the other. (*See below*, Canon.)

APPARATUS CRITICUS.—This means, firstly, the whole stock of documents containing the text of an author's writings; secondly, the list of such documents given by an editor; thirdly, and more loosely, the collection or selection of readings from such documents which is published in an edition, in the margin, at the foot of the page, or elsewhere. These readings are called 'variants' or 'various readings'. An edition containing these is often spoken of as a 'critical' edition. A 'variorum' edition is one which gives the opinions or comments of several editors or authorities.

AQUILA.—See p. 38.

ARAMAIC.—*See* Semitic Languages.

ARCHETYPE.—A MS. (extant or lost) from which later MSS. or groups of MSS. are derived; relatively, if not absolutely, their original.

ATBASH, ALBAM.—*See* Cipher.

AUGUSTINE.—*See* Fathers.

BIBLICAL GREEK.—A term used for the language in which the LXX. and N.T. generally are written. Some critics, especially Professors Deissmann and Moulton, condemn it strongly; it is certainly a question-begging term, but hardly worse than many others (see Salmon's *Thoughts on the Textual Criticism of N.T.*, p. 49). It is, no doubt, dangerous to represent the language of the LXX. and N.T. as all alike, and different from all other Greek: yet it has a character of its own.

BIBLIOGRAPHY.—Properly, the study and knowledge of books, especially of those bearing on a given subject; commonly used for a mere list of such.

BOHAIRIC.—The Northern Egyptian dialect, named from the Bohairah district, near Alexandria; also called Memphitic, from Memphis. The Egyptian dialects are now classed as Hamitic; the relation between them and the Semitic languages has not been determined. The alphabet is the Greek, with some additional letters, chiefly aspirates and sibilants, derived probably from the older Egyptian. The Egyptian versions, from their early date and freedom from later corruptions, are important witnesses to the text, but more so in the N.T. than for criticism of the LXX.

CANON.—Word means a 'rule', *i.e.* (1) a rod to keep things straight, (2) in our usual metaphorical sense. Hence the *C.* of the Scriptures, or rather, here, of the O.T., means the collection of books accepted by the Church as having authority. (Once definitely so accepted, the books become themselves a *C.*, a rule or standard of faith and conduct.) We must distinguish (i) the Hebrew Canon, (ii) the Greek, (iii) the Christian.

(i) The process of fixing the Hebrew *C.* was gradual. The writing of the books extended over several centuries; moreover they fell into three well-marked divisions: Law, Prophets, and 'Hagiographa'. (The Jews classed the Historical books as the 'former Prophets': the 'Hagiographa' included the Poetical books with Dan., Eccles., Esther, Lam., Ruth, and Chron.); cf. Luke xxiv. 44. The Law was complete and recognised as authoritative at any rate by the time of Ezra and Nehemiah; see Neh. viii. 1–14; Ezra iii. 1, 2, vii. 6, 10, 12, 26. According to 2 Macc. ii. 13, 14, Nehemiah collected a library, in which the 'acts of the kings, and the prophets, and of David' found a place; and Judas Maccabaeus collected 'the things that were lost by reason of the war'. The prologue to Ecclesiasticus refers to 'the law itself, and the prophets, and the rest of the books'; and Ecclus. xlviii., xlix., mention Isa., Jer., Ezek., and the twelve prophets. Thus the Law, from its age, the way in which it was promulgated, and its direct commands, forming the constitution of the Israelite theocracy, was earliest recognised, and maintained, among the Jews, a kind of pre-eminence. The Prophets were fully recognised, but it took time for their written works to be collected and consolidated; the Hagiographa, miscellaneous in character, and some, at least, comparatively late in date, were the last to receive acknowledgment. The prologue to Ecclesiasticus cannot be said positively to imply that this division was then complete. But we may say broadly that the Law was canonised during the Exile; the Prophets accepted, though not complete, by the time of Nehemiah; their completion accomplished, and the Hagiographa becoming recognised, by the time of the author of Ecclesiasticus. The later traditions of 2 Esdras xiv. and the 'Men of the Great Synagogue', must not be taken as history, whatever amount of truth may underlie them; on the other hand, those who adhere to traditional views may easily assign a much earlier date to the establishment of the Law; see Josh. i. 7, 8, xxiii. 6, Deut. xxxiii. 4. Josephus (contra Apion. 1. 8) reckons thirteen prophetical books to the time of Artaxerxes; five of Moses, and four poetical; it is not quite certain how he reckoned the thirteen and the four.

More important than the exact dates, for our purpose, is the fact that whatever the date or method of the formation of the Hebrew *C.*, there is very little doubt as to its contents. The N.T. references to every group, and to most of the books, makes this, in the main, secure; but except for Ecclesiastes and Solomon's Song, and Esther (see below), there is no serious question.

(ii) The Greek O.T., as we have seen, contained several books which stand quite outside the Hebrew *C.* They need not be recapitulated here. It is hard to say what agency, or what principle, further than their vogue among the Jews at Alexandria, brought some books of this class into the MSS. of the LXX., and excluded others. They were not, we may perhaps say could not be, canonised at Alexandria, nor does there seem to have been any attempt to do so. In fact there were no Greek additions to the *C.*, nor, properly, a Greek *C.* at all.

(iii) The Christian *C.*, however important, must be treated shortly, as having less direct concern with our work. The Church appears to have accepted the books of the Hebrew *C.* entire and unreservedly, with one exception—Esther. The list of Melito, Bp. of Sardis, about A.D. 170, gives them all, excluding Esther, in the Greek order, 'Esdras' standing last. Eusebius preserves this list, and that of Origen, who, favouring the Hebrew *C.*, inserts Esdras A, B, after Chronicles, attaches Lam. and the Ep. to Jer., inserts Esther last, and adds the 'Maccabaica' as 'outside'. Athanasius further adds Baruch to Jer., and gives more 'outside' books, Esther among them. In the East, the books of the 'Apocrypha' were read, but the Hebrew *C.* was generally upheld. The Westerns, on the other hand, excepting always Jerome, almost ceased to draw a hard and fast line, and accepted the 'Apocrypha' as well as the books of the Hebrew *C.* At the Reformation, the Council of Trent (not without opposition) pronounced Tobit, Judith, Wisdom, Ecclus., 1 and 2 Macc., and the additions to Esther and Daniel to be of equal inspiration and authority with the Hebrew canonical books. The curious omission of Esdras A, it is suggested, happened by inadvertence, some confusion perhaps arising among the numbers of the books under that name. The Reformed English Church, following Jerome, relegated the Apocrypha to a subordinate place (see Art. VI.); including among the Apocrypha '1 Esdras' (=Esdras A), 2 Esdras (=4 Ezra with the later beginning and end), and 1 and 2 Maccabees.

CANTICLES.—Solomon's Song is sometimes so called, from the Latin. In dealing with the LXX., the name is often used for the hymns, ᾠδαί, or poetical passages, extracted from the O.T. and N.T. for liturgical use, and written after the Psalter in many Greek MSS., including Cod. A and the uncial Psalters of Verona and Zurich (R, T).

CAPITULATION.—*See* Text-divisions.

CATENA.—A commentary, compiled from early writers, such as accompanies the Biblical text in many MSS. The name dates from end of the fifteenth century, when it is applied to a compilation of this kind upon the Gospels by Thomas Aquinas, which an early edition calls the C. Aurea. Earlier, they were called ἐκλογαί, or ἐπιτομαὶ (ἑρμηνειῶν). *C.* were compiled from the fifth century onward, out of the Fathers, sometimes also Philo, Josephus, and others; but usually within a certain limited range. Sometimes the commentary of the ancient writer refers to an older text than that given in the MS.; sometimes the work thus preserved is not found elsewhere; occasionally its matter is valuable. The compiler's object was mainly the commentary, not the text; but there seems to be ground for thinking that these MSS. with *c.* have some text-character of their own. Some *c.* have been published, as that of Nicephorus on the Octateuch and Historical books; but much remains to be done, and the workers since Ittig and Wolf (1742) have been but few. The chief modern authorities on the subject are H. Lietzmann and M. Faulhaber.

CIPHER.—A system by which words or sentences are expressed by different letters or symbols, so as to hide the meaning from all but those who know the system (possess the 'key' to the *c.*) or can detect it. The Hebrew alphabet consists of consonants only, any of which can stand practically anywhere in the word, which is usually a framework of three consonants (a tri-literal root). Thus simple ciphers involving mere substitution of letters are easily arranged in it. A few, hardly open to doubt, occur in the O.T.; others have been suspected. In Jeremiah, 'Sheshak', xxv. 26, li. 41, is, according to Jerome, and doubtless rightly, *Babel* in *c.* This is simply taking the alphabet in reverse order, Tau for Aleph, Sheth for Beth, and so on; hence this cipher is known as Atbash. It occurs again in li. 1, 'against them that dwell *in the midst of them that rise up against me*'; lit., 'in the heart of my uprisers', *leb qamai.* Here LBQ = KSD, *i.e.*, Kasdim, the Chaldaeans. The LXX. (refer to xxxii. 12, xxviii. 41) omits 'Sheshak' in both passages; the Hexaplaric matter in margin of Cod. Q gives Σησαχ and Εἰσαχ. The point may be of importance, because these passages occur in that part of Jeremiah where M.T.'s and LXX.'s arrangements differ, and critics are not agreed as to which is the older. In li. 1, LXX. render, by the cipher, 'Chaldaeans'; but Aquila has καρδίαν ἐπεγειρόντων, and Symm., perhaps following Theod., transliterates, with B for the second M, Λεβκαβη. Another simple form of *c.* is Albam, interchanging the two halves of the alphabet, A = L, B = M, etc.

By this the Jews are said to have interpreted Tabeal (with Teth, not Tau), Isa. vii. 6, as Remalia (Aramaic form). This is not, however, universally accepted.

CLEMENTINE VULGATE.—Pope Sixtus V., besides the great edition of the LXX. (1586–7), undertook an edition of the Vulgate, which appeared in 1590, commended by a Papal Bull. But Sixtus died in the same year, and Clement VII., succeeding in 1592, proceeded to call in the copies of the Sixtine text, and replaced it with a new edition, which, though hastily printed, corrected many blunders, and restored some better readings, though opinions differ as to the general merits of the two texts. Clement, however, published his edition under the name of Sixtus, it is said, to avoid the appearance of dissension; but it is not known whether the Sixtin copies were called in because the text was faulty, or for reasons of policy. The student must distinguish between the Sixtine Vulgate and the Latin edition of the Sixtine LXX.; the latter is a compilation from O.L. sources, by Nobilius and others, under Cardinal Carafa (1588).

CONFLATION.—The combination or fusing of two variant texts into one. It is a characteristic practice of Lucian in his revision of the LXX., and Hort claimed it to be similarly characteristic of later ('Syrian' or 'Antiochene') texts of the N.T.

COPTIC VERSIONS.—*See* Bohairic, Sahidic.

CORRECTORS.—When MSS. were written, they were generally checked, and mistakes corrected, by a *diorthōtes*, as he was called. After this, the possessor or student of a MS. often marked, and, according to his ideas, corrected it from available sources. In the case of the great uncials, this has been done several times, at intervals extending over centuries. The Sinaitic, in particular, is full of corrections by different hands. Readings due to these correctors are usually noted by small index letters, as B , B^{ab}; the original hand, if distinction is necessary, as B*. Some early corrections are valuable; but if nearly of the same age as the MS., it is not easy to distinguish the work of the *diorthōtes* from that of others.

CORRUPTION.—*See* Criticism.

CRITICISM.—(*a*) Textual *C.* (occasionally called 'lower') is the examination of all available materials (*see* Apparatus Criticus), in order to determine, as far as possible, the actual words of the author, or of that form of the writing which is, relatively, the original. *E.g.*, it may be applied to determine the first form of a version, or of a type or recension of a version; as the 'Lucianic' text of the LXX., or the 'African' type of Old Latin in the N.T. The need for Textual *C.* is caused by texts becoming corrupted. *Corruption* is the spoiling of a text by mistakes in copying, or by deliberate alteration. *Glosses* are intended explanations, usually in the form of added words, and these, by accident or intention, are frequently inserted from the margin into the text, instead of, or in addition to, the original wording.

(*b*) 'Higher' Criticism is the examination of the subject-matter of a writing, primarily to gain light upon it from internal evidence, especially as to its authorship and date. The name is unfortunate; and owing, apparently, to the tendencies of some who have attempted it, it has been loosely applied to what is more strictly 'destructive' criticism, *i.e.*, the examination of writings to detect mistakes and inconsistencies, and by exposing these to discredit the character and authenticity of the work, or of parts of it. 'Higher' *C.*, dealing with workings of the mind, can hardly be as scientifically exact in its procedure as Textual *C.*, which deals in part with semi-mechanical operations.

CURSIVE.—*See* Manuscripts.

CYPRIAN.—*See* Fathers.

DEMOTIC. The Egyptian alphabet, if it may be so called, was first written in picture signs (Hieroglyphic writing); then in a modified form, called Hieratic; then in an easier script, called Demotic. From this the later Coptic, adopting the Greek alphabet, borrowed some additional letters.

DIASPORA, DISPERSION.—When the LXX. was made, the Jews were already widely scattered through the world. Cf. John vii. 35; Acts ii. 5, 9-11; James i. 1; 1 Pet. i. 1. This process had begun long before, when the Assyrian kings, and afterwards Nebuchadnezzar, transplanted large numbers of the conquered Israelites to regions on Euphrates and Tigris, W. of Nineveh, and to the neighbourhood of Babylon on the N. Many of the descendants of these took no part in the collective Return to Palestine. Helped, perhaps, by the presence of Semitic kinsmen in some regions, many settled permanently, and others filtered gradually through the East. Some, as Mordecai, attained high positions in their adopted countries; the bulk of the people, traders by acquired instinct, were often protected, sometimes persecuted by the rulers, and seldom popular with the other inhabitants, so that racial riots were not unknown. In some cities, however, they formed a strong element, and were usually organised; living chiefly in a quarter of their own, as often happens to this day. In other directions than the East the *D.* was mostly voluntary, Jews settling in Syria, Asia Minor, even Greece, and especially Egypt. Alexander, who generally favoured them, opened a way by his conquests not merely to their spread, but also to some intercourse, though not as a rule intermarriage, with other peoples. As trade developed, the Jews naturally made their way where their maritime neighbours the Phoenicians sailed and traded; so also they accompanied the Greek 'dispersion' of colonists. Though hardly themselves seafarers, the story of Jonah, the voyages of Aquila, Priscilla, and Paul, seem to show that they had no objection to travel by sea. At Rome, from the days of Julius Caesar at least, they became numerous, though from time to time 'commanded . . . to depart' (Acts xviii. 2): and so they spread into Gaul, and later especially into Spain; also into Arabia, where they are found in Mohammed's day. In some cities, as Antioch, and at one time Ephesus, they were admitted to citizenship. So it was at Alexandria, where they lived in great numbers, with their own quarter, and a kind of local self-government. These settlements in Asia Minor and Egypt were forcibly assisted by Antiochus the Great, and by the first Ptolemy. The Egyptian Jews throve and increased, and Alexandria became almost the capital, so to speak, of the *D.*, especially of the Hellenised portion of it which lay between the far East and the western portion of the Roman Empire. Thus it is easy to understand how the Septuagint came to be made there, where also several of the Hellenistic books of the Apocrypha were written. There was something of a barrier, if not an impassable one, between Alexandria and Palestine; their views of life were rather different. The city's great influence was affected elsewhere also by distance; the Hellenism of Asia Minor was not exactly that of Egypt. But nearly all were devout in their way. Not all, even in Galilee, can have gone up to Jerusalem regularly to the feasts (Luke ii. 41, John v. 1, cf. Acts xxiv. 17); from further regions they went probably on a few great occasions, or once, or never. On the other hand, Paul found synagogues almost wherever he travelled; in nearly all these places Greek was spoken; and in them the LXX. must have been used, as the only common form in which these Jews, partly but almost never entirely denationalised, could read the 'oracles of God'.

DITTOGRAPHY.—A mistake in writing, when a copyist, generally confused by similarity of words or letters, wrote twice what should have been written once; the opposite error, which results in an omission, is called haplography.

DOUBLET.—A duplicate version of a word or clause: not uncommon in LXX., where a variant, or a phrase from a later version, is sometimes copied into the text in addition to the true rendering.

EUSEBIUS.—*See* Fathers.

EXEGESIS.—Explanation of the meaning of passages or books, and might almost as well be called so.

FATHERS.—The writers of the Christian Church, from those who were younger contemporaries of the Apostles onward. The later limit is difficult to fix, and may be carried down as late as the fifteenth century; but in practice the earlier writers, down to about the eighth century, are more usually so termed; even among these, the earlier are the more important, especially to students of the LXX. The name does not seem to have been used specially in this sense before the time of Athanasius. Strictly, it belongs only to orthodox Catholic teachers; but several writers, whose orthodoxy was called in question, or who lapsed into heresy, are often included, *e.g.*, Tertullian and Origen; so that, loosely, the term is used to cover ancient Christian writers generally. The student of the LXX. is more immediately concerned with the writers of the first five centuries; both those who wrote in Greek, and those, chiefly from Africa, who wrote in Latin; the Old Latin version being so literal and close that, as we have seen, it is of first-rate importance for the text of the LXX. These *F.* are important, firstly for their quotations and references to the text itself, which, where their own text can be trusted, gives us witness to what was read in the LXX. at fixed dates and in fixed places; secondly, for their interpretation, as they nearly all used the LXX. or the O.L., and were ignorant of Hebrew; so that the very precarious nature of interpretation on such lines can be seen; thirdly, for the historical information given by a few of them as to the LXX. Version, especially by Origen and Jerome, who actually worked upon it. A brief list of the writers most often referred to in connexion with the LXX. is added: the Jewish writers Philo and Josephus are included for convenience; while some great names, such as Ignatius and Polycarp, are absent, as not directly concerning us here.

AMBROSE (S.), 334–397.—Bp. of Milan, 364. Augustine's teacher. Wrote commentaries on the O.T., in Latin, using the O.L.; but it is not found in his text in an ancient form.

ATHANASIUS, 396?–373.—Abp. of Alexandria, upholder of Catholic faith against Arianism. Wrote in Greek, on the Psalms. The *synopsis* of the books of Scripture is not his, but he gives a list in *Ep.* xxxix.

AUGUSTINE.—Aurelius Augustinus, 354–430, Bp. of Hippo, near Carthage. Upheld the value and authority of the LXX. The *Speculum*, very doubtfully ascribed to him, gives valuable quotations from the O.L.

BARNABAS.—Not the Apostle, it is mostly agreed; his Epistle (Greek), probably 1st or 2nd century, quotes largely, but not always exactly, from the O.T.; important, especially for Psalms and Prophets; text often with ℵAQ. Probably Alexandrian. See Hatch, *Essays in Bib. Greek*, pp. 180 ff.

BASIL, 326–379?—Bp. of Caesarea. Shared in compilation of *Philocalia* from works of Origen. Wrote in Greek: not important for LXX.'s text.

CHRYSOSTOM, JOHN, 344–407.—Bp. of Constantinople. His writings (Greek) give a text of the kind used in his day at Constantinople, and traced from Antioch; *i.e.*, in the LXX., Lucianic.

CLEMENT OF ALEXANDRIA.—T. Flavius Clemens, 2nd–3rd century. Chief works (Greek), *Logos protrepticos*, *Paedagogus*, and *Stromateis*. Quotes freely, but sometimes loosely; his text, when itself secure, is Alexandrian, and therefore valuable.

CLEMENT OF ROME.—Another T. Flavius Clemens, 1st–2nd century. Traditionally Bp. of Rome, and author of an Epistle (Greek) from the Church of Rome to that of Corinth, about A.D. 96. His quotations from the LXX. are therefore of high value; his text is curious, mixed in character, apparently corrected from an uncertain source; agreeing frequently with A, sometimes with B.

CYPRIAN.—Thascius Caecilius Cyprianus, 200–258, Bp. of Carthage. Quotes freely; his *Testimonia* a series of quotations, and of special importance for the O.L., especially as Cyprian's text is fairly well preserved.

DAMASCUS, JOHN OF.—8th century, Greek. Sums up Eastern views on the Canon.

EUSEBIUS, 267–338.—Bp. of Caesarea. Wrote in Greek, *Ecclesiastical History*, ten books, from the beginning of the Church to his own day. Preserves invaluable extracts from older writers; has much to say of Origen; shared in issuing text of LXX. from the Hexapla, which continued in use in Palestine.

HIPPOLYTUS OF PORTUS.—Date and position uncertain; but connected with Rome, 2nd–3rd century. Quotes from the LXX.; text sometimes with A, sometimes quite independent. Works (Greek) edited by Lagarde.

IRENAEUS, 120–200.—Came from Asia Minor, became Bp. of Lyons. His treatise, *Adv. omnes haereses*, quotes largely. The original Greek mostly lost, but literal Latin version extant. His text, if to be trusted, frequently supports ℵAQ in the Prophets; in earlier books resembles that of the older element in Lucian. In Daniel sometimes agrees with Theodotion, sometimes shows mixture or independence.

JEROME.—Sophronius Eusebius Hieronymus, 346?–420. Educated in Rome, travelled in Gaul and the East, lived at Bethlehem mainly from 384 onward. Recognised before this as leading scholar of his time in the Church. For his work as reviser and translator, see pp. 56 ff. His commentaries are important textually, and for the boldness with which he opposes what he considers ill-grounded views.

JOSEPHUS, FLAVIUS, A.D. 37–95?—A Jew, whose part as historian of the revolt against Rome faintly resembles that of Polybius in the Achaean War. His character is variously estimated. Wrote, besides his history of the war, a history of his people, the *Antiquities*. Apparently familiar with Hebrew and Aramaic; later learnt Greek thoroughly, and writes a fair style. Uses the LXX.; his text, especially in the Historical books, is chiefly akin to that of Lucian; which is noteworthy in the case of a Palestinian Jew.

JUSTIN, commonly called Martyr, 103?–165.—Born at Shechem, of Greek descent; went to Ephesus, thence to Rome. Wrote Apologies, *i.e.*, defences of Christianity against unbelievers. The *Dialogue with Trypho* is similar, but against Judaism. Quotes much from LXX., and his text is interesting; apparently of mixed character, often with A and its associates, sometimes with D in Genesis; in Daniel varies between LXX. and Theod. Sometimes discusses the text; gives the remarkable reading, found only in Codd. R and 156 among Greek MSS., in Ps. xcvi. 10, familiar in the Latin hymn, *Regnavit* a ligno *Deus*.

LUCIFER.—Bp. of Caglian in Sardinia, 4th century; a witness to the O.L. text (African).

NOVATIAN, 3rd century, became schismatic and anti-pope. Wrote before this, a treatise, *De Trinitate*, of some value for the text of its quotations.

ORIGEN, 185?–254.—Lived at Alexandria, with an interval at Caesarea; scholar and teacher. Portions of his commentaries are extant. The most learned Christian writer before Jerome. On his great work, the Hexapla, see pp. 42, 57.

PHILO.—Alexandrian Jew, wrote in former half of 1st century. Quotes largely from LXX., but with freedom; text often with D in Genesis, B in other books; sometimes with Lucian. Discusses the O.T. Scriptures philosophically but reverently.

TERTULLIAN.—Q. Septimius Florens Tertullianus. Born about A.D. 160, or earlier. Well educated, versed in law and rhetoric. Converted about 190–195, became a presbyter. Lived at Carthage, but spent some time at Rome. Wrote fiercely against heretics, but himself became a Montanist, perhaps shortly after A.D. 200. The first and most powerful of the great African writers. Cyprian was greatly influenced by his works, and Minucius Felix, author of the charming little book *Octavius*, most classical in style of ancient Christian writings, seems to owe him much. Tert.'s best-known works are the *Apology* and *Adv. Marcionem.* He quotes the O.T. frequently, and would be a principal authority for the O.L., but that his text is so independent that it is even doubted whether he used a Latin Bible, or translated for himself: still, his quotations should always be studied and compared with other sources.

THEODORE, 358?–428.—Bp. of Mopsuestia, bred at Antioch. Commentaries extant, partly in a Latin translation, partly in Greek. Text Lucianic. Important for the Minor Prophets.

THEODORET, 386–457.—Bp. of Cyrrhus; also of the school of Antioch (Lucianic text).

TYCONIUS.—4th century (latter part), an African and a Donatist. Wrote a Latin commentary on the Apocalypse, itself lost, but largely used by later authors, as Primasius; also the *Book of Rules*, which deals curiously with the interpretation of prophecy. Quotes largely, and uses an O.L. version of pure and early character: so that the *Rules*, edited by Prof. Burkitt, are now recognised as a chief textual authority for the O.L., especially of the Major Prophets.

FAYUMIC.—A name sometimes given to a dialect of Middle Egypt.

GEMĀRA.—*See* Talmud.
GLOSS.—*See* Criticism.

HAGIOGRAPHA.—*See* Canon.
HALĀKHA.—*See* Talmud.
HAPHTAROTH.—*See* Text-division.

HEBRAICA VERITAS.—The true text, in the view of those who held it to be Hebrew, the LXX. and other versions being wrong wherever they departed from it.

HEBRAISM (Semitism, Aramaism).—An idiom of the Hebrew, or another Semitic language, rendered literally in Greek words, without regard to the spirit of the Greek language. Some object to the term, or rather almost deny the existence of Hebraisms, now that they can produce so many parallel expressions from the papyri.

HEBREW ACCENTS.—The system of these in the O.T. is very elaborate: there is an accent upon practically every word, the complete unit being the verse, with a division half-way. The accents are numerous, classed according to strength. They serve (*a*) to guide the reader in his 'cantillation' or intoning; (*b*) to show the sense, as an elaborate punctuation, connecting or separating the words. Consequently they may affect the way in which a sentence is to be understood, and are therefore often referred to in commentaries, so that a student of the LXX. needs some idea of what is implied. The accent-system is the invention of the Massoretes, and must be dated from the fifth to the eighth century; the underlying tradition, as in the case of the vowel-points, may be much older. Jerome often, but not always, agrees with it, but seems to have had no knowledge of any written vowel-points or accents; the LXX. had clearly, as shown by many instances, either a different tradition, or none, to follow. The Massoretic accents should always be respectfully considered; but it cannot be laid down as a rule that they should be followed without exception. They frequently affect the length of syllables: but this matter belongs to Hebrew grammar. The Poetical books (Job, Psalms, Proverbs) have a special system of accentuation.

HELLENIST, HELLENISTIC.—A 'Hellenist' Jew was one who had so far relaxed his nation's abhorrence of foreign ways as to adopt some degree of Greek culture, at any rate the Greek language. Those of the 'dispersion' were more likely, and sometimes they were practically compelled, by their situation and circumstances, to do this. Other peoples became thus Hellenised, especially after Alexander's conquests, explorations, and resettlements of the population. Thus Greek became widely spoken (see pp. 36, 50); and from the third century B.C. one form of it prevailed, the κοινὴ διάλεκτος, sometimes called 'Hellenistic' Greek.

HEXAPLA.—See p. 42 ff., 57.

HEXAPLARIC SIGNS.—In the critical work of the Hexapla, Origen found it necessary to indicate omissions and additions of the LXX., as compared with the Hebrew, by signs or marks; which he borrowed from the work of Aristarchus, the Alexandrian librarian and editor of Homer. Origen chose the *asterisk* to mark places where a Hebrew passage was absent from the LXX., and the *obelus* ('spear' or 'dagger') to mark passages in the LXX. which the Hebrew did not contain. The *metobelus*, generally in form like a colon, showed the end of the passage concerned; other forms of this were a sloping line with dots, or a 'mallet', also sloping downward from the right. This is used in the Syro-hexaplar, and may be seen in Field's *Hexapla*. The *obelus* was sometimes replaced by a horizontal line, with or without dots; sometimes like the sign of division, ÷, called *lemniscus*; or if with a dot under the line, *hypolemniscus*.

LACUNA.—A gap in a MS., where a portion is missing.

LAODICENE CANON.—The list of books (see above, Canon) recognised by the Council of Laodicea, A.D. 363 (a local Synod, not a general Council). The order is Gen.–Ruth, Esther, 1–4 Kingdoms, Chron., 150 Psalms (excluding the 151st and Ps. Sol.), Prov., Eccles., Song of Sol., Job, xii. Proph., Isa., Jer. (with Bar., Lam., Ep.), Ezek., Daniel.

LECTIONS, LECTIONARIES.—The early Church, as the Jewish Church (in the synagogues) before it, appointed portions of the O.T. to be read in the service: 'lections' or 'lessons'. This practice must soon have come into use: Justin Martyr appears to allude to it; Origen seems to base many of his homilies on the lesson for the day when they were to be delivered. Lessons seem to have been taken from almost every book of the O.T., excepting perhaps Esther (see above, Canon); the Psalms being differently used, as with us. The O.T. lesson was sometimes called 'the Prophet'; the Church, very naturally, emphasising this aspect, though of course the books of Moses were read. The N.T. once recognised as canonical, lessons from it also were read, and 'the apostle' followed 'the prophet'.

Just as in some copies of the Bible used in churches to-day, the appointed lessons were marked in the margins of MSS. to guide the reader. There marks are, however, sometimes doubtful in meaning, and possibly refer to divisions, in some cases, for other purposes than church reading (see below, Text-division). Later—as it would appear from the age of the specimens now remaining—it became customary to copy out the lessons alone (as in the books commonly known as 'Church Services'). MSS. containing these lessons are known as Lectionaries; they are often finely written, but seldom of early date. They have not as yet been fully studied; and from them it may be possible to gain evidence as to the local use of different types of text.

LITURGY, LITURGICAL NOTES.—As with Lections (see above), the Christian Church had, at an early date, forms of prayer and of praise for worship in its assemblies. These tended to become fixed, but at the same time varied in different places; for the Christians, widely if at first thinly diffused over the world, with comparatively scanty means of communication, could hardly in early days have secured uniformity, if indeed they desired to establish it; and the final separation of East and West arrived before they reached it. But in fact, the forms of service were left to the several Bishops. There was, of course, a general resemblance; usually, the service or Liturgy included reading of the Scriptures; prayers; a discourse, homily, or sermon; and the Eucharist. (Cf. Acts ii. 42.) To this we may add the singing of Psalms and Hymns; the writing or adaptation of the latter can be traced back to very early times. In essentials, the resemblance of the ancient forms of worship to those which still obtain is striking.

In the East, Liturgies bore the names of St. Clement, St. Mark, St. James, St. Basil, St. Chrysostom, and Serapion of Thmuis. In the West, Milan had the Ambrosian Rite (dated about A.D. 374), Rome the Sacramentary attributed to Pope Leo I. (440–461), which may at any rate contain some of his compositions; Gelasius (492) and Pope Gregory the Great (590) carried on the work. Gaul had its own 'use', and Britain perhaps obtained a form from thence; Augustine's aim at enforcing the Roman liturgy was modified by Gregory's advice (600). Variations continued, as our Prayer Book—'Concerning the Services of the Church'—reminds us, referring to the 'uses' of Salisbury (Sarum), Hereford, Bangor, York, and Lincoln. The Greek Liturgies of the East make great use of the language of the LXX.; the Westerns, similarly, of the Latin Version, that is, until Jerome's day (and even later), of the LXX. in a close-fitting Latin dress. In our own Prayer Book, apart from the passages of Scripture definitely introduced as such, notice the language of the O.T. pervading the versicles and responses, the Litany (esp. Pss. xliv., ciii.), the Te Deum, the Gloria in excelsis, the blessing from Num. vi. 24–26, and numerous passages in the prayers (as, *e.g.*, in the 'Forms of Prayer to be used at Sea'). In many of these the wording of the LXX. can be recognised. Thus the study of the LXX. throws light on the sources of the Liturgies, and on phrases, allusions, and terms employed in them. Conversely, it is as well to be on the watch for traces of the influence of liturgical use upon the text of MSS. of the LXX. itself. There is no reason why a liturgical note might not, as well as any other marginal note, intrude into the text by a copyist's mistake; and Mr. H. St. J.

Thackeray has made out a strong case for interpreting the obscure Hebrew of Hab. iii. 9 as an embodied lectionary note of the synagogue, using the evidence of the LXX. as part of his proof. Also, passages adapted to liturgical use might become familiar to copyists in that form, and corruptions in MSS. might thus arise. The titles in the Greek Psalter may be partly due to similar causes, and investigation of texts on these lines may produce further results. (See Swete, *Introd. to O.T. in Greek*, pp. 471 ff.; Thackeray in *Journ. Th. Stud.*, Jan. 1911.)

MANUSCRIPTS.—Greek MSS. of the LXX. fall into two main divisions, generally known as 'uncials' and 'cursives', according to the letters in which they are written. More strictly, 'uncial' letters are a modification of capitals, introducing curves freely; and the small letters are properly called 'minuscules', 'cursive' meaning a running hand with letters joined. But practically it is usual to speak of 'uncial' and 'cursive' MSS., according as they are written in these modified capitals or in small letters. The shapes of the letters vary somewhat at different dates. Some hands show a mixture of the forms, but those in which minuscules are found are classed as cursives. Cursive writing existed from a very early date; but in literary, and especially ecclesiastical MSS., uncials are found chiefly from the fourth to the ninth century, cursives from the ninth onward, with a little overlapping.

(In *Latin* MSS. the difference between capitals and uncials is more marked, and there are also 'half-uncial' and 'mixed' hands.)

A list is given, p. 240, of the principal uncial MSS.

of the LXX., with some of the more important cursives. The uncials number about thirty ; the cursives may amount to between four and five hundred ; but many contain only a few books, or even a single book of the O.T. The uncials are usually referred to, for convenience, by capital letters, English, Greek, and occasionally Hebrew ; the cursives by numbers, in Holmes and Parsons' great edition, and generally since ; the new Cambridge edition is substituting small letters for a select list.

Most MSS. of the LXX. are written on parchment or vellum. This material, made of the prepared skins of animals, was unrivalled for strength and durability, but decidedly expensive. It could, however, be used on both sides, and bound into book shape ('codex'), instead of the more cumbrous roll. The name 'parchment' comes from Pergamum, the headquarters of the manufacture, which was a necessity when (if the story be true which Pliny, following Varro, tells) the jealousy of Egypt, under Ptolemy Epiphanes, restricted the export of papyrus, in order to hamper the library of Pergamum, and prevent its becoming a rival to Alexandria. The Christian Church is said to have favoured the use of vellum, which was for many centuries the usual material for MSS. Paper, coming from China, reached the Nearer East in the eighth or ninth century, but was not much used in Europe till the fourteenth, when it began to supersede vellum.

Papyrus, the writing material of Egypt, was used there, it is said, as early as the third millennium B.C., and imported to other countries, where it was only occasionally grown and manufactured. The plant has now ceased to grow in many of the districts which formerly produced it. It is less durable, in use, than vellum, which would account for the Church's preference for the latter. Of late years, skilled searchers have recovered many writings on papyrus in Egypt; among them several Biblical and Apocryphal fragments of value and interest, besides a great store of local, official, and private documents and correspondence. The oldest MS. connected with the Bible is an Aramaic papyrus fragment of the Story of Aḥiḳar, apparently the original version, and dated by experts about 450 B.C.

Vellum MSS. could be washed, or more usually scraped, to erase the writing, that the material might be used again. A MS. so treated is called a 'palimpsest'. As a rule, the first writing was not thoroughly destroyed; and many MSS.—as Cod. C, and the fragments of Aquila recovered in 1897—are palimpsests, of which the under writing, still more or less readable, is to us the more valuable part. Papyrus could not be scraped, but only washed; so treated, it was loosely called a palimpsest also.

MASSORAH, MASSORETIC TEXT.—The Hebrew text of the O.T., as found in MSS., and as printed, has, comparatively speaking, very few variants. It is, substantially, the 'Massoretic Text', *i.e.*, the text as carefully edited, the work extending over several generations, by a school of Jewish students known as the Massoretes, *Massorah* meaning 'tradition'. The date of this school may be placed from about the seventh to the ninth century. Two schools, in fact, may be distinguished: the Western centred at

Tiberias, the Eastern in Babylonia. Even between these, though their vowel-systems differed, the variation of text is not great. The Massoretes, working by the traditions embodied in the Talmud, did their best to fix the consonantal text, and introduced (probably under Syriac influence) the dots or 'points' which now show the vowels.[1] They preserved this consonantal text with the greatest care, and when they found it quite unsatisfactory, they still left it untouched, but added a marginal note (Q'ri, 'read', the text being K'thib, 'written') of the reading preferred. They furnished also a mass of notes on the text, as distinguished from the subject-matter; a very short epitome of this is found in printed Hebrew Bibles. They also arranged the order of the books, some of their divisions (see Text-division), and the system of accents; the punctuators and the commentators may not have been the same set of men. The Massoretic text is generally referred to as 𝔐 or M.T.

MEMPHITIC VERSION.—*See* Bohairic.

MESROP (354–441).—To him is attributed the invention of the Armenian alphabet, and at least the superintendence of the Armenian version; perhaps also of the Georgian.

MINUSCULES.—*See* Manuscripts.

MISHNAH.—*See* Talmud.

MUSEUM.—The Museum at Alexandria was a great

[1] This point may be regarded as settled, though it was vehemently contested as late as the seventeenth century. Even the Buxtorfs, who were skilled Hebrew scholars, maintained that the vowel-points were far older. But it is clear that Jerome, for instance, knew nothing of them.

college, founded by Ptolemy Soter, who also began the great Library. Here began the secondary age of Greek literature, in which we find men of plentiful ability; but they were mostly conscious students rather than spontaneous creators. They gained their new mental material chiefly from without: Oriental or semi-Oriental ideas, philosophical and religious. They studied, and skilfully imitated, the old styles; but the living fire was flickering out. Museum and Library, however, were in a way a new departure, and were magnificently carried out.

OLD LATIN VERSION.—Made, in the case of the O.T., from the LXX.: literal and close. From its early date (possibly second century) a most important witness to the text of the LXX. before the Hexapla and its after-effects, and before the date of our earliest MSS. (See p. 52.)

PALAEOGRAPHY.—The study of the handwriting of ancient documents. Its object is the recovery of the true text; it is, in fact, the department of textual criticism which is concerned with the outward presentation of the text as written in the MSS., but the term is often loosely used almost as equivalent to textual criticism generally. In practice, most palaeographists are highly trained scholars, and deal more or less with the whole subject. Palaeography is a study which requires considerable natural gifts as well as training. By it mistakes in MSS. are detected, and often set right; the age of MSS. is estimated, as well as the district where they were written, and the knowledge of the history of the text thus greatly increased. The trained student works largely by recognised rules, but it remains still a field for the exercise of personal gifts rather than a rigidly exact science. See p. 85 ff.

PALESTINIAN SYRIAC.—*See* Peshiṭta.

PALIMPSEST, PAPYRUS.—*See* Manuscripts.

PARASHAH.—*See* Text-division.

PATRISTIC.—Adjective, 'of the Fathers'. *See* Fathers.

PESHIṬTA.—The common or Vulgate Syriac version of the Bible. In the O.T. it was made from the Hebrew; but some books, as Isaiah and Psalms, were either translated or altered with some reference to the LXX. In the N.T. it is generally held to be a revision of older versions, though the point is still argued whether its original basis is to be found in the Sinaitic and Curetonian versions or not. The *Palestinian* Syriac, on the other hand, was made from the LXX. It is extant in considerable fragments, and (thanks to the labours of Land, Gwilliam, Mrs. Lewis, Prof. Rendel Harris, and others) is now recognised as an important, though not very early, witness to the Greek text. *See also* Syro-hexaplar.

PSEUDEPIGRAPHA.—Writings more or less connected with, or distantly resembling, the books of the Bible, but not admitted to the Canon, nor ranking, as a rule, even with the Apocrypha. The name was applied because several of them were fathered upon earlier characters, as Ezra, Baruch, and Enoch. They are not usually found in MSS. of the LXX. or Vulgate, though this is not an absolute rule by which writings can be classified.

QUINTA, SEXTA, SEPTIMA.—Greek versions of the O.T., in addition to the LXX., Aquila, Theodotion, and Symmachus. They are chiefly known as fragments in the Hexapla (and Syro-hexaplar). Quinta and Sexta, as we learn from Eusebius (*H.E.*, vi. 16), were found by Origen; we do not know how much he found, and they may never have been entire versions. Fragments now remain of Psalms, and some other books; notably of Quinta in 2 Kings, where Prof. Burkitt thinks they may be genuine readings of the LXX., placed in the margin. *Septima* is so lost to knowledge that is is even doubted whether it existed at all.

RECENSION.—An edition of an ancient work, involving working over of the text; though, if this has been done, an edition preserving the original text is likely enough to be loosely called a 'recension' too, especially as it may long remain uncertain which edition is really the original or the nearest to it.

ROMAN EDITION.—The Sixtine edition of the LXX., 1586–7. *See* Clementine Vulgate.

SAHIDIC, also called THEBAIC.—The dialect of Upper Egypt. A good deal of the O.T. exists in a Sahidic version, perhaps as old as the third or early fourth century, and sometimes representing an early Greek text.

SAMARITAN PENTATEUCH.—What is usually meant, when this name is used, is the Hebrew Pentateuch in the Samaritan characters, which is in a recension differing from the M.T.., and not infrequently agreeing with the LXX. against it. At one time there was an idea that its text might prove superior to the M.T.; Gesenius, about a century ago, crushed this completely for the time, but something has been heard of it again recently. It is, however, impossible to maintain the extreme antiquity of the recension, or of the MSS. of it, as dating from the settlement of the Samaritans in Palestine. The Samaritan *translation* of this recension exists, but is considered less important.

SEMITIC LANGUAGES.—These, like the Indo-Germanic (Aryan) languages, fall into groups; the local and philological divisions, on the whole, agree. It cannot be said that any philological connexion between Semitic and Indo-Germanic languages has as yet been made clear.

Starting at the E. and N.E., we have (i) Assyrian and Babylonian; (ii) Aramaic; (iii) Canaanite (almost = Palestinian); (iv) to the S., Arabic; (v) proceeding W. into Africa, Ethiopic. Of these all but (i) have left later descendants; there are various subdivisions.

Hebrew belongs, with Phoenician and the Moabite language, to the Canaanite division.

Classical Arabic has passed into the modern language, spoken, with dialectic varieties, in Syria, Egypt, Arabia, and, to a greater or less extent, in many Mohammedan countries. Arabic also intruded as a mixture, into Persian (an Indo-Germanic language), and so into the compound dialect Urdu or Hindustani, and even into purer Indian languages. Its alphabet is very widely used, even for non-Semitic tongues (as Turkish); similarly, some Mongol languages use a script derived from the Syriac alphabet, written perpendicularly.

Ethiopic, in the wider sense, includes many modern dialects or languages, such as Amharic; and some relation is thought to exist between it and the Coptic languages, sometimes classed as Hamitic.

It would seem that the original speech of Abraham and his immediate ancestors was Aramaic, of the Eastern division; and that he and his descendants adopted Hebrew on coming into Canaan, and maintained it until after the return from the Captivity. Laban's surroundings seem to have been still Aramaic (Gen. xxxi. 47). In later times, the central position of the people who spoke Aramaic, extending from the borders of Palestine to Babylonia, made this the general language for communication between the various Semitic peoples from Egypt eastward. It even affected Persian in the Pahlavi stage, as Assyrian did in a former period. When, therefore, the Jews, on their return from the Captivity, found Aramaic useful in intercourse with the peoples who now surrounded them closely, they gradually adopted it, at first side by side with Hebrew, and then, except as the language of their sacred books, instead of it. Parts of Ezra and Daniel are written in Aramaic, and traces occur elsewhere in the O.T. It was the language, apparently, of diplomacy, as in Hezekiah's time (2 Kings xviii. 26). It was formerly called 'Chaldee', as in the margin of the A.V., as the Jews were supposed to have adopted it during the Captivity, and brought it back with them. It is called 'Hebrew' in the N.T. (as John xix. 13, 20, Acts xxi. 40, xxii. 2), having more or less usurped the name.

Syriac, as a literary language, is developed from an Eastern form of Aramaic; the Babylonian Talmud is in another dialect of this, the Palestinian Talmud and the Targums in Western Aramaic. Some knowledge of the Semitic idioms, especially Hebrew and Aramaic, is necessary for the thorough study of the LXX., in order that expressions akin to these idioms may be properly estimated; moreover, many peculiarities in the LXX. are probably due to the translators' mistakes or difficulties in reading the Hebrew before them.

SEXTA, SEPTIMA.—*See* Quinta.

SIXTINE.—*See* Roman Edition.

STICHOMETRY.—*See* Text-division.

SYMMACHUS.—See p. 40.

SYRO-HEXAPLAR VERSION.—Made by Paul, Bp. of Tella, about A.D. 616–8, from the Hexaplar text of the LXX. Very literal, and preserves most of the critical signs, as well as marginal notes. Regarded as extremely valuable for its textual evidence. Except for one Greek MS., it is the only extant authority for the *Septuagint* version of Daniel. The poetical books and the Prophets are complete; some of the historical books also remain.

TALMUD.—A body of Jewish literature which grew up around the Hebrew Scriptures. The name means 'teaching' or 'doctrine'. In the Talmud are contained the precepts of the oral Law ('Torah by mouth'), which was not at first written. It may be said that there are two Talmuds: the Eastern or Babylonian, and the Palestinian or Jerusalem Talmud, of somewhat lower importance. The main division of the Talmud is into Mishna and Gemāra. The Mishna, written in New-Hebrew, the name meaning 'repetition', is the teaching of the oral Law, and became a recognised textbook of it, consisting of 63 tracts, arranged in six 'orders'. (Pirkē-Aboth, mentioned among the Pseudepigrapha, is Tract ix. of Order IV.) These fall into chapters and paragraphs, each paragraph being sometimes called a Mishna (or in the Palestinian T., halākha). The Palestinian T. is complete for four orders, with part of the sixth; the Babylonian has the Mishna entire, but 26 tracts lack the Gemāra or additional matter. The term halākha is also used for such parts of the T. as furnish rules on legal and ritual points, while spiritual exhortations conveyed by stories, explanations, and moral precepts, are haggāda. In the Babylonian T. the Gemāra follows the Mishna by paragraphs, in the Palestinian by chapters. The Mishna, completed not long after A.D. 200, resulted from the labours of the Jewish students from the days of Hillel and Shammai, shortly before the Christian era. This was the age of the Tannaim or 'teachers', who were followed, till about A.D. 500, by the Amoraim or 'speakers', whose explanations and discourses went to form the Gemāra. The age of the Talmudists thus precedes that of the Massoretes.

A Midrash was an interpretation of a text; the verb meaning 'to examine' ('commentary' in marg. of 2 Chron. xiii. 22, xxiv. 27). Midrashic matter is divided, as above, into halākha and haggāda. The great time for the production of Midrashim was from the time of the completion of the Talmud till about the eleventh century. But, in a sense, the Mishna is Midrash; so are Tobit and Judith, as illustrative tales; possibly even Chronicles might be so considered.

TARGUM.—A paraphrase, in (Western) Aramaic, of the books of the O.T., to render them more easily intelligible to the Palestinian Jews. Explanations and Midrashic stories sometimes accompany the paraphrase. The Targum of Onkelos (sometimes, but on no convincing grounds, identified with Aquila) on the Pentateuch, and that of Jonathan, traditionally a disciple of Hillel, are the best known. In their present form, however, the Targums bearing these names are said to date only from the fourth to the fifth century, and cannot be the actual works; though the real Onkelos was perhaps known and used by Pseudo-Jonathan.

TETRAGRAMMATON.—The four letters of the Divine Name, usually, till of late, Englished as Jehovah, but more properly as Jahveh (JHVH). Out of reverence for its sacredness, writers of MSS. treated it in special ways, which resulted, perhaps, at times in defeating their intentions. Hebrew scribes, after the vowel-points were introduced, wrote it with the vowels, usually, of *Adonai* (Lord). In the LXX. it is usually rendered by Κύριος, abbreviated by $\overline{\text{KC}}$ ($\overline{\kappa\varsigma}$); but in old MSS., such as the palimpsest fragments of Aquila identified and edited by Prof. Burkitt and the late Dr. Taylor in 1897, the name was generally written in old Hebrew characters. In the margin of Cod. Q and some other MSS. it is represented by Greek letters of similar appearance, ΠΙΠΙ. This is even transliterated again into Syriac. An Oxyrhynchus papyrus of the third century (1007) has ƵƵ.

In the English version 'Lord' generally stands for

Adonai in the O.T., 'LORD' for Jahveh; 'Lord GOD' for Adonai Jahveh; 'LORD God' for Jahveh Elohim.

TEXT-DIVISION.—The systems on which the books of the O.T. were divided into portions of convenient length are important for various reasons. They are obviously useful, almost necessary, for purposes of reference; they afford clues to the history of MSS., and in cases where gaps occur, they help the calculation of the amount that is missing.

In some cases the Hebrew, Greek, and English Bibles differ (as a rule, slightly) in the divisions of chapters and verses. The Cambridge LXX. shows these differences, as between Hebrew and Greek. The margin of the Revised Version shows at any rate the chief differences between the Hebrew and the English version. When it is said that the differences between the Hebrew and Greek are slight, this is not taking account of those passages (see p. 102 ff.) where the Hebrew and Greek texts diverge specially in contents and arrangement.

Roughly, it may be said, for a starting-point, that the verse-division of the O.T. is ancient, and the chapter-division mediaeval, and therefore relatively very late.

The Hebrew Bible had verse-divisions, practically those now existing, certainly before the time of the Massoretes, who counted the number of them; perhaps a good deal before. There was also a division into sections (parashôth), greater and smaller; each longer portion of the Law, read as a lesson in the Synagogue, was also called a parashah; the Prophetical lessons were called haphtarôth. The printed Hebrew Bible still marks these in the Pentateuch: three letters for the end of a Synagogue lesson, one for a section. The chapter-division is generally said to have been invented by Abp. Stephen Langton in the thirteenth century, and applied firstly to the Vulgate; the Jews, later, used it for reference, and it was also used for the English translations of the Bible. (The printer-editor, Stephanus, first broke up the New Testament into verses; but besides the mediaeval chapter-division, there were ancient chapter-divisions, of which indications are found even in early MSS.

The oldest MSS. of the LXX., however, contain none of these divisions, except as supplied by later hands, sometimes of quite modern date. The copyist worked as a rule by *στίχοι*, 'lines' or rows, the length of which might depend on their writing material; if not, the verse became, naturally, the unit in the case of poetry, and in prose, as soon as the convenience of it was discovered, a standard line was set up, about equal to an ordinary hexameter, reckoned at 16 syllables, or 37–38 letters. (Homer's hexameter varies from 13 —very rarely 12—to 17 syllables, and from about 30 to 40 letters; *Il.* xxiii. 644, the line which can be scanned either as hexameter or iambic, has 31; English has more letters to a syllable than Greek.) By this conventional length of line, besides the convenience for reference, the quantity of a book, and so the copyist's pay, could be reckoned. This may sometimes account for the cases where the 'stichometry' (measurement or reckoning of lines) has been falsified, as sometimes appears to have been the case. There arose, however, another system, of regulating the lines by the sense, and not mechanically by mere length. This was well suited to the poetical books, in particular, of the O.T., where the parallelism and other characteristics of the style made distinct natural breaks; and it had already been applied to classical prose authors, who, with their rhetorical training, constructed their clauses with symmetry and balance. These clauses were known as the 'colon' (longer) and 'comma' (shorter). In Cod. B, which generally has three columns, and in the Sinaitic, which has four, the poetical books, written by *cola*, can be written only in two columns. When MSS. are thus written, the term 'colometry' is sometimes used. The reckoning of lines (stichometry) is sometimes inserted in MSS. of the LXX., either by hundreds in the margin, or by the total at the end of the book. In the poetical books these are given at the foot of the page in the Cambridge manual LXX.; but by actual counting of the lines (due to Dr. Nestle, see Swete, *Introd. to O.T. in Greek*, p. 349, note) and not from statements in the MSS. A few lists of the Canon also give the stichometry of the books. These vary considerably; sometimes by errors of the copyists, sometimes because the texts differed in actual length. Some MSS. of the LXX. have also traces of systems of 'capitulation' or chapter-division, either derived from earlier sources, or contemporary with the scribe, but quite different from the modern chapters. In some cases these ancient chapters have titles, showing the nature of their contents, rather like the page-headings in printed Bibles of to-day. Divisions into lessons for reading are sometimes marked, but these have not yet been fully studied. Later, special Lectionaries were generally used (*see above*,

Lections, Lectionaries). When printing came into use, the mediaeval chapter-division was soon adopted; it appears in the Complutensian and Aldine editions, and in some fifteenth century MSS. The verse-division was soon added, as in the Sixtine edition. The differences between the Hebrew, Greek, and English Bibles, as they stand, are probably, in the main, accidental.

THEBAIC.—*See* Sahidic.

THEODOTION.—See p. 39.

TRANSLITERATION.—Copying out the letters of a word, as from Hebrew into Greek, instead of translating it. Occasionally this is done in LXX.; it is regarded as a special practice of Theodotion, whatever his reasons.

TRIFARIA VARIETAS.—The three texts of the LXX. as edited by Eusebius and Pamphilus in Palestine, Hesychius in Egypt, and Lucian in Syria. Jerome uses the phrase, complaining of the differences, in his preface to Chronicles (Swete, *Introd.*, p. 86). He contrasts this with the *Hebraica veritas*, in which, like Origen, he firmly believed.

UNCIALS.—*See* Manuscripts.

VULGATE.—Jerome's translation direct from the Hebrew into Latin, which eventually superseded the Old Latin Version made from the LXX., and became the Bible of Western Christendom through the Middle Ages, down to Reformation times, when Protestant communities began to read the Bible in their own languages, and new translations were made. Attempts at this had been made before, partly in connexion with early reforming tendencies, *e.g.*, by Wiclif; but specimens of early translations exist, or are known to have existed, apparently unconnected with any such movements. Thus Burke (*History of Spain*, vol. i. p. 259, note) gives a specimen of an early translation, of which a MS. is preserved in the Escorial, and refers to Castilian translations of the thirteenth to fifteenth centuries (Muñoz, *Diccionario-historico de los antiguos Reinos y Provincias de España*, part ii. p. 27) and Catalan translations, possibly the work of reformers (Menendez y Pelayo, *Hist. de los Heterodoxos Españoles*, i. p. 435, ii. p. 700).

Jerome, however, did not translate all the Apocrypha afresh; and his second revised Psalter, the 'Gallican', still stands in the Vulgate, which is thus to some extent composite and incomplete. See above, p. 56ff.

APPENDIX.—THE

	Name.	Sign.	Equivalent (English).
1.	Aleph	א	—, (')
2.	Beth	ב	b (bh, v)
3.	Gimel	ג	g (gh)
4.	Daleth	ד	d (dh)
5.	He	ה	h, —
6.	Vav (waw)	ו	v, u (w)
7.	Zayin	ז	z
8.	Ḥeth	ח	h (ḥ, gutt. ch)
9.	Ṭeth	ט	t (ṭ, lingual)
10.	Yod (jod)	י	i, j (y, ye-)
11.	Kaph	כ (final ך)	c, ch (k, kh)
12.	Lamed	ל	l
13.	Mem	מ (final ם)	m
14.	Nun	נ (final ן)	n
15.	Samech	ס	s (ṣ)
16.	Ayin	ע	—, g, h (')
17.	Pe	פ (final ף)	p, ph (f)
18.	Tzade	צ (final ץ)	z (tz, ç, ss)
19.	Qoph	ק	k, c hard (q)
20.	Resh	ר	r
21.	{Sin	שׂ	s
21a.	{Shin	שׁ	sh, s
22.	Tau	ת	t, th

These letters are all consonants, though Aleph is a weak breath-
(i.) the resemblance between certain letters in form ; (ii.) the English
sibilants ; (iii.) the double use of 2, 3, 4, 11, 17, and 22 (**Begadke-**
three.

The equivalents are given, roughly, in order of frequency of use ;

The corresponding letters in the examples, if not initial, are in
vowels are those following the Heb. consonant. A line / marks the

HEBREW ALPHABET

Equivalent (Greek).	Examples.
ʾ, α, —	Adam, Ebenezer, Ishbosheth, Jezebel, On (Num. xvi. 1), Uriah, Asa, Joab, Kabzeel.
β	Babylon.
γ	Gilgal, Agag.
δ	Dan, Eldad.
ʿ, ʾ, —	Abel, Hor, Haran (Gen. xi. 26), Abraham, A/aron.
ου, ο, υ (ω)	Vophsi (Num. xiii. 14), Uphaz, David, Hur, Esau.
ζ	Zechariah, Azariah, Uzziah, Kenaz.
χ, ʿ, —	Hannah, Haggai, Eve, Haran (Gen. xi. 31, 32), Ahab, Nehemiah, Rachel, Is/aac (or Isaac), Ezekiel = Iᵉhezqel.
τ	Tabrimmon, Atad, Lot.
ι, ει	Jezreel, Isaiah, Benjamin.
χ (rarely κ)	Cush, Chedorlaomer, Milcah, Machir, Abimelech.
λ	Lebanon, Elimelech, Lemuel.
μ	Mamre, Mahanaim.
ν	Noah, Hanan.
σ	Sisera, Phinehas, Amos (-ως).
ʿ, , γ	Ammon, Obed, Og, Gomorrah, Hebrew, Bal/aam (or Balaam), Cana/an, Ja/cob.
φ, π (rare)	Pathrusim, Pisgah (Φ.), Potiphar, Pharpar, Zippor, Joseph.
σ (ζ exceptional)	Zephaniah, Tyre, Zidon, Tirzah, Amoz (-ως), Nebuchadnezzar.
κ (χ rare)	Cain, Keturah (X.), Jokshan, Rebekah, Balak.
ρ	Ruth, Gerar.
σ	Sarah, Israel.
σ	Shaphat, Seth, Tarshish, Jerusalem.
θ (τ)	Taanach, Tidal, Terah, Anathoth, Ephratah.

ing, and Vav and Yod have a kind of semi-vowel character. Note and Greek equivalents, or want of them, for gutturals, aspirates, and **phath**), and the general preference of Greek for χ, φ, θ for the last

the more scientific English equivalents sometimes follow in brackets. heavier type. In the case of Aleph, He, Ḥeth, Ayin, the varying place of a letter not represented.

INDEX

PRINTED BY MORRISON AND GIBB LTD. EDINBURGH

A SELECTION OF BOOKS PUBLISHED BY METHUEN AND CO. LTD. LONDON 36 ESSEX STREET W.C. 2

CONTENTS

A SELECTION OF

MESSRS. METHUEN'S PUBLICATIONS

IN this Catalogue the order is according to authors.

Colonial Editions are published of all Messrs. METHUEN'S Novels issued at a price above 4*s*. net, and similar editions are published of some works of General Literature. Colonial Editions are only for circulation in the British Colonies and India.

All books marked net are not subject to discount, and cannot be bought at less than the published price. Books not marked net are subject to the discount which the bookseller allows.

The prices in this Catalogue are liable to alteration without previous notice.

Messrs. METHUEN'S books are kept in stock by all good booksellers. If there is any difficulty in seeing copies, Messrs. Methuen will be very glad to have early information, and specimen copies of any books will be sent on receipt of the published price *plus* postage for net books, and of the published price for ordinary books.

This Catalogue contains only a selection of the more important books published by Messrs. Methuen. A complete catalogue of their publications may be obtained on application.

Andrewes (Lancelot). PRECES PRIVATAE. Translated and edited, with Notes, by F. E. BRIGHTMAN. *Cr. 8vo. 7s. 6d. net.*

Aristotle. THE ETHICS. Edited, with an Introduction and Notes, by JOHN BURNET. *Demy 8vo. 15s. net.*

Atkinson (T. D.). ENGLISH ARCHITECTURE. Illustrated. *Fourth Edition. Fcap. 8vo. 6s. net.*

A GLOSSARY OF TERMS USED IN ENGLISH ARCHITECTURE. Illustrated. *Second Edition. Fcap. 8vo. 6s. net.*

Atteridge (A. H.). FAMOUS LAND FIGHTS. Illustrated. *Cr. 8vo. 7s. 6d. net.*

Baggally (W. Wortley). TELEPATHY: GENUINE AND FRAUDULENT. *Cr. 8vo. 3s. 6d. net.*

Bain (F. W.). A DIGIT OF THE MOON: A HINDOO LOVE STORY. *Twelfth Edition. Fcap. 8vo. 5s. net.*

THE DESCENT OF THE SUN: A CYCLE OF BIRTH. *Seventh Edition. Fcap. 8vo. 5s. net.*

A HEIFER OF THE DAWN. *Ninth Edition. Fcap. 8vo. 5s. net.*

IN THE GREAT GOD'S HAIR. *Sixth Edition. Fcap 8vo. 5s. net.*

A DRAUGHT OF THE BLUE. *Sixth Edition. Fcap. 8vo. 5s. net.*

AN ESSENCE OF THE DUSK. *Fourth Edition. Fcap. 8vo. 5s. net.*

AN INCARNATION OF THE SNOW. *Fourth Edition. Fcap. 8vo. 5s. net.*

A MINE OF FAULTS. *Fourth Edition. Fcap. 8vo. 5s. net.*

THE ASHES OF A GOD. *Second Edition. Fcap. 8vo. 5s. net.*

BUBBLES OF THE FOAM. *Second Edition. Fcap. 4to. 7s. 6d. net. Also Fcap. 8vo. 5s. net.*

A SYRUP OF THE BEES. *Fcap. 4to. 7s. 6d. net. Also Fcap. 8vo. 5s. net.*

THE LIVERY OF EVE. *Second Edition. Fcap. 4to. 7s. 6d. net. Also Fcap. 8vo. 5s. net.*

AN ECHO OF THE SPHERES. Rescued from Oblivion by F. W. BAIN. *Wide Demy 8vo. 10s. 6d. net.*

Balfour (Graham). THE LIFE OF ROBERT LOUIS STEVENSON. *Fifteenth Edition. In one Volume. Cr. 8vo. Buckram, 7s. 6d. net.*

Baring (Hon. Maurice). LANDMARKS IN RUSSIAN LITERATURE. *Third Edition. Cr. 8vo. 7s. 6d. net.*

THE RUSSIAN PEOPLE. *Second Edition. Demy 8vo. 15s. net.*

Lane-Poole (Stanley). A HISTORY OF EGYPT IN THE MIDDLE AGES. Illustrated. *Second Edition, Revised. Cr. 8vo.* 9*s. net.*

Lankester (Sir Ray). SCIENCE FROM AN EASY CHAIR. Illustrated. *Eighth Edition. Cr. 8vo.* 7*s.* 6*d. net.*

SCIENCE FROM AN EASY CHAIR. *Second Series.* Illustrated. *First Edition. Cr. 8vo.* 7*s.* 6*d. net.*

DIVERSIONS OF A NATURALIST. Illustrated. *Second Edition. Cr. 8vo.* 7*s.* 6*d. net.*

Lewis (Edward). EDWARD CARPENTER: AN EXPOSITION AND AN APPRECIATION. *Second Edition. Cr. 8vo.* 6*s. net.*

Lock (Walter). ST. PAUL, THE MASTER BUILDER. *Third Edition. Cr. 8vo.* 5*s. net.*

THE BIBLE AND CHRISTIAN LIFE. *Cr. 8vo.* 6*s. net.*

Lodge (Sir Oliver). MAN AND THE UNIVERSE: A STUDY OF THE INFLUENCE OF THE ADVANCE IN SCIENTIFIC KNOWLEDGE UPON OUR UNDERSTANDING OF CHRISTIANITY. *Ninth Edition. Crown 8vo.* 7*s.* 6*d. net.*

THE SURVIVAL OF MAN: A STUDY IN UNRECOGNISED HUMAN FACULTY. *Seventh Edition. Cr. 8vo.* 7*s.* 6*d. net.*

MODERN PROBLEMS. *Cr. 8vo.* 7*s.* 6*d. net.*

RAYMOND; OR, LIFE AND DEATH. Illustrated. *Eleventh Edition. Demy 8vo.* 15*s. net.*

THE WAR AND AFTER: SHORT CHAPTERS ON SUBJECTS OF SERIOUS PRACTICAL IMPORT FOR THE AVERAGE CITIZEN IN A.D. 1915 ONWARDS. *Eighth Edition. Fcap. 8vo.* 2*s. net.*

Loreburn (Earl). CAPTURE AT SEA. *Second Edition. Cr. 8vo.* 2*s.* 6*d. net.*

HOW THE WAR CAME. With a Map. *Cr. 8vo.* 7*s.* 6*d. net.*

Lorimer (George Horace). LETTERS FROM A SELF-MADE MERCHANT TO HIS SON. Illustrated. *Twenty-fourth Edition. Cr. 8vo.* 6*s. net.*

OLD GORGON GRAHAM. Illustrated. *Second Edition. Cr. 8vo.* 6*s. net.*

Lorimer (Norma). BY THE WATERS OF EGYPT. Illustrated. *Third Edition. Cr. 8vo.* 7*s.* 6*d. net.*

Lucas (E. V.). THE LIFE OF CHARLES LAMB. Illustrated. *Sixth Edition. Demy 8vo.* 10*s.* 6d. *net.*

A WANDERER IN HOLLAND. Illustrated. *Sixteenth Edition. Cr. 8vo.* 8*s.* 6*d. net.*

A WANDERER IN LONDON. Illustrated. *Eighteenth Edition, Revised. Cr. 8vo.* 8*s.* 6*d. net.*

LONDON REVISITED. Illustrated. *Third Edition. Cr. 8vo.* 8*s.* 6*d. net.*

A WANDERER IN PARIS. Illustrated. *Thirteenth Edition. Cr. 8vo.* 8*s.* 6*d. net. Also Fcap. 8vo.* 6*s. net.*

A WANDERER IN FLORENCE. Illustrated. *Sixth Edition. Cr. 8vo.* 8*s.* 6*d. net.*

A WANDERER IN VENICE. Illustrated. *Second Edition. Cr. 8vo.* 8*s.* 6*d. net.*

THE OPEN ROAD: A LITTLE BOOK FOR WAYFARERS. *Twenty-seventh Edition. Fcap. 8vo.* 6*s.* 6*d. net. India Paper,* 7*s.* 6*d. net.*
Also Illustrated. Cr. 4to. 15*s. net.*

THE FRIENDLY TOWN: A LITTLE BOOK FOR THE URBANE. *Ninth Edition. Fcap. 8vo.* 6*s. net.*

FIRESIDE AND SUNSHINE. *Ninth Edition. Fcap. 8vo.* 6*s. net.*

CHARACTER AND COMEDY. *Eighth Edition. Fcap. 8vo.* 6*s. net.*

THE GENTLEST ART: A CHOICE OF LETTERS BY ENTERTAINING HANDS. *Tenth Edition. Fcap. 8vo.* 6*s. net.*

THE SECOND POST. *Fifth Edition. Fcap. 8vo.* 6*s. net.*

HER INFINITE VARIETY: A FEMININE PORTRAIT GALLERY. *Eighth Edition. Fcap. 8vo.* 6*s. net.*

GOOD COMPANY: A RALLY OF MEN. *Fourth Edition. Fcap. 8vo.* 6*s. net.*

ONE DAY AND ANOTHER. *Seventh Edition. Fcap. 8vo.* 6*s. net.*

OLD LAMPS FOR NEW. *Sixth Edition. Fcap. 8vo.* 6*s. net.*

LOITERER'S HARVEST. *Third Edition. Fcap. 8vo.* 6*s. net.*

CLOUD AND SILVER. *Third Edition. Fcap. 8vo.* 6*s. net.*

LISTENER'S LURE: AN OBLIQUE NARRATION. *Twelfth Edition. Fcap. 8vo.* 6*s. net.*

OVER BEMERTON'S: AN EASY-GOING CHRONICLE. *Sixteenth Edition. Fcap. 8vo.* 6*s. net.*

MR. INGLESIDE. *Twelfth Edition. Fcap. 8vo.* 6*s. net.*

LONDON LAVENDER. *Twelfth Edition. Fcap. 8vo.* 6*s. net.*

LANDMARKS. *Fifth Edition. Fcap. 8vo.* 6*s. net.*

THE BRITISH SCHOOL: AN ANECDOTAL GUIDE TO THE BRITISH PAINTERS AND PAINTINGS IN THE NATIONAL GALLERY. *Fcap.* 8*vo.* 6*s. net.*

A BOSWELL OF BAGHDAD, AND OTHER ESSAYS. *Third Edition. Fcap.* 8*vo.* 6*s. net.*

'TWIXT EAGLE AND DOVE. *Third Edition. Fcap.* 8*vo.* 6*s. net.*

Lydekker (R.). THE OX AND ITS KINDRED. Illustrated. *Cr.* 8*vo.* 7*s.* 6*d. net.*

Macaulay (Lord). CRITICAL AND HISTORICAL ESSAYS. Edited by F. C. MONTAGUE. *Three Volumes. Cr.* 8*vo.* 18*s. net.*

Macdonald (J. R. M.). A HISTORY OF FRANCE. *Three Volumes. Cr.* 8*vo. Each* 10*s.* 6*d. net.*

McDougall (William). AN INTRODUCTION TO SOCIAL PSYCHOLOGY. *Twelfth Edition. Cr.* 8*vo.* 7*s.* 6*d. net.*

BODY AND MIND: A HISTORY AND A DEFENCE OF ANIMISM. *Fourth Edition. Demy* 8*vo.* 12*s.* 6*d. net.*

Maeterlinck (Maurice). THE BLUE BIRD: A FAIRY PLAY IN SIX ACTS. Translated by ALEXANDER TEIXEIRA DE MATTOS. *Fcap.* 8*vo.* 6*s. net. Also Fcap.* 8*vo.* 2*s. net.* Of the above book Forty-one Editions in all have been issued.

MARY MAGDALENE: A PLAY IN THREE ACTS. Translated by ALEXANDER TEIXEIRA DE MATTOS. *Third Edition. Fcap.* 8*vo.* 5*s. net. Also Fcap.* 8*vo.* 2*s. net.*

DEATH. Translated by ALEXANDER TEIXEIRA DE MATTOS. *Fourth Edition. Fcap.* 8*vo.* 3*s.* 6*d. net.*

OUR ETERNITY. Translated by ALEXANDER TEIXEIRA DE MATTOS. *Second Edition. Fcap.* 8*vo.* 6*s. net.*

THE UNKNOWN GUEST. Translated by ALEXANDER TEIXEIRA DE MATTOS. *Third Edition. Cr.* 8*vo.* 6*s. net.*

POEMS. Done into English Verse by BERNARD MIALL. *Second Edition. Cr.* 8*vo.* 5*s. net.*

THE WRACK OF THE STORM. *Third Edition. Cr.* 8*vo.* 6*s. net.*

THE MIRACLE OF ST. ANTHONY: A PLAY IN ONE ACT. Translated by ALEXANDER TEIXEIRA DE MATTOS. *Fcap.* 8*vo.* 3*s.* 6*d. net.*

THE BURGOMASTER OF STILEMONDE: A PLAY IN THREE ACTS. Translated by ALEXANDER TEIXEIRA DE MATTOS. *Fcap.* 8*vo.* 5*s. net.*

THE BETROTHAL; OR, THE BLUE BIRD CHOOSES. Translated by ALEXANDER TEIXEIRA DE MATTOS. *Fcap.* 8*vo.* 6*s. net.*

MOUNTAIN PATHS. Translated by ALEXANDER TEIXEIRA DE MATTOS. *Fcap.* 8*vo.* 6*s. net.*

Mahaffy (J. P.). A HISTORY OF EGYPT UNDER THE PTOLEMAIC DYNASTY. Illustrated. *Second Edition. Cr.* 8*vo.* 9*s. net.*

Maitland (F. W.). ROMAN CANON LAW IN THE CHURCH OF ENGLAND. *Royal* 8*vo.* 10*s.* 6*d. net.*

Marett (R. R.). THE THRESHOLD OF RELIGION. *Third Edition. Cr.* 8*vo.* 7*s.* 6*d. net.*

Marriott (J. A. R.). ENGLAND SINCE WATERLOO. With Maps. *Second Edition, Revised. Demy* 8*vo.* 12*s.* 6*d. net.*

Masefield (John). A SAILOR'S GARLAND. Selected and Edited. *Second Edition. Cr.* 8*vo.* 6*s. net.*

Masterman (C. F. G.). TENNYSON AS A RELIGIOUS TEACHER. *Second Edition. Cr.* 8*vo.* 7*s.* 6*d. net.*

Medley (D. J.). ORIGINAL ILLUSTRATIONS OF ENGLISH CONSTITUTIONAL HISTORY. *Cr.* 8*vo.* 8*s.* 6*d. net.*

Miles (Eustace). LIFE AFTER LIFE; OR, THE THEORY OF REINCARNATION. *Cr.* 8*vo.* 3*s.* 6*d. net.*

THE POWER OF CONCENTRATION: HOW TO ACQUIRE IT. *Fifth Edition. Cr.* 8*vo.* 6*s. net.*

PREVENTION AND CURE. *Second Edition. Crown* 8*vo.* 5*s. net.*

Miles (Mrs. Eustace). HEALTH WITHOUT MEAT. *Sixth Edition. Fcap.* 8*vo.* 1*s.* 6*d. net.*

Millais (J. G.). THE LIFE AND LETTERS OF SIR JOHN EVERETT MILLAIS. Illustrated. *Third Edition. Demy* 8*vo.* 12*s.* 6*d. net.*

Milne (J. G.). A HISTORY OF EGYPT UNDER ROMAN RULE. Illustrated. *Second Edition. Cr.* 8*vo.* 9*s. net.*

Money (Sir Leo Chiozza). RICHES AND POVERTY, 1910. *Eleventh Edition. Demy* 8*vo.* 5*s. net.*

Montague (C. E.). DRAMATIC VALUES. *Second Edition. Fcap.* 8*vo.* 5*s. net.*

Myers (Charles S.). PRESENT-DAY APPLICATIONS OF PSYCHOLOGY. *Third Edition. Fcap. 8vo. 1s. 3d. net.*

[N]oyes (Alfred). A SALUTE FROM THE FLEET, AND OTHER POEMS. *Third Edition. Cr. 8vo. 7s. 6d. net.*

[R]ADA: A BELGIAN CHRISTMAS EVE. Illustrated. *Fcap. 8vo. 5s. net.*

[Oma]n (C. W. C.). A HISTORY OF THE [AR]T OF WAR IN THE MIDDLE [AG]ES. Illustrated. *Demy 8vo. 15s. net.*

[EN]GLAND BEFORE THE NORMAN [CO]NQUEST. With Maps. *Third Edition, Revised. Demy 8vo. 12s. 6d. net.*

[O]xenham (John). BEES IN AMBER: A LITTLE BOOK OF THOUGHTFUL VERSE. *228th Thousand. Small Pott 8vo. Paper 1s. 3d. net; Cloth Boards, 2s. net.*
Also Illustrated. Fcap. 8vo. 3s. 6d. net.

[A]LL'S WELL: A COLLECTION OF WAR POEMS. *175th Thousand. Small Pott 8vo. Paper, 1s. 3d. net; Cloth Boards, 2s. net.*

THE KING'S HIGH WAY. *120th Thousand. Small Pott 8vo. 1s. 3d. net; Cloth Boards, 2s. net.*

THE VISION SPLENDID. *100th Thousand. Small Pott 8vo. Paper, 1s. 3d. net; Cloth Boards, 2s. net.*

THE FIERY CROSS. *80th Thousand. Small Pott 8vo. Paper, 1s. 3d. net; Cloth Boards, 2s. net.*

HIGH ALTARS: THE RECORD OF A VISIT TO THE BATTLEFIELDS OF FRANCE AND FLANDERS. *40th Thousand. Small Pott 8vo. 1s. 3d. net; Cloth Boards, 2s. net.*

HEARTS COURAGEOUS. *Small Pott 8vo. 1s. 3d net. Cloth Boards, 2s. net.*

ALL CLEAR. *Small Pott 8vo. 1s. 3d. net. Cloth Boards, 2s. net.*

WINDS OF THE DAWN. *Small Pott 8vo. 2s. net.*

Oxford (M. N.). A HANDBOOK OF NURSING. *Seventh Edition, Revised. Cr. 8vo. 5s. net.*

Pakes (W. C. C.). THE SCIENCE OF HYGIENE. Illustrated. *Second and Cheaper Edition.* Revised by A. T. NANKIVELL. *Cr. 8vo. 6s. net.*

Petrie (W. M. Flinders.) A HISTORY OF EGYPT. Illustrated. *Six Volumes Cr. 8vo. Each 9s. net.*

VOL. I. FROM THE IST TO THE XVITH DYNASTY. *Eighth Edition.*

VOL. II. THE XVIITH AND XVIIITH DYNASTIES. *Sixth Edition.*

VOL. III. XIXTH TO XXXTH DYNASTIES. *Second Edition.*

VOL. IV. EGYPT UNDER THE PTOLEMAIC DYNASTY. J. P. MAHAFFY. *Second Edition.*

VOL. V. EGYPT UNDER ROMAN RULE. J. G. MILNE. *Second Edition.*

VOL. VI. EGYPT IN THE MIDDLE AGES. STANLEY LANE POOLE. *Second Edition.*

RELIGION AND CONSCIENCE IN ANCIENT EGYPT. Illustrated. *Cr. 8vo. 5s. net.*

SYRIA AND EGYPT, FROM THE TELL EL AMARNA LETTERS. *Cr. 8vo. 5s. net.*

EGYPTIAN TALES. Translated from the Papyri. First Series, IVth to XIIth Dynasty. Illustrated. *Third Edition. Cr. 8vo. 5s. net.*

EGYPTIAN TALES. Translated from the Papyri. Second Series, XVIIIth to XIXth Dynasty. Illustrated. *Second Edition. Cr. 8vo. 5s. net.*

Pollard (Alfred W.). SHAKESPEARE FOLIOS AND QUARTOS. A Study in the Bibliography of Shakespeare's Plays, 1594-1685. Illustrated. *Folio. £1 1s. net.*

Porter (G. R.). THE PROGRESS OF THE NATION. A New Edition. Edited by F. W. HIRST. *Demy 8vo. £1 1s. net.*

Power (J. O'Connor). THE MAKING OF AN ORATOR. *Cr. 8vo.* 6s. net.

Price (L. L.). A SHORT HISTORY OF POLITICAL ECONOMY IN ENGLAND FROM ADAM SMITH TO ARNOLD TOYNBEE. *Ninth Edition. Cr. 8vo. 5s. net.*

Rawlings (Gertrude B.). COINS AND HOW TO KNOW THEM. Illustrated. *Third Edition. Cr. 8vo. 7s. 6d. net.*

Regan (C. Tate). THE FRESHWATER FISHES OF THE BRITISH ISLES. Illustrated. *Cr. 8vo. 7s. 6d. net.*

Reid (G. Archdall). THE LAWS OF HEREDITY. *Second Edition. Demy 8vo. £1 1s. net.*

Robertson (C. Grant). SELECT STATUTES, CASES, AND DOCUMENTS, 1660-1832. *Second Edition, Revised and Enlarged. Demy 8vo. 15s. net.*

ENGLAND UNDER THE HANOVERIANS. Illustrated. *Third Edition. Demy 8vo. 12s. 6d. net.*

Rolle (Richard). THE FIRE OF LOVE AND THE MENDING OF LIFE. Edited by FRANCES M. COMPER. *Cr. 8vo. 6s. net.*

Ryley (A. Beresford). OLD PASTE. Illustrated. *Royal 4to. £2 2s. net.*

'Saki' (H. H. Munro). REGINALD. *Fourth Edition. Fcap. 8vo. 3s. 6d. net.*

REGINALD IN RUSSIA. *Fcap. 8vo.* 3*s.* 6*d. net.*

Schidrowitz (Philip). RUBBER. Illustrated. *Second Edition. Demy 8vo.* 15*s. net.*

Selous (Edmund). TOMMY SMITH'S ANIMALS. Illustrated. *Sixteenth Edition. Fcap. 8vo.* 3*s.* 6*d. net.*

TOMMY SMITH'S OTHER ANIMALS. Illustrated. *Seventh Edition. Fcap. 8vo.* 3*s.* 6*d. net.*

TOMMY SMITH AT THE ZOO. Illustrated. *Second Edition. Fcap. 8vo.* 2*s.* 9*d.*

TOMMY SMITH AGAIN AT THE ZOO. Illustrated. *Fcap. 8vo.* 2*s.* 9*d.*

JACK'S INSECTS. Illustrated. *Cr. 8vo.* 6*s. net.*

Shakespeare (William).

THE FOUR FOLIOS, 1623; 1632; 1664; 1685. Each £4 4*s. net*, or a complete set, £12 12*s. net.*

THE POEMS OF WILLIAM SHAKESPEARE. With an Introduction and Notes by GEORGE WYNDHAM. *Demy 8vo. Buckram*, 12*s.* 6*d. net.*

Shelley (Percy Bysshe). POEMS. With an Introduction by A. CLUTTON-BROCK and notes by C. D. LOCOCK. *Two Volumes. Demy 8vo.* £1 1*s. net.*

Sladen (Douglas). SICILY: THE NEW WINTER RESORT. An Encyclopædia of Sicily. With 234 Illustrations, a Map, and a Table of the Railway System of Sicily. *Second Edition, Revised. Cr. 8vo.* 7*s.* 6*d. net.*

Slesser (H. H.). TRADE UNIONISM. *Cr. 8vo.* 5*s. net.*

Smith (Adam). THE WEALTH OF NATIONS. Edited by EDWIN CANNAN. *Two Volumes. Demy 8vo.* £1 5*s. net.*

Smith (G. F. Herbert). GEM-STONES AND THEIR DISTINCTIVE CHARACTERS. Illustrated. *Second Edition. Cr. 8vo.* 7*s.* 6*d. net.*

Stancliffe. GOLF DO'S AND DONT'S. *Sixth Edition. Fcap. 8vo.* 2*s. net.*

Stevenson (R. L.). THE LETTERS OF ROBERT LOUIS STEVENSON. Edited by Sir SIDNEY COLVIN. *A New Rearranged Edition in four volumes. Fourth Edition. Fcap. 8vo. Each* 6*s. net. Leather, each* 7*s.* 6*d. net.*

Surtees (R. S.). HANDLEY CROSS. Illustrated. *Eighth Edition. Fcap. 8vo.* 7*s.* 6*d. net.*

MR. SPONGE'S SPORTING TOUR. Illustrated. *Fourth Edition. Fcap. 8vo.* 7*s.* 6*d. net.*

ASK MAMMA; OR, THE RICHEST COMMONER IN ENGLAND. Illustrated. *Second Edition. Fcap. 8vo.* 7*s.* 6*d. net.*

JORROCKS'S JAUNTS AND JOLLITIES. Illustrated. *Sixth Edition. Fca[p.]* *8vo.* 6*s. net.*

MR. FACEY ROMFORD'S HOUN[DS.] Illustrated. *Third Edition. Fcap.* [8vo.] 7*s.* 6*d. net.*

HAWBUCK GRANGE; OR, THE SP[ORT]ING ADVENTURES OF THO[MAS] SCOTT, ESQ. Illustrated. *Fcap.* [8vo.] 6*s. net.*

PLAIN OR RINGLETS? Illustra[ted.] *Fcap. 8vo.* 7*s.* 6*d. net.*

HILLINGDON HALL. With 12 Coloure[d] Plates by WILDRAKE, HEATH, and JELL[I]COE. *Fcap. 8vo.* 7*s.* 6*d. net.*

Suso (Henry). THE LIFE OF TH[E] BLESSED HENRY SUSO. By HIMSELF. Translated by T. F. KNOX. With an Intro[]duction by DEAN INGE. *Second Edition. Cr. 8vo.* 6*s. net.*

Swanton (E. W.). FUNGI AND HOW TO KNOW THEM. Illustrated. *Cr. 8vo.* 10*s.* 6*d. net.*

BRITISH PLANT-GALLS. *Cr. 8vo.* 10*s.* 6*d. net.*

Tabor (Margaret E.). THE SAINTS IN ART. With their Attributes and Symbols Alphabetically Arranged. Illustrated. *Third Edition. Fcap. 8vo.* 5*s. net.*

Taylor (A. E.). ELEMENTS OF METAPHYSICS. *Fourth Edition. Demy 8vo.* 12*s.* 6*d. net.*

Taylor (J. W.). THE COMING OF THE SAINTS. *Second Edition. Cr. 8vo.* 6*s. net.*

Thomas (Edward). MAURICE MAETERLINCK. Illustrated. *Second Edition. Cr. 8vo.* 6*s. net.*

A LITERARY PILGRIM IN ENGLAND. Illustrated. *Demy 8vo.* 12*s.* 6*d. net.*

Tileston (Mary W.). DAILY STRENGTH FOR DAILY NEEDS. *Twenty-fifth Edition. Medium 16mo.* 3*s.* 6*d. net.*

Toynbee (Paget). DANTE ALIGHIERI. HIS LIFE AND WORKS. With 16 Illustrations. *Fourth and Enlarged Edition. Cr. 8vo.* 6*s. net.*

Trevelyan (G. M.). ENGLAND UNDER THE STUARTS. With Maps and Plans. *Seventh Edition. Demy 8vo.* 12*s.* 6*d. net.*

Triggs (H. Inigo). TOWN PLANNING: PAST, PRESENT, AND POSSIBLE. Illustrated. *Second Edition. Wide Royal 8vo.* 16*s. net.*

Underhill (Evelyn). MYSTICISM. A Study in the Nature and Development of Man's Spiritual Consciousness. *Seventh Edition. Demy 8vo.* 15*s. net.*

Vardon (Harry). HOW TO PLAY GOLF. Illustrated. *Eleventh Edition. Cr. 8vo.* 5*s. net.*

Vernon (Hon. W. Warren). READINGS ON THE INFERNO OF DANTE. With an Introduction by the Rev. Dr. MOORE. *Two Volumes. Second Edition, Rewritten. Cr. 8vo.* 15*s. net.*

READINGS ON THE PURGATORIO OF DANTE. With an Introduction by the late DEAN CHURCH. *Two Volumes. Third Edition, Revised. Cr. 8vo.* 15*s. net.*

READINGS ON THE PARADISO OF DANTE. With an Introduction by the BISHOP OF RIPON. *Two Volumes. Second Edition, Revised. Cr. 8vo.* 15*s. net.*

Vickers (Kenneth H.). ENGLAND IN THE LATER MIDDLE AGES. With Maps. *Second Edition, Revised. Demy 8vo.* 12*s.* 6*d. net.*

Waddell (L. A.). LHASA AND ITS MYSTERIES. With a Record of the Expedition of 1903-1904. Illustrated. *Third Edition. Medium 8vo.* 12*s.* 6*d. net.*

Wade (G. W. and J. H.). RAMBLES IN SOMERSET. Illustrated. *Cr. 8vo.* 7*s.* 6*d. net.*

Wagner (Richard). RICHARD WAGNER'S MUSIC DRAMAS. Interpretations, embodying Wagner's own explanations. By ALICE LEIGHTON CLEATHER and BASIL CRUMP. *Fcap. 8vo. Each* 4*s. net.*

THE RING OF THE NIBELUNG. *Sixth Edition.*

LOHENGRIN AND PARSIFAL. *Third Edition.*

TRISTAN AND ISOLDE. *Second Edition.*

TANNHÄUSER AND THE MASTERSINGERS OF NUREMBURG.

Waterhouse (Elizabeth). WITH THE SIMPLE-HEARTED. Little Homilies. *Third Edition. Small Pott 8vo.* 3*s.* 6*d. net.*

THE HOUSE BY THE CHERRY TREE. A Second Series of Little Homilies. *Small Pott 8vo.* 3*s.* 6*d. net.*

COMPANIONS OF THE WAY. Being Selections for Morning and Evening Reading. *Cr. 8vo.* 7*s.* 6*d. net.*

THOUGHTS OF A TERTIARY. *Second Edition. Small Pott 8vo.* 1*s.* 6*d. net.*

VERSES. *Second Edition, Enlarged. Fcap. 8vo.* 2*s. net.*

A LITTLE BOOK OF LIFE AND DEATH. *Nineteenth Edition. Small Pott 8vo. Cloth,* 2*s.* 6*d. net.*

Waters (W. G.). ITALIAN SCULPTORS. Illustrated. *Cr. 8vo.* 7*s.* 6*d. net.*

Watt (Francis). CANTERBURY PILGRIMS AND THEIR WAYS. With a Frontispiece in Colour and 12 other Illustrations. *Demy 8vo.* 10*s.* 6*d. net.*

Weigall (Arthur E. P.). A GUIDE TO THE ANTIQUITIES OF UPPER EGYPT: FROM ABYDOS TO THE SUDAN FRONTIER. Illustrated. *Second Edition. Cr. 8vo.* 10*s.* 6*d. net.*

Wells (J.). A SHORT HISTORY OF ROME. *Sixteenth Edition.* With 3 Maps. *Cr. 8vo.* 6*s.*

Wilde (Oscar). THE WORKS OF OSCAR WILDE. *Thirteen Volumes. Fcap. 8vo. Each* 6*s.* 6*d. net.*

I. LORD ARTHUR SAVIL[illegible] CRIME AND THE PORTRAIT OF MR. W. [illegible]. II. THE DUCHESS OF PADUA. III. P[illegible]MS. IV. LADY WINDERMERE'S FAN. V. [illegible] WOMAN OF NO IMPORTANCE. VI. AN IDEAL HUSBAND. VII. THE IMPORTANCE OF BEING EARNEST. VIII. A HOUSE OF POMEGRANATES. IX. INTENTIONS. X. DE PROFUNDIS AND PRISON LETTERS. XI. ESSAYS. XII. SALOMÉ, A FLORENTINE TRAGEDY, and LA SAINTE COURTISANE. XIV. SELECTED PROSE OF OSCAR WILDE.

A HOUSE OF POMEGRANATES. Illustrated. *Cr. 4to.* 21*s. net.*

Wilding (Anthony F). ON THE COURT AND OFF. With 58 Illustrations. *Seventh Edition. Cr. 8vo.* 6*s. net.*

Wilson (Ernest H.). A NATURALIST IN WESTERN CHINA. Illustrated. *Second Edition.* 2 Vols. *Demy 8vo.* £1 10*s. net.*

Wood (Sir Evelyn). FROM MIDSHIPMAN TO FIELD-MARSHAL. Illustrated. *Fifth Edition. Demy 8vo.* 12*s.* 6*d. net.*

THE REVOLT IN HINDUSTAN (1857-59). Illustrated. *Second Edition. Cr. 8vo.* 7*s.* 6*d. net.*

Wood (Lieut. W. B.) and Edmonds (Col. J. E.). A HISTORY OF THE CIVIL WAR IN THE UNITED STATES (1861-65). With an Introduction by SPENSER WILKINSON. With 24 Maps and Plans. *Third Edition. Demy 8vo.* 15*s. net.*

Wordsworth (W.). POEMS. With an Introduction and Notes by NOWELL C. SMITH. *Three Volumes. Demy 8vo.* 18*s. net.*

Yeats (W. B.). A BOOK OF IRISH VERSE. *Third Edition. Cr. 8vo.* 6*s. net.*

PART II.—A SELECTION OF SERIES

Ancient Cities

General Editor, SIR B. C. A. WINDLE

Cr. 8vo. 6*s. net each volume*

With Illustrations by E. H. NEW, and other Artists

BRISTOL. Alfred Harvey.

CANTERBURY. J. C. Cox.

CHESTER. Sir B. C. A. Windle.

DUBLIN. S. A. O. Fitzpatrick.

EDINBURGH. M. G. Williamson.

LINCOLN. E. Mansel Sympson.

SHREWSBURY. T. Auden.

WELLS and GLASTONBURY. T. S. Holmes.

The Antiquary's Books

General Editor, J. CHARLES COX

Demy 8vo. 10*s.* 6*d. net each volume*

With Numerous Illustrations

ANCIENT PAINTED GLASS IN ENGLAND. Philip Nelson.

ARCHÆOLOGY AND FALSE ANTIQUITIES. R. Munro.

BELLS OF ENGLAND, THE. Canon J. J. Raven. *Second Edition.*

BRASSES OF ENGLAND, THE. Herbert W. Macklin. *Third Edition.*

CASTLES AND WALLED TOWNS OF ENGLAND, THE. A. Harvey.

CELTIC ART IN PAGAN AND CHRISTIAN TIMES. J. Romilly Allen. *Second Edition.*

CHURCHWARDENS' ACCOUNTS. J. C. Cox.

DOMESDAY INQUEST, THE. Adolphus Ballard.

ENGLISH CHURCH FURNITURE. J. C. Cox and A. Harvey. *Second Edition.*

ENGLISH COSTUME. From Prehistoric Times to the End of the Eighteenth Century. George Clinch.

ENGLISH MONASTIC LIFE. Cardinal Gasquet. *Fourth Edition.*

ENGLISH SEALS. J. Harvey Bloom.

FOLK-LORE AS AN HISTORICAL SCIENCE. Sir G. L. Gomme.

GILDS AND COMPANIES OF LONDON, THE. George Unwin.

HERMITS AND ANCHORITES OF ENGLAND, THE. Rotha Mary Clay.

MANOR AND MANORIAL RECORDS, THE. Nathaniel J. Hone. *Second Edition.*

MEDIÆVAL HOSPITALS OF ENGLAND, THE. Rotha Mary Clay.

OLD ENGLISH INSTRUMENTS OF MUSIC. F. W. Galpin. *Second Edition.*

The Antiquary's Books—*continued*

OLD ENGLISH LIBRARIES. Ernest A. Savage.

OLD SERVICE BOOKS OF THE ENGLISH CHURCH. Christopher Wordsworth, and Henry Littlehales. *Second Edition.*

PARISH LIFE IN MEDIÆVAL ENGLAND. Cardinal Gasquet. *Fourth Edition.*

PARISH REGISTERS OF ENGLAND, THE. J. C. Cox.

REMAINS OF THE PREHISTORIC AGE IN ENGLAND. Sir B. C. A. Windle. *Second Edition.*

ROMAN ERA IN BRITAIN, THE. J. Ward.

ROMANO-BRITISH BUILDINGS AND EARTHWORKS. J. Ward.

ROYAL FORESTS OF ENGLAND, THE. J. C. Cox.

SCHOOLS OF MEDIEVAL ENGLAND, THE. A. F. Leach. *Second Edition.*

SHRINES OF BRITISH SAINTS. J. C. Wall.

The Arden Shakespeare

General Editor—R. H. CASE

Demy 8vo. 6s. net each volume

An edition of Shakespeare in Single Plays; each edited with a full Introduction, Textual Notes, and a Commentary at the foot of the page

ALL'S WELL THAT ENDS WELL.
ANTONY AND CLEOPATRA. *Third Edition.*
AS YOU LIKE IT.
CYMBELINE. *Second Edition.*
COMEDY OF ERRORS, THE.
HAMLET. *Fourth Edition.*
JULIUS CAESAR. *Second Edition.*
KING HENRY IV. PT. I.
KING HENRY V. *Second Edition.*
KING HENRY VI. PT. I.
KING HENRY VI. PT. II.
KING HENRY VI. PT. III
KING HENRY VIII.
KING LEAR. *Second Edition.*
KING RICHARD II.
KING RICHARD III. *Second Edition.*
LIFE AND DEATH OF KING JOHN, THE.
LOVE'S LABOUR'S LOST. *Second Edition.*
MACBETH. *Second Edition.*
MEASURE FOR MEASURE.
MERCHANT OF VENICE, THE. *Fourth Edition.*
MERRY WIVES OF WINDSOR, THE.
MIDSUMMER NIGHT'S DREAM, A.
OTHELLO. *Second Edition.*
PERICLES.
ROMEO AND JULIET. *Second Edition.*
SONNETS AND A LOVER'S COMPLAINT.
TAMING OF THE SHREW, THE.
TEMPEST, THE. *Second Edition.*
TIMON OF ATHENS.
TITUS ANDRONICUS.
TROILUS AND CRESSIDA.
TWELFTH NIGHT. *Third Edition.*
TWO GENTLEMEN OF VERONA, THE.
VENUS AND ADONIS.
WINTER'S TALE, THE.

Classics of Art

Edited by DR. J. H. W. LAING

With numerous Illustrations. Wide Royal 8vo

ART OF THE GREEKS, THE. H. B. Walters. *15s. net.*

ART OF THE ROMANS, THE. H. B. Walters. *16s. net.*

CHARDIN. H. E. A. Furst. *15s. net.*

DONATELLO. Maud Cruttwell. *16s. net.*

FLORENTINE SCULPTORS OF THE RENAISSANCE. Wilhelm Bode. Translated by Jessie Haynes. *15s. net.*

GEORGE ROMNEY. Arthur B. Chamberlain. *15s. net.*

Classics of Art—*continued*

GHIRLANDAIO. Gerald S. Davies. *Second Edition.* 15*s. net.*

LAWRENCE. Sir Walter Armstrong. 25*s. net.*

MICHELANGELO. Gerald S. Davies. 15*s. net.*

RAPHAEL. A. P. Oppé. 15*s. net.*

REMBRANDT'S ETCHINGS. A. M. Hind. Two Volumes. 25*s. net.*

RUBENS. Edward Dillon. 30*s. net.*

TINTORETTO. Evelyn March Phillipps. 16*s. net.*

TITIAN. Charles Ricketts. 16*s. net.*

TURNER'S SKETCHES AND DRAWINGS. A. J. Finberg. *Second Edition.* 15*s. net.*

VELAZQUEZ. A. de Beruete. 15*s. net.*

The 'Complete' Series

Fully Illustrated. Demy 8vo

COMPLETE AMATEUR BOXER, THE. J. G. Bohun Lynch. 10*s.* 6*d. net.*

COMPLETE ASSOCIATION FOOTBALLER, THE. B. S. Evers and C. E. Hughes-Davies. 10*s.* 6*d. net.*

COMPLETE ATHLETIC TRAINER, THE. S. A. Mussabini. 10*s.* 6*d. net.*

COMPLETE BILLIARD PLAYER, THE. Charles Roberts. 12*s.* 6*d. net.*

COMPLETE COOK, THE. Lilian Whitling. 10*s.* 6*d. net.*

COMPLETE CRICKETER, THE. Albert E. KNIGHT. *Second Edition.* 10*s.* 6*d. net.*

COMPLETE FOXHUNTER, THE. Charles Richardson. *Second Edition.* 16*s. net.*

COMPLETE GOLFER, THE. Harry Vardon. *Fifteenth Edition, Revised.* 12*s.* 6*d. net.*

COMPLETE HOCKEY-PLAYER, THE. Eustace E. White. *Second Edition.* 10*s.* 6*d. net.*

COMPLETE HORSEMAN, THE. W. Scarth Dixon. *Second Edition.* 12*s.* 6*d. net.*

COMPLETE JUJITSUAN, THE. W. H. Garrud. 5*s. net.*

COMPLETE LAWN TENNIS PLAYER, THE. A. Wallis Myers. *Fourth Edition.* 12*s.* 6*d. net.*

COMPLETE MOTORIST, THE. Filson Young and W. G. Aston. *Revised Edition.* 10*s.* 6*d. net.*

COMPLETE MOUNTAINEER, THE. G. D. Abraham. *Second Edition.* 16*s. net.*

COMPLETE OARSMAN, THE. R. C. Lehmann. 12*s.* 6*d. net.*

COMPLETE PHOTOGRAPHER, THE. R. Child Bayley. *Fifth Edition, Revised.* 12*s.* 6*d. net.*

COMPLETE RUGBY FOOTBALLER, ON THE NEW ZEALAND SYSTEM, THE. D. Gallaher and W. J. Stead. *Second Edition.* 12*s.* 6*d. net.*

COMPLETE SHOT, THE. G. T. Teasdale-Buckell. *Third Edition.* 16*s. net.*

COMPLETE SWIMMER, THE. F. Sachs. 10*s.* 6*d. net.*

COMPLETE YACHTSMAN, THE. B. Heckstall-Smith and E. du Boulay. *Second Edition, Revised.* 16*s. net.*

The Connoisseur's Library

With numerous Illustrations. Wide Royal 8vo. 25s. net each volume

ENGLISH COLOURED BOOKS. Martin Hardie.

ENGLISH FURNITURE. F. S. Robinson. *Second Edition.*

ETCHINGS. Sir F. Wedmore. *Second Edition.*

EUROPEAN ENAMELS. Henry H. Cunynghame.

FINE BOOKS. A. W. Pollard.

GLASS. Edward Dillon.

GOLDSMITHS' AND SILVERSMITHS' WORK. Nelson Dawson. *Second Edition.*

ILLUMINATED MANUSCRIPTS. J. A. Herbert. *Second Edition.*

IVORIES. Alfred Maskell.

JEWELLERY. H. Clifford Smith. *Second Edition.*

MEZZOTINTS. Cyril Davenport.

MINIATURES. Dudley Heath.

PORCELAIN. Edward Dillon.

SEALS. Walter de Gray Birch.

WOOD SCULPTURE. Alfred Maskell.

Handbooks of English Church History

Edited by J. H. BURN. *Crown 8vo.* 5*s. net each volume*

FOUNDATIONS OF THE ENGLISH CHURCH, THE. J. H. Maude.

SAXON CHURCH AND THE NORMAN CONQUEST, THE. C. T. Cruttwell.

MEDIÆVAL CHURCH AND THE PAPACY, THE. A. C. Jennings.

REFORMATION PERIOD, THE. Henry Gee.

STRUGGLE WITH PURITANISM, THE. Bruce Blaxland.

CHURCH OF ENGLAND IN THE EIGHTEENTH CENTURY, THE. Alfred Plummer.

Handbooks of Theology

Demy 8vo

DOCTRINE OF THE INCARNATION, THE. R. L. Ottley. *Fifth Edition.* 15*s. net.*

HISTORY OF EARLY CHRISTIAN DOCTRINE, A. J. F. Bethune-Baker. 15*s. net.*

INTRODUCTION TO THE HISTORY OF RELIGION, AN. F. B. Jevons. *Seventh Edition.* 12*s.* 6*d. net.*

INTRODUCTION TO THE HISTORY OF THE CREEDS, AN. A. E. Burn. 12*s.* 6*d. net.*

PHILOSOPHY OF RELIGION IN ENGLAND AND AMERICA, THE. Alfred Caldecott. 12*s.* 6*d. net.*

XXXIX ARTICLES OF THE CHURCH OF ENGLAND, THE. Edited by E. C. S. Gibson. *Ninth Edition.* 15*s. net.*

Health Series

Fcap. 8vo. 2*s.* 6*d. net*

BABY, THE. Arthur Saunders.

CARE OF THE BODY, THE. F. Cavanagh.

CARE OF THE TEETH, THE. A. T. Pitts.

EYES OF OUR CHILDREN, THE. N. Bishop Harman.

HEALTH FOR THE MIDDLE-AGED. Seymour Taylor. *Third Edition.*

HEALTH OF A WOMAN, THE. R. Murray Leslie.

HEALTH OF THE SKIN, THE. George Pernet.

HOW TO LIVE LONG. J. Walter Carr.

PREVENTION OF THE COMMON COLD, THE. O. K. Williamson.

STAYING THE PLAGUE. N. Bishop Harman.

THROAT AND EAR TROUBLES. Macleod Yearsley. *Third Edition.*

TUBERCULOSIS. Clive Riviere.

HEALTH OF THE CHILD, THE. O. Hilton. *Second Edition.* 2*s. net.*

The 'Home Life' Series

Illustrated. Demy 8vo.

HOME LIFE IN AMERICA. Katherine G. Busbey. *Second Edition.* 12*s.* 6*d. net.*

HOME LIFE IN CHINA. I. Taylor Headland. 12*s.* 6*d. net.*

HOME LIFE IN FRANCE. Miss Betham Edwards. *Sixth Edition.* 7*s.* 6*d. net.*

HOME LIFE IN GERMANY. Mrs. A. Sidgwick. *Third Edition.* 12. 6*d. net.*

HOME LIFE IN HOLLAND. D. S. Meldrum. *Second Edition.* 12*s.* 6*d. net.*

HOME LIFE IN ITALY. Lina Duff Gordon. *Third Edition.* 12*s.* 6*d. net.*

HOME LIFE IN NORWAY. H. K. Daniels. *Second Edition.* 12*s.* 6*d. net.*

HOME LIFE IN SPAIN. S. L. Bensusan. *Second Edition.* 12*s.* 6*d. net.*

BALKAN HOME LIFE. Lucy M J. Garnett. 12*s.* 6*d. net.*

Leaders of Religion

Edited by H. C. BEECHING. *With Portraits*

Crown 8vo. 3*s.* *net each volume*

AUGUSTINE OF CANTERBURY. E. L. Cutts.

BISHOP BUTLER. W. A. Spooner.

BISHOP WILBERFORCE. G. W. Daniell.

CARDINAL MANNING. A. W. Hutton. *Second Edition.*

CARDINAL NEWMAN. R. H. Hutton.

CHARLES SIMEON. H. C. G. Moule.

GEORGE FOX, THE QUAKER. T. Hodgkin. *Third Edition.*

JOHN DONNE. Augustus Jessop.

JOHN HOWE. R. F. Horton.

JOHN KEBLE. Walter Lock. *Seventh Edition.*

JOHN KNOX. F. MacCunn. *Second Edition.*

JOHN WESLEY. J. H. Overton.

LANCELOT ANDREWES. R. L. Ottley. *Second Edition.*

LATIMER. R. M. and A. J. Carlyle.

THOMAS CHALMERS. Mrs. Oliphant. *Second Edition.*

THOMAS CRANMER. A. J. Mason.

THOMAS KEN. F. A. Clarke.

WILLIAM LAUD. W. H. Hutton. *Fourth Edition.*

The Library of Devotion

With Introductions and (where necessary) Notes

Small Pott 8vo, cloth, 3*s. net; also some volumes in leather,* 3*s.* 6*d. net each volume*

BISHOP WILSON'S SACRA PRIVATA.

BOOK OF DEVOTIONS, A. *Second Edition.*

CHRISTIAN YEAR, THE. *Fifth Edition.*

CONFESSIONS OF ST. AUGUSTINE, THE. *Ninth Edition.* 3*s.* 6*d. net.*

DAY BOOK FROM THE SAINTS AND FATHERS, A.

DEATH AND IMMORTALITY.

DEVOTIONS FROM THE APOCRYPHA.

DEVOTIONS OF ST. ANSELM, THE.

DEVOTIONS FOR EVERY DAY IN THE WEEK AND THE GREAT FESTIVALS.

GRACE ABOUNDING TO THE CHIEF OF SINNERS.

GUIDE TO ETERNITY, A.

HORAE MYSTICAE. A Day Book from the Writings of Mystics of Many Nations.

IMITATION OF CHRIST, THE. *Eighth Edition.*

INNER WAY, THE. *Third Edition.*

INTRODUCTION TO THE DEVOUT LIFE, AN.

LIGHT, LIFE, and LOVE. A Selection from the German Mystics.

LITTLE BOOK OF HEAVENLY WISDOM, A. A Selection from the English Mystics.

LYRA APOSTOLICA.

LYRA INNOCENTIUM. *Third Edition.*

LYRA SACRA. A Book of Sacred Verse. *Second Edition.*

MANUAL OF CONSOLATION FROM THE SAINTS AND FATHERS, A.

ON THE LOVE OF GOD.

PRECES PRIVATAE.

PSALMS OF DAVID, THE.

SERIOUS CALL TO A DEVOUT AND HOLY LIFE, A. *Fifth Edition.*

SONG OF SONGS, THE.

SPIRITUAL COMBAT, THE.

SPIRITUAL GUIDE, THE. *Third Edition.*

TEMPLE, THE. *Second Edition.*

THOUGHTS OF PASCAL, THE. *Second Edition.*

Little Books on Art

With many Illustrations. Demy 16mo. 5s. net each volume

Each volume consists of about 200 pages, and contains from 30 to 40 Illustrations, including a Frontispiece in Photogravure

ALBRECHT DÜRER. L. J Allen.

ARTS OF JAPAN, THE. E. Dillon. *Third Edition.*

BOOKPLATES. E. Almack.

BOTTICELLI. Mary L. Bonnor.

BURNE-JONES. F. de Lisle. *Third Edition.*

CELLINI. R. H. H. Cust.

CHRISTIAN SYMBOLISM. Mrs. H. Jenner.

CHRIST IN ART. Mrs. H. Jenner.

CLAUDE. E. Dillon.

CONSTABLE. H. W. Tompkins. *Second Edition.*

COROT. A. Pollard and E. Birnstingl.

EARLY ENGLISH WATER-COLOUR. C. E. Hughes.

ENAMELS. Mrs. N. Dawson. *Second Edition.*

FREDERIC LEIGHTON. A. Corkran.

GEORGE ROMNEY. G. Paston.

GREEK ART. H. B. Walters. *Fifth Edition.*

GREUZE AND BOUCHER. E. F. Pollard.

HOLBEIN. Mrs. G. Fortescue.

JEWELLERY. C. Davenport. *Second Edition.*

JOHN HOPPNER. H. P. K. Skipton.

SIR JOSHUA REYNOLDS. J. Sime. *Second Edition.*

MILLET. N. Peacock. *Second Edition.*

MINIATURES. C. Davenport, V.D., F.S.A. *Second Edition.*

OUR LADY IN ART. Mrs. H. Jenner.

RAPHAEL. A. R. Dryhurst. *Second Edition*

RODIN. Muriel Ciolkowska.

TURNER. F. Tyrrell-Gill.

VANDYCK. M. G. Smallwood.

VELAZQUEZ. W. Wilberforce and A. R. Gilbert.

WATTS. R. E. D. Sketchley. *Second Edition.*

The Little Guides

With many Illustrations by E. H. NEW and other artists, and from photographs

Small Pott 8vo. 4s. net each volume

The main features of these Guides are (1) a handy and charming form; (2) illustrations from photographs and by well-known artists; (3) good plans and maps; (4) an adequate but compact presentation of everything that is interesting in the natural features, history, archæology, and architecture of the town or district treated.

CAMBRIDGE AND ITS COLLEGES. A. H. Thompson. *Fourth Edition, Revised.*

CHANNEL ISLANDS, THE. E. E. Bicknell.

ENGLISH LAKES, THE. F. G. Brabant.

ISLE OF WIGHT, THE. G. Clinch.

LONDON. G. Clinch.

MALVERN COUNTRY, THE. Sir B. C. A. Windle. *Second Edition.*

NORTH WALES. A. T. Story.

OXFORD AND ITS COLLEGES. J. Wells. *Tenth Edition.*

ST. PAUL'S CATHEDRAL. G. Clinch.

SHAKESPEARE'S COUNTRY. Sir B. C. A. Windle. *Fifth Edition.*

SOUTH WALES. G. W. and J. H. Wade.

TEMPLE, THE. H. H. L. Bellot.

WESTMINSTER ABBEY. G. E. Troutbeck. *Second Edition.*

The Little Guides—*continued*

BEDFORDSHIRE AND HUNTINGDONSHIRE. H. W. Macklin.

BERKSHIRE. F. G. Brabant.

BUCKINGHAMSHIRE. E. S. Roscoe. *Second Edition, Revised.*

CAMBRIDGESHIRE. J. C. Cox.

CHESHIRE. W. M. Gallichan.

CORNWALL. A. L. Salmon. *Second Edition.*

DERBYSHIRE. J. C. Cox. *Second Edition.*

DEVON. S. Baring-Gould. *Fourth Edition.*

DORSET. F. R. Heath. *Fourth Edition.*

DURHAM. J. E. Hodgkin.

ESSEX. J. C. Cox. *Second Edition.*

GLOUCESTERSHIRE. J. C. Cox. *Second Edition.*

HAMPSHIRE. J. C. Cox. *Third Edition.*

HEREFORDSHIRE. G. W. and J. H. Wade.

HERTFORDSHIRE. H. W. Tompkins.

KENT. J. C. Cox. *Second Edition, Rewritten.*

KERRY. C. P. Crane. *Second Edition.*

LEICESTERSHIRE AND RUTLAND. A. Harvey and V. B. Crowther-Beynon.

LINCOLNSHIRE. J. C. Cox.

MIDDLESEX. J. B. Firth.

MONMOUTHSHIRE. G. W. and J. H. Wade.

NORFOLK. W. A. Dutt. *Fourth Edition, Revised.*

NORTHAMPTONSHIRE. W. Dry. *Second Edition, Revised.*

NORTHUMBERLAND. J. E. Morris. 5*s. net.*

NOTTINGHAMSHIRE. L. Guilford.

OXFORDSHIRE. F. G. Brabant. *Second Edition.*

SHROPSHIRE. J. E. Auden. *Second Edition.*

SOMERSET. G. W. and J. H. Wade. *Fourth Edition.*

STAFFORDSHIRE. C. Masefield. *Second Edition.*

SUFFOLK. W. A. Dutt. *Second Edition.*

SURREY. J. C. Cox. *Third Edition, Rewritten.*

SUSSEX. F. G. Brabant. *Fifth Edition.*

WARWICKSHIRE. J. C. Cox.

WILTSHIRE. F. R. Heath. *Third Edition.*

YORKSHIRE, THE EAST RIDING. J. E. Morris.

YORKSHIRE, THE NORTH RIDING. J. E. Morris.

YORKSHIRE, THE WEST RIDING. J. E. Morris. 5*s. net.*

BRITTANY. S. Baring-Gould. *Second Edition.*

NORMANDY. C. Scudamore. *Second Edition.*

ROME. C. G. Ellaby.

SICILY. F. H. Jackson.

The Little Library

With Introduction, Notes, and Photogravure Frontispieces

Small Pott 8vo. Each Volume, cloth, 2s. 6d. net; also some volumes in leather at 3s. 6d. net

Anon. A LITTLE BOOK OF ENGLISH LYRICS. *Second Edition.* 3*s.* 6*d. net.*

Austen (Jane). PRIDE AND PREJUDICE. *Two Volumes.*

NORTHANGER ABBEY.

Bacon (Francis). THE ESSAYS OF LORD BACON.

Barnett (Annie). A LITTLE BOOK OF ENGLISH PROSE. *Third Edition.*

Beckford (William). THE HISTORY OF THE CALIPH VATHEK.

Blake (William). SELECTIONS FROM THE WORKS OF WILLIAM BLAKE.

Browning (Robert). SELECTIONS FROM THE EARLY POEMS OF ROBERT BROWNING.

Canning (George). SELECTIONS FROM THE ANTI-JACOBIN: With some later Poems by GEORGE CANNING.

Cowley (Abraham). THE ESSAYS OF ABRAHAM COWLEY.

The Little Library—*continued*

Crabbe (George). SELECTIONS FROM THE POEMS OF GEORGE CRABBE.

Crashaw (Richard). THE ENGLISH POEMS OF RICHARD CRASHAW.

Dante Alighieri. PURGATORY.
PARADISE.

Darley (George). SELECTIONS FROM THE POEMS OF GEORGE DARLEY.

Kinglake (A. W.). EOTHEN. *Second Edition.* 2*s.* 6*d. net.*

Locker (F.). LONDON LYRICS.

Marvell (Andrew). THE POEMS OF ANDREW MARVELL.

Milton (John). THE MINOR POEMS OF JOHN MILTON.

Moir (D. M.). MANSIE WAUCH.

Nichols (Bowyer). A LITTLE BOOK OF ENGLISH SONNETS.

Smith (Horace and James). REJECTED ADDRESSES.

Sterne (Laurence). A SENTIMENTAL JOURNEY.

Tennyson (Alfred, Lord). THE EARLY POEMS OF ALFRED, LORD TENNYSON.
IN MEMORIAM.
THE PRINCESS.
MAUD.

Vaughan (Henry). THE POEMS OF HENRY VAUGHAN.

Waterhouse (Elizabeth). A LITTLE BOOK OF LIFE AND DEATH. *Nineteenth Edition.*

Wordsworth (W.). SELECTIONS FROM THE POEMS OF WILLIAM WORDSWORTH.

Wordsworth (W.) and Coleridge (S. T.). LYRICAL BALLADS. *Third Edition.*

The Little Quarto Shakespeare

Edited by W. J. CRAIG. With Introductions and Notes

Pott 16*mo.* 40 *Volumes. Leather, price* 1*s.* 9*d. net each volume*

Miniature Library

Demy 32*mo. Leather,* 3*s.* 6*d. net each volume*

EUPHRANOR: A Dialogue on Youth. Edward FitzGerald.

POLONIUS; or, Wise Saws and Modern Instances. Edward FitzGerald.

THE RUBAIYÁT OF OMAR KHAYYÁM. Edward FitzGerald. *Fifth Edition. Cloth,* 1*s. net.*

The New Library of Medicine

Edited by C. W. SALEEBY. *Demy* 8*vo*

AIR AND HEALTH. Ronald C. Macfie. *Second Edition.* 10*s.* 6*d. net.*

CARE OF THE BODY, THE. F. Cavanagh. *Second Edition.* 10*s.* 6*d. net.*

CHILDREN OF THE NATION, THE. The Right Hon. Sir John Gorst. *Second Edition.* 10*s.* 6*d. net.*

DRUGS AND THE DRUG HABIT. H. Sainsbury. 10*s.* 6*d. net.*

FUNCTIONAL NERVE DISEASES. A. T. Schofield. 10*s.* 6*d. net.*

HYGIENE OF MIND, THE. Sir T. S. Clouston. *Sixth Edition.* 10*s.* 6*d. net.*

INFANT MORTALITY. Sir George Newman. 10*s.* 6*d. net.*

PREVENTION OF TUBERCULOSIS (CONSUMPTION), THE. Arthur Newsholme. *Second Edition.* 12*s.* 6*d. net.*

The New Library of Music

Edited by ERNEST NEWMAN. *Illustrated. Demy 8vo.* 10*s.* 6*d. net*

BRAHMS. J. A. Fuller-Maitland. *Second Edition.*

HANDEL. R. A. Streatfeild. *Second Edition.*

HUGO WOLF. Ernest Newman.

Oxford Biographies

Illustrated. Fcap. 8vo. Each volume, cloth, 4*s. net; also some in leather,* 5*s. net*

DANTE ALIGHIERI. Paget Toynbee. *Fifth Edition.*

GIROLAMO SAVONAROLA. E. L. S. Horsburgh. *Sixth Edition.*

JOHN HOWARD. E. C. S. Gibson.

SIR WALTER RALEIGH. I. A. Taylor.

CHATHAM. A. S. McDowall.

CANNING. W. Alison Phillips.

Nine Plays

Fcap. 8vo. 3*s.* 6*d. net*

ACROSS THE BORDER. Beulah Marie Dix.

HONEYMOON, THE. A Comedy in Three Acts. Arnold Bennett. *Third Edition.*

GREAT ADVENTURE, THE. A Play of Fancy in Four Acts. Arnold Bennett. *Fourth Edition.*

MILESTONES. Arnold Bennett and Edward Knoblock. *Eighth Edition.*

IDEAL HUSBAND, AN. Oscar Wilde. *Acting Edition.*

KISMET. Edward Knoblock. *Third Edition.*

TYPHOON. A Play in Four Acts. Melchior Lengyel. English Version by Laurence Irving. *Second Edition.*

WARE CASE, THE. George Pleydell.

GENERAL POST. J. E. Harold Terry. *Second Edition.*

Sport Series

Illustrated. Fcap. 8vo. 2*s. net*

FLYING, ALL ABOUT. Gertrude Bacon.

GOLF DO'S AND DONT'S. 'Stancliffe.' *Sixth Edition.*

GOLFING SWING, THE. Burnham Hare. *Fourth Edition.*

HOW TO SWIM. H. R. Austin.

WRESTLING. P. Longhurst.

The States of Italy

Edited by E. ARMSTRONG and R. LANGTON DOUGLAS

Illustrated. Demy 8vo

MILAN UNDER THE SFORZA, A HISTORY OF. Cecilia M. Ady. 12*s.* 6*d. net.*

VERONA, A HISTORY OF. A. M. Allen. 15*s. net.*

PERUGIA, A HISTORY OF. W. Heywood. 15*s. net.*

The Westminster Commentaries

General Editor, WALTER LOCK

Demy 8vo

ACTS OF THE APOSTLES, THE. R. B. Rackham. *Seventh Edition.* 16*s. net.*

AMOS. E. A. Edghill. 8*s.* 6*d. net.*

CORINTHIANS, I. H. L. Goudge. *Fourth Edition.* 8*s.* 6*d. net.*

EXODUS. A. H. M'Neile. *Second Edition.* 15*s. net.*

EZEKIEL. H. A. Redpath. 12*s.* 6*d. net.*

GENESIS. S. R. Driver. *Tenth Edition.* 16*s. net.*

HEBREWS. E. C. Wickham. 8*s.* 6*d. net.*

ISAIAH. G. W. Wade. 16*s. net.*

JEREMIAH. L. E. Binns. 16*s. net.*

JOB. E. C. S. Gibson. *Second Edition* 8*s.* 6*d. net.*

PASTORAL EPISTLES, THE. E. F. BROWN. 8*s.* 6*d. net.*

PHILIPPIANS, THE. Maurice Jones. 8*s.* 6*d. net.*

ST. JAMES. R. J. Knowling. *Second Edition.* 8*s.* 6*d. net.*

ST. MATTHEW. P. A. Micklem. 15*s. net.*

The 'Young' Series

Illustrated. Crown 8vo

YOUNG BOTANIST, THE. W. P. Westell and C. S. Cooper. *6s. net.*

YOUNG CARPENTER, THE. Cyril Hall. *6s. net.*

YOUNG ELECTRICIAN, THE. Hammond Hall. *Second Edition. 6s. net.*

YOUNG ENGINEER, THE. Hammond Hall. *Third Edition. 6s. net.*

YOUNG NATURALIST, THE. W. P. Westell. *7s. 6d. net.*

YOUNG ORNITHOLOGIST, THE. W. P. Westell. *6s. net.*

Methuen's Cheap Library

Fcap. 8vo. 2s. net

ALL THINGS CONSIDERED. G. K. Chesterton.

BEST OF LAMB, THE. Edited by E. V. Lucas.

BLUE BIRD, THE. Maurice Maeterlinck.

CHARLES DICKENS. G. K. Chesterton.

CHARMIDES, AND OTHER POEMS. Oscar Wilde.

CHITRÀL: The Story of a Minor Siege. Sir G. S. Robertson.

CUSTOMS OF OLD ENGLAND, THE. F. J. Snell.

DE PROFUNDIS. Oscar Wilde.

FAMOUS WITS, A BOOK OF. W. Jerrold.

FROM MIDSHIPMAN TO FIELD-MARSHAL. Sir Evelyn Wood, F.M., V.C.

HARVEST HOME. E. V. Lucas.

HILLS AND THE SEA. Hilaire Belloc.

IDEAL HUSBAND, AN. Oscar Wilde.

IMPORTANCE OF BEING EARNEST, THE. Oscar Wilde.

INTENTIONS. Oscar Wilde.

JANE AUSTEN AND HER TIMES. G. E. MITTON.

JOHN BOYES, KING OF THE WA-KIKUYU. John Boyes.

LADY WINDERMERE'S FAN. Oscar Wilde.

LETTERS FROM A SELF-MADE MERCHANT TO HIS SON. George Horace Lorimer.

LIFE OF JOHN RUSKIN, THE. W. G. Collingwood.

LIFE OF ROBERT LOUIS STEVENSON, THE. Graham Balfour.

LITTLE OF EVERYTHING, A. E. V. Lucas.

LORD ARTHUR SAVILE'S CRIME. Oscar Wilde.

LORE OF THE HONEY-BEE, THE. Tickner Edwardes.

MAN AND THE UNIVERSE. Sir Oliver Lodge.

MARY MAGDALENE. Maurice Maeterlinck.

MIRROR OF THE SEA, THE. J. Conrad.

MIXED VINTAGES. E. V. Lucas.

MODERN PROBLEMS. Sir Oliver Lodge.

MY CHILDHOOD AND BOYHOOD. Leo Tolstoy.

MY YOUTH. Leo Tolstoy.

OLD COUNTRY LIFE. S. Baring-Gould.

OLD TIME PARSON, THE. P. H. Ditchfield.

ON EVERYTHING. Hilaire Belloc.

ON NOTHING. Hilaire Belloc.

OSCAR WILDE: A Critical Study. Arthur Ransome.

PICKED COMPANY, A. Hilaire Belloc.

REASON AND BELIEF. Sir Oliver Lodge.

R. L. S. Francis Watt.

SCIENCE FROM AN EASY CHAIR. Sir Ray Lankester.

SELECTED POEMS. Oscar Wilde.

SELECTED PROSE. Oscar Wilde.

SHEPHERD'S LIFE, A. W. H. Hudson.

SHILLING FOR MY THOUGHTS, A. G. K. Chesterton.

SOCIAL EVILS AND THEIR REMEDY. Leo Tolstoy.

SOME LETTERS OF R. L. STEVENSON. Selected by Lloyd Osbourne.

SUBSTANCE OF FAITH, THE. Sir Oliver Lodge.

SURVIVAL OF MAN, THE. Sir Oliver Lodge.

TOWER OF LONDON, THE. R. Davey.

TWO ADMIRALS. Admiral John Moresby.

VAILIMA LETTERS. Robert Louis Stevenson.

VARIETY LANE. E. V. Lucas.

VICAR OF MORWENSTOW, THE. S. Baring-Gould.

WOMAN OF NO IMPORTANCE, A. Oscar Wilde.

A Selection only

Books for Travellers

Crown 8vo. 8s. 6d. net each

Each volume contains a number of Illustrations in Colour

AVON AND SHAKESPEARE'S COUNTRY, THE. A. G. Bradley. *Second Edition.*

BLACK FOREST, A BOOK OF THE. C. E. Hughes.

CITIES OF LOMBARDY, THE. Edward Hutton.

CITIES OF ROMAGNA AND THE MARCHES, THE. Edward Hutton.

CITIES OF SPAIN, THE. Edward Hutton. *Fifth Edition.*

CITIES OF UMBRIA, THE. Edward Hutton. *Fifth Edition.*

FLORENCE AND NORTHERN TUSCANY, WITH GENOA. Edward Hutton. *Third Edition.*

LAND OF PARDONS, THE (Brittany). Anatole Le Braz. *Fourth Edition.*

LONDON REVISITED. E. V. Lucas. *Third Edition.* *8s. 6d. net.*

NAPLES. Arthur H. Norway. *Fourth Edition.* *8s. 6d. net.*

NAPLES AND SOUTHERN ITALY. Edward Hutton.

NAPLES RIVIERA, THE. H. M. Vaughan. *Second Edition.*

NEW FOREST, THE. Horace G. Hutchinson. *Fourth Edition.*

NORWAY AND ITS FJORDS. M. A. Wyllie.

ROME. Edward Hutton. *Third Edition.*

ROUND ABOUT WILTSHIRE. A. G. Bradley. *Third Edition.*

SIENA AND SOUTHERN TUSCANY. Edward Hutton. *Second Edition.*

SKIRTS OF THE GREAT CITY, THE. Mrs. A. G. Bell. *Second Edition.*

VENICE AND VENETIA. Edward Hutton.

WANDERER IN FLORENCE, A. E. V. Lucas. *Sixth Edition.*

WANDERER IN PARIS, A. E. V. Lucas. *Thirteenth Edition.*

WANDERER IN HOLLAND, A. E. V. Lucas. *Sixteenth Edition.*

WANDERER IN LONDON, A. E. V. Lucas. *Eighteenth Edition.*

WANDERER IN VENICE, A. E. V. Lucas. *Second Edition.*

Some Books on Art

ART, ANCIENT AND MEDIEVAL. M. H. Bulley. Illustrated. *Crown 8vo.* 7s. 6d. *net.*

BRITISH SCHOOL, THE. An Anecdotal Guide to the British Painters and Paintings in the National Gallery. E. V. Lucas. Illustrated. *Fcap. 8vo.* 6s. *net.*

DECORATIVE IRON WORK. From the XIth to the XVIIIth Century. Charles ffoulkes. *Royal 4to.* £2 2s. *net.*

FRANCESCO GUARDI, 1712–1793. G. A. Simonson. Illustrated. *Imperial 4to.* £2 2s. *net.*

ILLUSTRATIONS OF THE BOOK OF JOB. William Blake. *Quarto.* £1 1s. *net.*

ITALIAN SCULPTORS. W. G. Waters. Illustrated. *Crown 8vo.* 7s. 6d. *net.*

OLD PASTE. A. Beresford Ryley. Illustrated. *Royal 4to.* £2 2s. *net.*

ONE HUNDRED MASTERPIECES OF SCULPTURE. With an Introduction by G. F. Hill. Illustrated. *Demy 8vo.* 12s. 6d. *net.*

ROYAL ACADEMY LECTURES ON PAINTING. George Clausen. Illustrated. *Crown 8vo.* 7s. 6d. *net.*

SAINTS IN ART, THE. Margaret E. Tabor. Illustrated. *Third Edition. Fcap. 8vo.* 5s. *net.*

SCHOOLS OF PAINTING. Mary Innes. Illustrated. *Second Edition. Cr. 8vo.* 8s. *net.*

CELTIC ART IN PAGAN AND CHRISTIAN TIMES. J. R. Allen. Illustrated. *Second Edition. Demy 8vo.* 10s. 6d. *net.*

GOD AND THE KING. *Sixth Edition. Cr. 8vo. 7s. net.*

PRINCE AND HERETIC. *Third Edition. Cr. 8vo. 7s. net.*

A KNIGHT OF SPAIN. *Third Edition. Cr. 8vo. 7s. net.*

THE QUEST OF GLORY. *Third Edition. Cr. 8vo. 7s. net.*

THE GOVERNOR OF ENGLAND. *Third Edition. Cr. 8vo. 7s. net.*

THE CARNIVAL OF FLORENCE. *Fifth Edition. Cr. 8vo. 7s. net.*

MR. WASHINGTON. *Third Edition. Cr. 8vo. 7s. net.*

"BECAUSE OF THESE THINGS. . . ." *Third Edition. Cr. 8vo. 7s. net.*

THE THIRD ESTATE. *Second Edition. Cr. 8vo. 7s. net.*

Burroughs (Edgar Rice). THE RETURN OF TARZAN. *Fcap. 8vo. 2s. net.*

THE BEASTS OF TARZAN. *Second Edition. Cr. 8vo. 6s. net.*

THE SON OF TARZAN. *Cr. 8vo. 7s. net.*

A PRINCESS OF MARS. *Cr. 8vo. 5s. net.*

Castle (Agnes and Egerton). THE GOLDEN BARRIER. *Third Edition. Cr. 8vo. 7s. net.*

Conrad (Joseph). A SET OF SIX. *Fourth Edition. Cr. 8vo. 7s. net.*

VICTORY: AN ISLAND TALE. *Sixth Edition. Cr. 8vo. 9s. net.*

Conyers (Dorothea). SANDY MARRIED. *Fifth Edition. Cr. 8vo. 7s. net.*

OLD ANDY. *Fourth Edition. Cr. 8vo. 7s. net.*

THE BLIGHTING OF BARTRAM. *Third Edition. Cr. 8vo. 7s. net.*

B. E. N. *Cr. 8vo. 7s. net.*

Corelli (Marie). A ROMANCE OF TWO WORLDS. *Thirty-fifth Edition. Cr. 8vo. 7s. 6d. net.*

VENDETTA; OR, THE STORY OF ONE FORGOTTEN. *Thirty-fifth Edition. Cr. 8vo. 8s. net.*

THELMA: A NORWEGIAN PRINCESS. *Fifty-ninth Edition. Cr. 8vo. 8s. 6d. net.*

ARDATH: THE STORY OF A DEAD SELF. *Twenty-fourth Edition. Cr. 8vo. 7s. 6d. net.*

THE SOUL OF LILITH. *Twentieth Edition. Cr. 8vo. 7s. net.*

WORMWOOD: A DRAMA OF PARIS. *Twenty-second Edition. Cr. 8vo. 8s. net.*

BARABBAS: A DREAM OF THE WORLD'S TRAGEDY. *Fiftieth Edition. Cr. 8vo. 8s. net.*

THE SORROWS OF SATAN. *Sixty-third Edition. Cr. 8vo. 7s. net.*

THE MASTER-CHRISTIAN. *Eighteenth Edition. 184th Thousand. Cr. 8vo. 8s. 6d. net.*

TEMPORAL POWER: A STUDY IN SUPREMACY. *Second Edition. 150th Thousand. Cr. 8vo. 6s. net.*

GOD'S GOOD MAN: A SIMPLE LOVE STORY. *Twentieth Edition. 159th Thousand. Cr. 8vo. 8s. 6d. net.*

HOLY ORDERS: THE TRAGEDY OF A QUIET LIFE. *Third Edition. 121st Thousand. Cr. 8vo. 8s. 6d. net.*

THE MIGHTY ATOM. *Thirty-sixth Edition. Cr. 8vo. 7s. 6d. net.*

BOY: A SKETCH. *Twentieth Edition. Cr. 8vo. 6s. net.*

CAMEOS. *Fifteenth Edition. Cr. 8vo. 6s. net.*

THE LIFE EVERLASTING. *Eighth Edition. Cr. 8vo. 8s. 6d. net.*

Crockett (S. R.). LOCHINVAR. Illustrated. *Fifth Edition. Cr. 8vo. 7s. net.*

THE STANDARD BEARER. *Second Edition. Cr. 8vo. 7s. net.*

Doyle (Sir A. Conan). ROUND THE RED LAMP. *Twelfth Edition. Cr. 8vo. 7s. net.*

Dudeney (Mrs. H.). THIS WAY OUT. *Cr. 8vo. 7s. net.*

Fry (B. and C. B.). A MOTHER'S SON. *Fifth Edition Cr. 8vo. 7s. net.*

Harraden (Beatrice). THE GUIDING THREAD. *Second Edition. Cr. 8vo. 7s. net.*

Hichens (Robert). THE PROPHET OF BERKELEY SQUARE. *Second Edition. Cr. 8vo. 7s. net.*

TONGUES OF CONSCIENCE. *Fourth Edition. Cr. 8vo. 7s. net.*

FELIX: THREE YEARS IN A LIFE. *Seventh Edition. Cr. 8vo. 7s. net.*

THE WOMAN WITH THE FAN. *Eighth Edition. Cr. 8vo. 7s. net.*

BYEWAYS. *Cr. 8vo. 7s. net.*

THE GARDEN OF ALLAH. *Twenty-sixth Edition.* Illustrated. *Cr. 8vo. 8s. 6d. net.*

THE CALL OF THE BLOOD. *Ninth Edition. Cr. 8vo. 8s. 6d. net.*

BARBARY SHEEP. *Second Edition. Cr. 8vo. 6s. net.*

THE DWELLER ON THE THRESHOLD. *Cr. 8vo. 7s. net.*

THE WAY OF AMBITION. *Fifth Edition. Cr. 8vo. 7s. net.*

IN THE WILDERNESS. *Third Edition. Cr. 8vo. 7s. net.*

Hope (Anthony). A CHANGE OF AIR. *Sixth Edition. Cr. 8vo. 7s. net.*

A MAN OF MARK. *Seventh Edition. Cr. 8vo. 7s. net.*

THE CHRONICLES OF COUNT ANTONIO. *Sixth Edition. Cr. 8vo. 7s. net.*

PHROSO. Illustrated. *Ninth Edition. Cr. 8vo. 7s. net.*

SIMON DALE. Illustrated. *Ninth Edition. Cr. 8vo. 7s. net.*

THE KING'S MIRROR. *Fifth Edition. Cr. 8vo. 7s. net.*

QUISANTÉ. *Fourth Edition. Cr. 8vo. 7s. net.*

THE DOLLY DIALOGUES. *Cr. 8vo. 7s. net.*

TALES OF TWO PEOPLE. *Third Edition. Cr. 8vo. 7s. net.*

A SERVANT OF THE PUBLIC. Illustrated. *Fourth Edition. Cr. 8vo. 7s. net.*

MRS. MAXON PROTESTS. *Third Edition. Cr. 8vo. 7s. net.*

A YOUNG MAN'S YEAR. *Second Edition. Cr. 8vo. 7s. net.*

Hyne (C. J. Cutcliffe). MR. HORROCKS, PURSER. *Fifth Edition. Cr. 8vo 7s. net.*

FIREMEN HOT. *Fourth Edition. Cr. 8vo. 7s. net.*

CAPTAIN KETTLE ON THE WARPATH. *Third Edition. Cr. 8vo. 7s. net.*

RED HERRINGS. *Cr. 8vo. 6s. net.*

Jacobs (W. W.). MANY CARGOES. *Thirty-third Edition. Cr. 8vo. 5s. net. Also Cr. 8vo. 2s. 6d. net.*

SEA URCHINS. *Nineteenth Edition. Cr. 8vo.* 5s. net.
Also Cr. 8vo. 3s. 6d. net.

A MASTER OF CRAFT. Illustrated. *Eleventh Edition. Cr. 8vo. 5s. net.*

LIGHT FREIGHTS. Illustrated. *Fifteenth Edition. Cr. 8vo. 5s. net.*

THE SKIPPER'S WOOING. *Twelfth Edition. Cr. 8vo. 5s. net.*

AT SUNWICH PORT. Illustrated. *Eleventh Edition. Cr. 8vo. 5s. net.*

DIALSTONE LANE. Illustrated. *Eighth Edition. Cr. 8vo 5s. net.*

ODD CRAFT. Illustrated. *Fifth Edition. Cr. 8vo. 5s. net.*

THE LADY OF THE BARGE. Illustrated. *Tenth Edition. Cr. 8vo. 5s. net.*

SALTHAVEN. Illustrated. *Fourth Edition. Cr. 8vo. 5s. net.*

SAILORS' KNOTS. Illustrated. *Sixth Edition. Cr. 8vo. 5s. net.*

SHORT CRUISES. *Third Edition. Cr 8vo. 5s. net.*

King (Basil). THE LIFTED VEIL. *Cr. 8vo. 7s. net.*

Lethbridge (Sybil C.). ONE WOMAN'S HERO. *Cr. 8vo. 7s. net.*

London (Jack). WHITE FANG. *Ninth Edition. Cr. 8vo. 7s. net.*

Lowndes (Mrs. Belloc). THE LODGER. *Third Edition. Cr. 8vo. 7s. net.*

Lucas (E. V.). LISTENER'S LURE: AN OBLIQUE NARRATION. *Twelfth Edition. Fcap. 8vo. 6s. net.*

OVER BEMERTON'S: AN EASY-GOING CHRONICLE. *Sixteenth Edition. Fcap. 8vo.* 6s. *net.*

MR. INGLESIDE. *Thirteenth Edition. Fcap. 8vo. 6s. net.*

LONDON LAVENDER. *Twelfth Edition. Fcap. 8vo. 6s. net.*

LANDMARKS. *Fifth Edition. Cr. 8vo. 7s. net.*

THE VERMILION BOX. *Fifth Edition. Cr. 8vo. 7s. net.*

Lyall (Edna). DERRICK VAUGHAN, NOVELIST. *44th Thousand. Cr. 8vo. 5s. net.*